ETHNICITY AND GLOBALIZATION

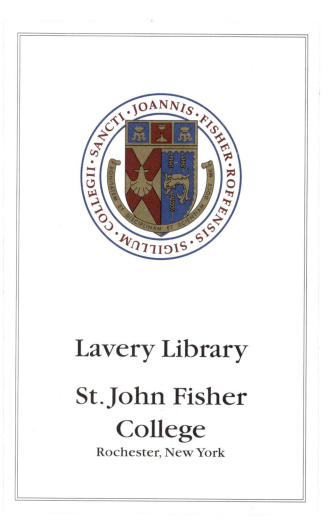

ETHNICITY AND GLOBALIZATION

From Migrant Worker to Transnational Citizen

Stephen Castles

SAGE Publications
London • Thousand Oaks • New Delhi

SAGE Publications Ltd
6 Bonhill Street
London EC2A 4PU

SAGE Publications Inc.
2455 Teller Road
Thousand Oaks, California 91320

SAGE Publications India Pvt Ltd
32, M-Block Market
Greater Kailash - I
New Delhi 110 048

British Library Cataloguing in Publication data

A catalogue record for this book is available from the British Library

ISBN 0 7619 5611 5
ISBN 0 7619 5612 3 (pbk)

Library of Congress catalog card number 00 132725

Typeset by SIVA Math Setters, Chennai, India
Printed and bound in Great Britain by
Athenaeum Press, Gateshead

For Freyja and Jenny

CONTENTS

TABLES

PREFACE

This book sums up over thirty years of research on international migration and how it has changed the world. The essays collected in this volume provide a running commentary on the ways in which migration – first to the older industrial countries and then as a more general phenomenon linked to globalization – has created multicultural societies and changed ideas on citizenship and identity. At the beginning of the new millennium, transnational communities and increasingly complex forms of identification are part of the growing challenge to the nation-state.

Chapter 2 was first published in 1972, while Chapters 3 and 4 sum up European developments of the 1970s and 1980s. However, most of the collection is much more recent, reflecting the global trends of the 1990s and looking beyond to perspectives for the next thirty years. Three of the essays – Chapters 1, 7 and 13 – have been especially written for this book. This edition keeps very closely to the original texts, with only minor editorial changes. A few cuts have been made to avoid repetition; these are marked by an ellipsis in square brackets […].

It is very hard to acknowledge all the people who have influenced and supported my work over so many years. One testimony is to be found in the references to the many important publications that have helped shape my own work, but it has always been the personal conversations, debates and arguments that have done most to advance my ideas. A few friends and colleagues should be mentioned specifically. The first is Godula Kosack, my collaborator in the late 1960s and 1970s, who is co-author of Chapter 2 of the present volume. As librarian and then director of the Institute of Race Relations (London), A. Sivanandan showed me and many other scholars how to combine the academic and the political. Wiebke Wüstenberg gave a great deal of encouragement and support in the late 1970s and early 1980s. Mark J. Miller persuaded me to take a global view. Carl-Ulrik Schierup, Aleksandra Ålund, Robin Cohen, Annie Phizacklea, John Solomos, Russell King, Klaus Bade, Catherine Wihtol de Wenden and Michael Bommes have helped me maintain my European involvement since coming to Australia in 1986. Many Australian colleagues have shared their ideas with me, among them Jock Collins, James Jupp, Alan Matheson, Robyn Iredale and Michael Morrissey. Rainer Bauböck and Alastair Davidson facilitated my access to the new area of citizenship studies. Supang Chantavanich, Diana Wong, Wong Siu-lun, Ron Skeldon, Ben Cariño, Paul Spoonley, Dick Bedford, Vijay Naidu and other colleagues in the Asia Pacific Migration Research Network have helped me to begin studying this huge and complex region. The support of the UNESCO-MOST (Management of Social

Transformations) programme, and particularly of Ali Kazancigil and Nadia Auriat, has been vital to developing my research in Asia and the Pacific. Ellie Vasta has been my close collaborator and strongest critic for many years.

I thank all the many publishers with whom I have worked over the years. Good publishers play a vital role in commissioning work, encouraging authors, helping to make complex ideas accessible and stimulating, and in choosing good titles for books. This is one reason why quick-fix electronic media will never replace the book. The idea for this book came from Chris Rojek of Sage Publications, who was highly encouraging (and patient) throughout the process of putting it together.

I also thank my colleagues at the University of Wollongong, especially within the Centre for Multicultural Studies and then the Migration and Multicultural Studies Program, for their great support. Kim Oborn helped make texts of diverse formats into a coherent manuscript. Colleen Mitchell did a wonderful job of editing and formatting the final text, despite persistent attacks by computer viruses.

ACKNOWLEDGEMENTS

The author and publishers wish to thank the following for permission to use copyright material:

Allen and Unwin for S. Castles, 'The racisms of globalisation', in E. Vasta and S. Castles (eds), *The Teeth are Smiling: the Persistence of Racism in Multicultural Australia* (Sydney, Allen and Unwin, 1996), pp. 17–45.

Berg for S. Castles, 'Migration and minorities in Europe: perspectives for the 1990s – eleven hypotheses', in J. Wrench and J. Solomos (eds), *Racism and Migration in Western Europe* (Oxford, Berg, 1993), pp. 17–34.

Blackwell Publishers and UNESCO (Paris) for S. Castles, 'Globalisation and migration: some pressing contradictions', *International Social Science Journal*, 156 (1998), pp. 179–86.

Cambridge University Press for S. Castles, 'Contract labour migration', in R. Cohen (ed.), *The Cambridge Survey of World Migration* (Cambridge, Cambridge University Press, 1995), pp. 510–14.

The Center for Migration Studies (New York) for S. Castles, 'The guest-worker in Western Europe: an obituary', *International Migration Review*, 20 (4) (1986), pp. 761–78.

The Guardian for S. Castles, 'Bidonville – a French word for Hell' (14 January 1970).

The Institute of Race Relations (London) for S. Castles, 'The social time-bomb: education of an underclass in West Germany', *Race and Class*, 21 (4) (1980), pp. 369–87.

Macmillan Press for S. Castles, 'Multicultural citizenship: the Australian experience', in V. Bader (ed.), *Citizenship and Exclusion* (London, Macmillan, and St. Martin's Press Inc., 1997), pp. 113–38, and for S. Castles, 'Citizenship and the Other in the age of migration', in A. Davidson and K. Weekley (eds), *Globalization and Citizenship in the Asia-Pacific* (London, Macmillan, 1999), pp. 27–48.

New Left Review for S. Castles and G. Kosack, 'The function of labour immigration in Western European capitalism', *New Left Review*, 73 (May/June 1972), pp. 3–21.

The University of Queensland and the Editors of *Social Alternatives* for S. Castles, 'Explaining racism in the new Germany', *Social Alternatives*, 12 (1993), pp. 9–12.

PART I

INTRODUCTION

1

THIRTY YEARS OF RESEARCH ON MIGRATION AND MULTICULTURAL SOCIETIES

I began researching international migration in 1968. As part of a masters course in contemporary European studies at the University of Sussex, I wrote a 35,000 word dissertation entitled 'Social aspects of the mobility of labour: foreign workers in the German Federal Republic' (Castles 1968). Gathering data in Frankfurt am Main and West Berlin was pretty exciting for this was the height of the May 1968 student movement, with daily demonstrations, sit-ins and mass meetings. I spent my days interviewing trade-union officials, employers and social workers, and my evenings attending teach-ins (and some very good parties) at Frankfurt University, which was occupied by the socialist students and surrounded by helmeted pickets to keep out possible right-wing intruders. These were heady days, marked by an innocence which was soon to be lost in the increasingly violent confrontations of the 1970s. Everything still seemed possible; one had only to blow away the 'mould of a thousand years' (as one famous poster put it) and a new society could emerge, bringing sexual emancipation, education and fulfilling employment for all.

It was typical of the time that southern European and Turkish foreign workers were seen by many on the left as a potential new working-class vanguard. Their militancy and spontaneity were a breath of fresh air, especially in West Germany, with its huge, centralized trade unions and ritualized annual industrial disputes. In the early 1970s, young intellectuals like Joschka Fischer (who was to become Germany's first Green Foreign Minister in 1998) went to work at the Opel-Rüsselsheim car factory to learn from the Italian militants of *Lotta Continua* and *Potere Operaio*. As important as the migrants' political culture was their colourful and gregarious lifestyle, as expressed in the street festivals they started in the 1970s. These were first viewed with suspicion by Germans, but by the 1980s they would be run by neighbourhood groups all over the country, as part of a rejuvenated urban culture. The roots of multiculturalism lie in such experiences.

Before going to Sussex University, I had studied sociology from 1963 to 1966 at the Frankfurt Institute of Social Research, then still run by the grand old men of the Frankfurt School, Max Horkheimer and Theodor Adorno, and their successor, Jürgen Habermas. In accordance with the Frankfurt School principle of analysing society as a totality, it seemed evident that labour migration to the Federal Republic of Germany (FRG) was a result of the dramatic economic and social changes brought about by the German economic miracle, and that it would in turn become a major factor of social and cultural change in itself. This was not a popular view in Germany, where policy-makers, employers and unions all saw the recruitment of 'guest-workers' as a temporary expedient – an economic buffer of labour which could be brought in as needed and sent away to 'export unemployment' if growth ever flagged. However, coming back to Sussex to write up my research, I soon came up against another conceptual issue. It seemed clear that foreign workers in Germany were doing the same unskilled and unpopular jobs as black workers in Britain. Yet British social scientists studying new Commonwealth immigration seemed totally uninterested in what was happening 'on the Continent' (of course, the British were notoriously insular and bad at foreign languages in those pre-European Union days). Comparative researchers took their evidence from South Africa or the southern states of the USA, rather than looking across the Channel. They therefore emphasized skin colour and used social-psychological concepts such as the 'dark stranger', prejudice or race relations, rather than looking at the socio-economic position of migrant workers within contemporary societies.

I and my then partner and collaborator Godula Kosack observed that immigrant workers were doing the same type of work and taking on similar societal positions throughout Western Europe. This led us to argue that immigration had structural causes inherent in the political economy of post-war capitalism, and was likely to have effects which transcended national differences. From this arose our interlinked Doctor of Philosophy (D Phil) projects, which involved a comparative study of immigrant workers and their effects on society in Britain, the German Federal Republic, France and Switzerland – the four main immigrant-receiving countries of Europe. This (in retrospect absurdly ambitious) project was a great deal of fun. We drove around Europe in an old van for months at a time, spending our mornings writing hundreds of index cards (this was before cheap photocopying) in the specialized libraries of ministries, research institutes, welfare organizations, trade unions and international organizations. The afternoons we spent visiting building sites, factories, workers' hostels or shanty-towns, in order to talk to migrant workers and their families. The long conversations over tea in Moroccan workers' shacks in the Parisian suburbs, or over a beer in a cheap bar near the depressing huts in which Spanish workers were housed in Geneva, gave human meaning to all the dry statistics and endless bureaucratic reports we had to work through. (A flavour of our experiences is given in the article 'Bidonville – a French word for Hell' published by the *Guardian* in January 1970, and reproduced on pp. 4–6). John Berger and Jean Mohr's famous portrayal of the migrant worker's condition through stories, photographs and poetry, *A Seventh Man* (Berger and Mohr 1975), is still worth reading today.

We also drove south to visit the countries of origin: a Spain still marked by grinding rural poverty, repression of urban workers and the constant terror of the Franco dictatorship; Algeria with its veiled women, unemployed youth and a pervading feeling of tension and aggression remaining from the recent war of liberation (reading Frantz Fanon helped us understand it, but did not make us feel any safer); southern Italy, with its railway stations crowded with departing men with cardboard suitcases, but also where the half-finished shells of migrant workers' houses built bit by bit during their holidays were beginning to sprout from the ground.

One result of all this was the book *Immigrant Workers and Class Structure in Western Europe* (Castles and Kosack 1973, 2nd edn 1985), which was to help change the way in which social scientists conceptualized migration. Another result was a strong and abiding interest on my part in international migration, as well as a passionate concern to expose the injustices brought about by exploitation of immigrants and racism against minorities. Since then, international migration and its consequences – the emergence of multicultural societies and transnational identities – has been the main theme of my work as a social scientist, whether in Britain, Germany, Australia or South-east Asia. Another continuity has been my use of an interdisciplinary comparative approach to understanding migration.

This book sums up my work on international migration, multicultural societies, racism and citizenship through a selection of essays written and published over three decades. The three chapters of Part II deal with the early period of migration and settlement after the Second World War, while the rest of the book is concerned with more recent developments, especially since the 1980s. The collection reflects the phases of development of global population mobility, as well as shifts in the social-scientific frameworks used to analyse these phenomena. Obviously, the essays also reflect my own intellectual development and the way in which this has been linked both to social change and paradigm shifts. The purpose of this Introduction is to trace these linkages. The next three sections contextualize the essays, roughly following the three main parts of the book, while the final section discusses some of the conceptual barriers which have bedevilled social-scientific research on migration and multicultural societies.

BIDONVILLE: A FRENCH WORD FOR HELL (1970)

The Ministry of the Interior has estimated that there are 75,346 people living in *bidonvilles* throughout France. A *bidonville* (the name comes from *bidons* – petrol cans – hammered flat to provide building material) is a 'group of light constructions erected on unprepared land, whether closed off or not, with materials found by chance'. The official figures probably underestimate the problem considerably because *bidonville* residents often do not give accurate answers to the census-takers as they are afraid of any form of officialdom and their papers are frequently not in order. *Bidonvilles* tend to spring up wherever there is a big building project, usually on the outskirts of cities. Thirty-five per cent of building workers in France are foreigners and normal housing is often unobtainable for them. This explains the paradox that *bidonvilles* are usually near modern housing developments.

When a homeless family or group of male immigrants moves into a *bidonville* their first dwelling is often an old truck or bus which has been dumped. At La Courneuve, in the northern suburbs of Paris, whole Yugoslav families with three or four children live in small delivery vans. These are the most recent arrivals. Once established, they collect building materials – corrugated iron, discarded planks, hardboard – and build a shack. Those who have been there longest (up to 15 years in some cases) even have some brick walls. From a high vantage point, the *bidonville* looks like a rubbish dump, for the inhabitants pile any available material round their walls and on their roofs in a vain attempt to keep out wet and cold. There are no sanitary amenities of any kind. The open sewers which develop are a constant danger to health. In some areas the local authorities have been persuaded to collect refuse from time to time; in others there is simply an ever-growing heap. At Nanterre one *bidonville* of more than 1,000 North Africans shares a single water tap with a nearby Portuguese 'village'.

Once a family has been reduced to living in a *bidonville*, a vicious circle tends to keep it there. Frequent illness caused by the bad housing conditions, and bad time-keeping caused by lack of transport, make it difficult for a man to keep a good job. Soon, employers come to know the addresses of *bidonvilles* and will not employ men giving them (which leads to a profitable trade in phoney domicile certificates issued by unscrupulous hoteliers).

Bidonvilles tend to develop their own forms of communal existence, which makes life somewhat less unbearable, but which, on the other hand, causes difficulties with regard to re-housing and integration into French society. To some extent, immigrants living in *bidonvilles* are able to maintain the patterns of life of their own countries. The men have to adapt to urban-industrial conditions at work, but the *bidonville* is a ghetto in which they and their families are completely isolated from other aspects of French society.

In an entirely North African *bidonville* it is possible to maintain the extended family structure with three generations (and sometimes animals) living under one roof. The high birth rate also persists – a child a year up to a total of six or eight children. So does the complete subordination of women, who are often not allowed to leave the *bidonville* even to go shopping, let alone to take a job. Many of them do not speak the language after several years in France.

At Champigny, about 10,000 Portuguese have a completely independent community. Here the shacks are fairly well built. Many have their own water taps outside and most have electricity. But even where communal solidarity has somewhat improved matters, nobody lives in a *bidonville* from choice. In the country with the worst housing shortage in Western Europe, the 2.5 million immigrants are at the end of the queue for every type of accommodation. Since the war, French government policy has encouraged large families and immigration, but has done little to provide housing for the resulting population growth. Today it is estimated that it would be necessary to build 600,000 dwellings (half of them with public money) a year for twenty years to make up the deficiency.

For several years the French government has carried out a programme for clearing away the *bidonvilles* through a special fund (*Le fonds d'action sociale pour les travailleurs migrants* – FAS). About two-thirds of the money for this fund comes from the immigrants themselves in the form of deductions from family allowances when the children remain in the country of origin. For example, in 1967 a French worker with five children got 531 francs a month in family allowances. His Portuguese colleague with five children at home got 89 francs, i.e. the amount he would have been entitled to if working in Portugal. The difference went to the FAS.

Since 1959, the FAS has helped to finance about 60,000 hostel beds for workers whose families are not in France. This is only a fraction of the number needed, but even if they do have the opportunity many immigrants are unwilling to move into such hostels. Apart from restrictions in some hostels (no visitors, lights out at a fixed time), the rent of between 60 and 120 francs a month is too high for men who have to support families at home. Some hostels are built much too far away from the places of work. Organizations representing immigrants have demanded a say in the running of the FAS, and protest at having to pay twice for the accommodation – once through their compulsory contributions to the FAS and again in the form of rent. The FAS housing programme for single men also creates racial segregation as there are separate hostels for black Africans.

> The FAS also gives subsidies to provide family housing for immigrants. But the proportion of foreigners in a housing development is not allowed to exceed 15 per cent to avoid conflict and the growth of separate communities. Often, foreigners from *bidonvilles* are not immediately re-housed in normal flats, but are sent first to *cités de transit* (transit centres). The idea is that they are unused to modern urban housing, having come straight from a backward rural area to the *bidonville*. In the *cité de transit* they are supposed to get used to modern sanitary facilities and housekeeping methods under the guidance of social workers, before moving on to normal flats after a year or two. In fact, immigrant families tend to stay much longer in the *cités*. New flats are just not available for them and there are not enough social workers. The *cités* – usually wooden huts – become forgotten ghettos, finally to form nuclei for new *bidonvilles*.
>
> *Guardian* (14 January 1970)

Western Europe: the guests who stayed

The period from 1945 to the mid-1970s (known in France by the evocative term of *les trente glorieuses* – the thirty glorious years) was a time of rapid growth and widespread prosperity for the old industrial nations. This was possible due to their financial and technological dominance and the lack of serious competition from the rest of the world. The need to main-tain legitimacy in the face of the alternative political model provided by the Soviet bloc led to Keynesian anti-cyclical policies, full employment and the construction of welfare states. After the trauma of the Great Depression, fascism and the war, everything had to be done to maintain economic growth and reduce class conflict. Under these conditions, employers faced serious difficulty in securing additional labour for expansion, while at the same time preventing wage inflation which might bring about recession. An important study in the mid-1960s showed the approaches used in various countries to obtain adequate labour supplies (Kindleberger 1967), such as the transfer of labour from agriculture to industry and increasing female labour force participation. The most suc-cessful economies were those with abundant labour supplies: the German economic miracle could partly be explained by the presence of some 9 million expellees from former eastern parts of Germany annexed by the Soviet Union and Poland. But Germany's labour surplus was soon absorbed into industry, and most Western European countries lacked such reserves.

The same solution was adopted everywhere: the import of labour from the less-developed European periphery (Mediterranean countries, Ireland and Finland), or from more distant Third World countries, became a cru-cial factor in economic growth in all the core industrial economies. However, the form taken by labour import varied according to historical circumstances. Britain, France and The Netherlands could make use of labour from their colonies or former colonies. The political and cultural linkages created by colonialism made it possible readily to obtain low-skilled labour, usually without the need for specific recruiting systems. Information on the work opportunities in the 'mother-country', together with the availability of transport and the right to free movement, were sufficient to start and sustain migratory flows. By contrast, such countries as Germany, Switzerland, Belgium and Sweden had no access to colonial labour. Instead they set up labour recruitment systems to bring in temporary foreign workers, who were given permission to stay only as long as their labour was needed. The most developed of all these arrangements was the German 'guest-worker' system. Even the post-colonial powers used Mediterranean workers when colonial workers were insufficient in number. By the 1960s, migrant labour had become a structural feature of Western European labour markets. Abundant labour with low social costs was a vital factor in the long boom. This paved the way for subsequent family reunion and permanent settlement that was to lead to the multi-cultural Europe we know today.

In retrospect the most surprising feature of all this was the fact that neither policy-makers nor social scientists showed much foresight or concern about possible long-term consequences. Foreign workers were not expected to settle, and it was assumed that they could easily be sent home in the event of a recession. The only exception was Britain, where economic stagnation, anti-immigrant movements and growing unrest (notably the Notting Hill Riots of 1958) led to the 1962 Commonwealth Immigrants Act, which severely curtailed labour migration from the West Indies, India and Pakistan. Chapter 2, 'The Function of Labour Migration in Western European Capitalism' (co-authored with Godula Kosack and originally published in *New Left Review* in 1972) can be seen as an overview of this period, and a summary of *Immigrant Workers and Class Structure in Western Europe* (Castles and Kosack 1973). Reflecting its time, the chapter uses the terminology of Marxist political economy and class analysis in a way that neither I nor most of my contemporaries would subscribe to today. None the less, the analysis makes some important points on the economic and societal functions of migrant labour, which are beginning to seem relevant again in the light of the current Asian crisis.

These early works focused on Western Europe. The USA, Canada and Australia also experienced considerable immigration in this period, though in rather different forms. Australia initiated a mass immigration programme after 1945 because policy-makers believed that the population of 7.5 million needed to be increased for both economic and strategic reasons. The initial target was 70,000 migrants per year and a ratio of ten British migrants to every 'foreigner'. However, it proved impossible to attract enough British migrants, and recruitment was extended first to northern and Eastern Europe, and then to southern Europe. Non-Europeans were not admitted at all: the White Australia policy was still in force, and Asian immigration was seen as a potential threat to Australia's survival as a 'European nation'. The policy was one of permanent immigration: newcomers were expected to bring in their families, settle and be assimilated into society as 'new Australians'. None the less, the aim of the immigration programme was primarily to recruit labour for Australia's new factories and infrastructure projects. By the 1970s, manufacturing industry relied heavily on migrant labour and factory jobs were popularly known as 'migrant work' (Collins 1991). Canada followed similar policies of mass immigration. At first only Europeans were admitted. Most entrants were British, but Eastern and southern Europeans soon played an increasing role. Family entry was encouraged, and immigrants were seen as settlers and future citizens.

Large-scale migration to the USA developed rather later, owing to the restrictive immigration laws enacted in the 1920s. Intakes averaged 250,000 persons annually in the period 1951–60, and 330,000 annually from 1961 to 1970 – far less than in the great immigration waves of the period 1870–1914. However, agricultural employers recruited temporary migrant workers from Mexico and the Caribbean. Government policies varied: at times, systems of temporary labour recruitment, such as the Mexican *bracero* programme of the 1940s, were introduced; in other periods, recruitment was formally prohibited, but tacitly tolerated, leading to the presence of a large number of illegal workers. The short-term perspective was very like that which governed European 'guest-worker' recruitment: the Mexican workers were seen as temporary flexible labour, and were not expected to settle. The big change in US immigration came with the 1965 amendments to the Immigration and Nationality Act. These were seen as part of the civil rights legislation of the period, designed to remove the discriminatory national-origins quota system. They were not expected or intended to lead to large-scale non-European immigration. In fact, the amendments created a system of worldwide immigration, in which the most important criterion for admission was kinship with US citizens or residents (Borjas 1990; Portes and Rumbaut 1990). The result was to be a dramatic upsurge in migration from Asia and Latin America.

The overwhelming impression of the period 1945–73 is thus of a short-term economic approach: migrants were seen simply as workers whose labour was needed, while their social needs and their potential impact on receiving societies were largely ignored. There was little understanding that migration was a social process that could develop its own dynamics, which might confound the expectations of even the most efficient states. The 'guest-worker' recruiting countries wanted labour, not people, but were to end up with new ethnic minorities. By contrast, both Europe's former colonial powers and the New World countries did see immigrants as settlers, but they did not expect migration to go on proliferating and diversifying. Australia, for instance, regarded immigration as a way of strengthening the population and economy, to keep the country white and British. As subsequent events were to show, the result was to be the opposite – one of the most ethnically diverse societies in the world.

Changes in migratory patterns were precipitated by the oil crisis of 1973, which marked the end of *les trente glorieuses* and the acceleration of major shifts in the global political economy. In the subsequent period, major corporations became transnational and moved their investments away from the high-wage economies of the old industrial heartland to low-wage export zones in the Third World. New industrial economies emerged in Asia and Latin America, while employment stagnated in the 'rustbelt' industries of the West. The electronic revolution and new modes of business organization changed the nature of work, eroding old skills and wiping out the security of the unionized blue-collar working class. The new casualized labour market pitted women and migrant workers against deskilled male workers, eroding wages and conditions for all. The victorious neo-classical ideology of monetarism preached deregulation, a small state and the demolition of welfare systems.

I spent most of the period from 1971 to 1986 teaching political economy at the *Fachhochschule* (polytechnic) of Frankfurt am Main. Migration remained my main interest, apart from a foray into the sociology of education which led to a book (Castles and Wüstenberg 1979), two years working in community education in Bristol and a year working for the Foundation for Education with Production in Botswana and Zimbabwe. Frankfurt was a good vantage point for observing changes in migratory patterns. Training social workers to work with immigrant youth quickly brought home the realities of settlement and minority formation. Much of my work at this time was concerned with Germany, although always in comparison with other European countries.

In November 1973, the German federal government abruptly stopped labour recruitment – an action to be followed by most Western European governments within the next twelve months. It was expected that large numbers of migrant workers would go home, allowing the export of unemployment – always seen as a potential benefit of the 'guest-worker' system. Although many did leave, the majority stayed. Family reunion gathered momentum and trends towards long-term settlement became obvious. Now attention shifted to the growing number of immigrant children entering European schools which were poorly prepared for this challenge. The media began to portray immigrant youth as a potential threat to public order. Chapter 3, 'The Social Time Bomb: Education of an Underclass in West Germany' (first published in *Race and Class* in 1980) uses the example of Germany to analyse trends in settlement, demographic normalization and intergenerational change among immigrant populations throughout Europe. The argument is that discriminatory educational policies were tending to reproduce the disadvantaged class position of immigrant workers for the next generation, providing European societies both with low-skilled labour and with scapegoats for the likely social problems of the future – an analysis which was to be confirmed by the events of the 1990s.

The final contribution in Part II is a retrospective analysis of the post-war labour recruitment system: 'The Guest-worker in Western Europe: an Obituary' (Chapter 4, first published in *International Migration Review* in 1986). This can be read as a summary of my book on the transition from labour migration to minority formation, *Here for Good: Western Europe's New Ethnic Minorities* (Castles et al. 1984). The chapter gives a country-by-country account of labour recruitment systems, showing how each one failed in its aim of preventing permanent settlement, paving the way for the multi-ethnic societies which were to prove so challenging for Western Europe. These developments are put in the context of a changing global political economy, already beginning to give rise to quite new forms of mobility.

The globalization of migration

In 1986 I moved to Australia to take up the post of director of the Centre for Multicultural Studies at the University of Wollongong. In a sense, I was a returning migrant myself, since I was born in Australia in 1944, but my parents had moved back to England in 1946, and I had grown up there. One reason for the move was my interest in the multicultural policies then being developed as a response to the failure of assimilationism and the emergence of a culturally diverse society in Australia. But the move also broadened my perspectives on migration, allowing me to compare the effects of permanent settler movements to Australia with European labour recruitment, and then to contrast both with the new forms of population mobility emerging in Asia and elsewhere. Like many observers at the time, I became increasingly aware that economic globalization also meant the globalization of population mobility. The four contributions in Part III describe and analyse various facets of the new migrations of the 1980s and 1990s.

'Migrations and Minorities in Europe: Perspectives for the 1990s – Eleven Hypotheses' (Chapter 5, originally published in Wrench and Solomos 1993) was written for a conference in 1991, and may be seen as a first draft for some of the ideas later developed by Mark Miller and myself in *The Age of Migration* (Castles and Miller 1993). The mid-1970s to the mid-1980s had been a time of stabilization of immigrant populations in Western Europe. Low levels of labour migration and trends to settlement and community formation had led to improvements in legal and social status, opening the way for debates on cultural pluralism and multicultural education. But events of the late 1980s and early 1990s were to change all this. The disintegration of the Soviet bloc and the end of the Cold War combined with rapid economic and social change in many Third World countries to produce vast new population flows. Some took the form of organized labour recruitment, but far more significant were the large flows of asylum-seekers and undocumented workers to

Western Europe and North America. The world's media showed dramatic scenes – such as the desperate attempts of Albanians to reach Italy in a flotilla of decrepit ships, or the interception by the US coastguard of Haitians trying to sail to Florida – which caused widespread fears of a mass influx of impoverished people who might undermine the prosperity of the West. This led to the emergence of anti-immigrant movements, tighter border controls and intergovernmental agreements to reduce the number of asylum-seekers and illegal entrants. Chapter 5 seeks to put all these developments into a global perspective, using the form of hypotheses to raise a wide range of questions in a speculative way.

Chapter 6 on 'Contract Labour Migration' (originally published in Cohen 1995) is a global overview of migrant labour recruitment systems. Such systems generally impose restrictions on the rights of migrants compared with other workers, and thus create a new form of 'unfree labour'. Historical antecedents include slavery, indentured labour and systems for control of foreign labour pioneered in Germany before the First World War. Western Europe's 'guest-workers' were contract labour – just like the Mexican *braceros* recruited for US agribusiness. The latter case shows the closeness between contract labour systems and undocumented flows: when the *bracero* programme was stopped in 1964, illegal migration quickly replaced it. Contract labour is a good example of the globalization of migration. This type of recruitment grew rapidly after 1973 as oil-rich countries hired ex-patriate experts and low-skilled manual workers to carry out their ambitious programmes of infrastructure development, construction and industrialization. Contract labour systems meant a very high degree of control over workers, designed to maintain a docile labour force and prevent settlement. Soon such contract labour systems spread to Asia's 'tiger economies', which were rapidly running into labour shortages as their economies soared. An important trend of the 1990s was the feminization of migrant labour: more and more women were recruited as domestic workers, entertainers and factory employees. The lack of rights typical of contract labour arrangements increased women's vulnerability to exploitation and sexual abuse, while conditions for undocumented women migrants were often even worse.

The growth of migration up to 1997 was a major factor in the 'Asian miracle'. Millions of Asians moved to North America, Australia, New Zealand and Europe, but even more migrated within Asia. Fast economic growth in certain countries was accompanied by declines in fertility and population growth. As opportunities for educational and occupational mobility for the populations of the 'tiger economies' grew, there was a lack of labour for the '3-D jobs' (dirty, difficult and dangerous). These were filled by migrant workers, both legal and illegal. Countries with slower economic growth but greater demographic growth became labour reserves. I became more deeply involved in the study of Asian migration through the establishment in 1995 of the Asia Pacific Migration Research Network (APMRN). This academic network, which covered eleven countries by 1998, is part of the UNESCO-MOST (Management of Social Transformations) programme, and is coordinated by myself and my colleagues at the University of Wollongong.

The rapid growth in Asian migration was inextricably linked to the rapid economic and social changes in the region connected with decolonization and globalization. When the 'Asian miracle' was suddenly interrupted in 1997 by a deep financial and economic crisis, this inevitably had serious repercussions for migrant workers and their families. However, the complete stop in labour migration and the mass repatriation of migrant workers expected by many did not take place. As in Western Europe a generation earlier, the results of the crisis look likely to be far more complex and ambiguous. Chapter 7, 'Migration in the Asian Pacific Region: Before and After the Crisis' (especially written for this volume, though partly based on an article published in UNESCO's *International Social Science Journal* in 1998) examines the development of Asian migration up to 1997 and discusses new trends in migration and settlement which may emerge from the crisis.

The brief essay which concludes Part III (Chapter 8, 'Globalization and Migration: Some Pressing Contradictions', first published in 1998 in the *International Social Science Journal*) is an attempt to link trends in international migration to some of the fundamental problems inherent in globalization. The argument is that migration plays a key part in most contemporary social transformations. It is both a result of economic, social, cultural and political change, and a powerful factor precipitating further change. The often disadvantaged position of migrant workers and their families reveals much about the dialectic of inclusion and exclusion, which is so typical of the new global (dis)order. Millions of people work and live in countries where they cannot become citizens. Often they have multiple identities and feel that they belong both in the country of origin and the country of residence. Such developments undermine the nation-state principle of singular and exclusive membership. These considerations form a bridge to the theme of Part IV of this book.

Multicultural societies as a challenge to the nation-state

When I arrived in Australia in 1986, I was fascinated by the way in which culture and identity were being reshaped in the highly diverse society that had resulted from post-war migration: 23 per cent of the population were immigrants from well over a hundred countries, while a further 20 per cent of the population were children of immigrants. My first attempt to analyse this, together with my colleagues at the Centre for Multicultural Studies, was the book *Mistaken Identity* (Castles et al. 1992), published as a critical contribution to the 1988 bicentenary of white settlement (see also Castles et al. 1988). At this time, Australia appeared to be not only one of the most ethnically diverse countries, but also one which had done much to recognize cultural diversity and to guarantee social justice for all members of society irrespective of their origins. There were major anomalies, such as the continuing marginalization of Aboriginal people and the persistence of racism against immigrants, but on the whole Australian multiculturalism seemed a model which could hold useful lessons for other countries looking for ways to manage diversity.

Parallel to my work on global migration, I therefore started to study multiculturalism and its meaning for citizenship and the nation-state. An important sub-theme was racism. The four chapters of Part IV are concerned with these issues. 'Multicultural Citizenship: the Australian Experience' (Chapter 9, first published in Bader 1997) starts by looking at differing models for managing diversity: differential exclusion (the German approach), assimilation (the French approach); and pluralism (as applied in classical immigration countries like Australia and the USA, but also in Sweden). The chapter goes on to examine the dilemmas posed for democracy by ethnic difference in view of the historical link between political membership and ethno-cultural belonging inherent in the nation-state. This discussion leads to a set of principles for 'multicultural citizenship'. An examination of the Australian situation shows that the policy statements of the 1983-96 Labor government embodied many of these principles, but that there was a big gap between the rhetoric and actual implementation: empirical data showed the continued exclusion of Aboriginal people and immigrants from positions of economic and political power. Since then, the Australian model has been much eroded as the Liberal–National coalition, which came to power in 1996, has abolished many of the agencies and social services vital to multiculturalism.

European debates on how to deal with the political and social exclusion of the new minorities took on a new character in the early 1990s as a result of the rise of extreme-right organizations, which used racism as their main instrument of mobilization. Similar trends were to appear in Australia from 1996 with the development of Pauline Hanson's One Nation Party. The anti-immigrant violence of neo-Nazis and skinheads in post-reunification Germany aroused international concern, although it was actually no worse than what had been happening in Britain and France for years. 'Explaining Racism in the New Germany' (Chapter 10, originally published in 1993 in *Social Alternatives*) seeks to understand the upsurge in racism by reviewing the explanations put forward by German social scientists. The chapter concludes that Germany, like other Western countries, is going through a 'crisis of modernization', which is partly expressed through racism and racist violence. However, Germany also has some unique features linked to its turbulent recent past and the sudden and poorly planned character of reunification. Racism has to be explained by a holistic analysis which includes the history of nationalism and the character of citizenship, as well as economic, social and cultural factors which lead to the alienation of large sections of youth.

Chapter 11, 'The Racisms of Globalization' (originally published in Vasta and Castles 1996), seeks to deepen the analysis of racism by linking it to global change and by examining its main forms throughout the world. Racism is examined as a set of practices and discourses deeply rooted in the history and culture of modernity. Racism plays a crucial role in consolidating nation-states and is closely linked to sexism and class domination. Racism does not contradict democracy – rather, it helps to consolidate the boundaries of democratic polities by defining who does not belong and can therefore be excluded from universalistic principles. That is why the nation-state finds it so hard to accept the principle of multicultural belonging. The central argument of the chapter is that globalization leads to fundamental societal changes, which are experienced as crises of the national economy and social relations, as crises of culture and identity, and as political crises. The groups most threatened by these crises – typically the poorer and less-educated strata of society – lack the information required to make sense of these developments and the political agency needed to take action to deal with them. Since most major political forces support the conventional wisdom of deregulation and economic restructuring, disadvantaged groups tend to turn their anger against the most visible signs of change: old and new ethnic minorities. Racism has thus become an emblem of resistance for disempowered groups in increasingly polarized societies. However, many political leaders are willing to make political capital out of racism, if it suits their aims.

Chapter 12, 'Citizenship and the Other in the Age of Migration' (first published in Davidson and Weekley 1999), is an attempt to work through the problems of citizenship at a time of erosion of nation-state boundaries. International migration is just one of the globalizing forces, but an important one because the 'immigration of the irreducible Other' exacerbates the already-existing contradictions of the nation-state model at a time when it is in any case under strong challenge. The chapter goes on to discuss the various responses to these dilemmas, including the reform of citizenship laws and new debates on the civil, political and social rights conferred by the status of citizenship. The argument is that, under conditions of global migration and increasing diversity, these traditional rights are no longer adequate, and new categories of gender rights and cultural rights need to be added. Multicultural societies are marked by simultaneous processes of racialization of difference and formation of minority communities as a basis for resistance and mobilization. The solution may lie in new forms of multicultural and transnational citizenship, but such principles often meet with bitter opposition. Change is likely to be a long-drawn-out and uneven process involving political mobilization by the new social groups now being constituted in multicultural societies. The outcome is uncertain, but it seems clear that the migrations and growing cultural diversity of the past half-century are not going to leave social relations and political institutions unchanged.

The fragmentation of research on migration and multicultural societies

This final section of the Introduction examines the way in which social scientists have responded to the changes outlined above. Perceptions and understandings of migration and its consequences have been shaped not only by actual patterns of population mobility, settlement and community formation, but also by powerful factors inherent in the way social-scientific research is organized, carried out and interpreted in contemporary societies. Entrenched (and sometimes unconscious) assumptions and preconceptions undermine claims to scientific objectivity and often constitute barriers to a full understanding of the phenomenon. The result is a fragmentation of research, which has several aspects:

- Loss of comprehension of the overall migratory process through its *division into a number of fields of study.*
- The *compartmentalization* of social-scientific and policy discourses.
- *National models* which shape underlying ideas on migration and its meaning for society, with the result that researchers tend to choose questions, methods and interpretations conducive to the reproduction of prevailing ideologies.
- *Disciplinary boundaries* which can lead to one-sidedness in choice of research topics, methods and interpretations.
- The *paradigmatic closure* often embodied in such approaches as functionalism, Marxist political economy, human capital theory or post-modern cultural theory.

These points all need more explanation.

Division into fields of study

This refers to the social-scientific division of labour between researchers who splinter an all-embracing human experience into relatively autonomous research areas such as migration, ethnicity, racism, multiculturalism, transnational communities, identity construction and citizenship. Each of these has become a field of study in its own right, with distinct theories, bodies of literature, research centres, journals and specialized courses at universities. Each of these fields claims to be multidisciplinary, although with certain disciplines playing a greater role than others: for instance, migration studies has been dominated by geography and economics, although with the increasing involvement of law, sociology and political science in recent years; ethnic studies has been the domain of anthropologists and sociologists; the study of multiculturalism has involved cultural studies, linguistics, philosophy and public policy.

This fragmentation into fields of study conflicts with the lived reality of migrants, who experience migration, settlement, ethnic relations, public policies, language issues and identity construction as closely related and overlapping segments of a single process. This dynamic whole may be referred to as the *migratory process*, a term which underlines the fact that migration is not a single event (i.e. the crossing of a border) but a life-long process which affects all aspects of a migrant's existence, as well as the lives of non-migrants and communities in both sending and receiving countries. The notion of the migratory process as a whole should be a basic epistemological principle and a starting-point for any study of migration, even if most specific pieces of empirical research only deal with one (or a few) segments of the process.

Fragmentation also results from discontinuities in migration research over time. Several observers point to the existence of 'waves' of comparative research, which correspond to different periods in the evolution of the migratory movements themselves (King 1996; Messina 1996). In the case of Western Europe, waves of major research activity were the early 1970s to the early 1980s, and then the beginning of the 1990s. Since research was driven by policy considerations as well as by public perceptions (for instance, fears of mass immigration), comparative study of international migration became a priority in certain periods, leading to a plethora of conferences, reports and books, but then went out of fashion once politics moved on to other issues. Such discontinuities hinder the emergence of an agreed body of knowledge and theory, with the result that new researchers often seem to be starting from scratch, with little awareness of previous work.

Compartmentalization

Literature and discourse on migration and its consequences are often divided up according to the purpose of research or the goals of funding bodies, so that researchers often have little interchange or even knowledge of each other's work. Messina refers to 'four distinct but clearly interrelated literatures' just for European migration in the 1990s: 'immigration policy studies, political economy of migration, immigration fallout and immigrant incorporation literature' (Messina 1996: 132). The net can be cast much wider. Researchers studying migration to developed countries often know little of the empirical and theoretical work being done on migration and development in Africa, Asia and Latin America. Although there are important differences, greater interchange of theoretical and methodological ideas would be fruitful. Similarly, many academics make little use of the valuable statistical material and analyses produced by national government agencies and international organizations such as the International Labour Office (ILO), the Organization for Economic Cooperation and Development (OECD) or the International Organization for Migration (IOM). In turn, the officials of governments and international organizations often make little use of academic work. This division is based partly on differing research goals: policy-makers seek primarily descriptive data which can readily inform administrative decisions, while academics are more interested in analytical and theoretical knowledge.

One of the most significant divisions in migration studies is that between internal and international migration. Skeldon argues that 'two almost separate traditions have evolved and those researching in one part of the subject rarely have anything to do with those in the other' (Skeldon 1997: 9–10). The reason for the split is that the two types of research are driven by differing policy considerations and use largely separate data sources, yet there is no doubt that it is an artificial division that hinders our understanding of the many cases in which international migration develops as a continuation of internal migration. As in so many aspects of migration research, the interests of the nation-state in controlling borders have set research priorities, with negative consequences for social-scientific understanding.

National models

Indeed, the tunnel vision brought about by national models appears as one of the main barriers to understanding in migration research. Fundamental ideas on the nature of migration and its consequences for society arise from nationally specific historical experiences of population mobility and cultural diversity. Past experiences with internal ethnic minorities, colo-nized peoples and migrant labour recruited during industrialization play a major role in shaping current attitudes and practices. Historical prece-dents lead to stereotypes and practices which are often deeply embedded in political and cultural discourses, so that they have become an unques-tioned 'common sense' (Goldberg 1993: 41–3), which affects even the most critical researchers. Such national ideologies affect government policies on migration research, shape the questions asked by migration researchers and influence modes of explanation and analysis. A look at any major migration country will show the importance of such national models, as I have discussed elsewhere (see Castles 1985, 1990, 1995; Castles and Miller 1998: chs 8 and 9; Castles et al. 1992). Each country has diverse and even contradictory elements in its perception of migration. There is no space for detailed accounts here but a few examples can be given.

France has a national myth of cultural homogeneity, which seeks to deny a long history of migration and cultural mixing (Noiriel 1988). From the late nineteenth century, the dominant approach has been 'the Republican model' of turning immigrants into French men and women through natu-ralization and powerful institutions of assimilation (especially language, civic culture, school and military service). This model has made it hard to face up to the reality of the linguistically, culturally and religiously hetero-geneous society that has emerged following post-1945 immigration. The focus of research has passed through phases of ethnological concern with the entry of the colonial Other (influenced by anthropologists, geogra-phers and demographers who had worked in the colonies), followed by a predominantly economic emphasis on the labour-market effects of immi-gration, and then a concentration on political tensions in an increasingly fragmented society (see Vuddamalay 1998). The principle of assimilation remains the conventional wisdom of mainstream France (Schnapper 1994), yet it is now being questioned by conservatives, who see Islam as incompatible with French citizenship, as well as by descendants of immigrants who want political and social rights without loss of their cultural heritage (Bouamama et al. 1992).

Most Germans, by contrast, have traditionally seen themselves as members of an ethno-cultural community (the *Volk*), defined through descent, to which foreigners could not normally be admitted (Hoffmann 1990). This model meant treating foreign residents as temporary sojourners and denying them citizenship, long after their permanent settlement had become evident. The focus of social-scientific research up to the mid-1970s was on labour-market integration and on containment of perceived threats to industrial peace and public order. In the 1980s, with growing trends to settlement, the emphasis shifted to policy-oriented studies of social and educational integration. The large influxes of the early 1990s led to a renewed emphasis on immigration control, combined with debates on how to manage growing xenophobia. However, community formation, the growing significance of Islam and the inescapable presence of new ethnic minorities now entering their third generation also led to debates on pluralism and citizenship that moved away from the old German model of nationality by descent (Castles 1996). Accordingly, the focus of research again shifted, with a flood of studies on the consequences of pluralism for German society (for instance, Cohn-Bendit and Schmid 1993; Habermas 1996; Oberndörfer 1993).

The so-called 'classical countries' of immigration have gone through rather different evolutions in their social-scientific models. Immigration was seen as an essential part of nation-building – to be managed by the state in the cases of Australia, Canada and New Zealand, and left to market forces in the USA. However, in all these countries it was seen as axiomatic from about the 1880s that their national identity could not cope with non-European immigration nor with cultural pluralism. After 1945, the governments of Australia and Canada began large-scale immigration programmes, but social scientists argued that non-Europeans (and sometimes even southern Europeans) could not be assimilated and had to be kept out. 'Acceptable' European immigrants, by contrast, were subjected to assimilation policies designed to turn them into citizens who shared the dominant culture – namely that of Britain, the imperial mother-country. The USA also enshrined the notion of the unacceptability of non-Europeans and certain Europeans in the restrictive immigration laws introduced in the 1920s. For acceptable immigrants, assimilation was the principle, but it was understood here as *Americanization*: the idea that everybody could become part of a new distinct nation through the opportunities offered by expanding free-market economics and through immersion in a democratic civic culture. Academics produced a vast body of work on the dynamics of assimilation (see, for example, Gordon 1964 and, for a recent re-evaluation, Alba and Nee 1997).

From the 1960s to the 1980s, major changes came about in the classical immigration countries, due partly to new forms of migration and partly to the emergence of minority movements which exposed the racism and cultural imperialism implicit in assimilationism. Overt racial discrimination in immigration policy was abandoned, while pluralism and multiculturalism became official policy. The focus of social-science research shifted to cultural diversity, intercultural relations and barriers to equal participation in society. However, by the 1990s, a new scepticism was emerging. Sociologists showed that pluralist ideas and social policies had done little to alleviate social divisions linked to race, ethnicity, gender and class (Carnoy 1994; Wilson 1987). Neo-classical economists argued that inclusive social policies and affirmative action were economically inefficient, while some political scientists claimed that multiculturalism was dividing the nation and undermining national identity. All this was linked to a popular backlash against multiculturalism, which arose in a context of growing fear of the consequences of economic deregulation and globalization.

Such differences and ambiguities in national traditions make it difficult to achieve the common social-scientific language needed for effective cross-national comparison and the advancement of theoretical understanding. Immigration and multicultural studies form an area where the implicit fixation of the social sciences upon the nation-state is particularly evident. Sociology, for example, has generally been seen as a discipline which arose with industrialization and which has always focused on national societies (that is, societies organized within nation-state boundaries) (Lapeyronnie et al. 1990). Sociological research and the recommendations which derive from this have been based on an unquestioning assumption that the national society was the fundamental unit for economic and social policy. Recently, Connell has questioned the conventional wisdom of the link between sociology and industrial society, arguing that much nineteenth-century sociology was actually concerned with understanding and controlling colonized peoples: 'Sociology's comparative method embodied the imperial gaze on the world' (Connell 1997: 1523). Even so, there was still an underlying assumption of the strength and relative autonomy of nation-states, which had the power to exclude or control the Other. Certainly, contemporary sociologists have been slow in responding to the new conditions created by globalization, large-scale cross-border migration and growing ethnic diversity within nation-states. In a period of 'decomposition of national societies' (Wieviorka 1994: 24) traditional social-scientific frameworks and policy models are no longer adequate and there is an urgent need for new approaches.

Disciplinary boundaries

The division of the social sciences into distinct disciplines is another source of fragmentation. Economists and sociologists, for instance, often differ with regard to choice of topics, methodological approaches, types of data and theoretical frameworks. They therefore frequently come to quite different conclusions and diverging policy recommendations. Most researchers claim to accept the need for cross-disciplinary cooperation, but in practice this is often missing. The result can be findings and analyses that make sense in terms of a single discipline, but appear misleading in the context of migrants' overall experience. An early example of this was the social-psychological 'immigrant–host' framework so popular in race-relations studies in Britain in the 1960s. Explanations of conflict were centred around 'strangeness' and 'colour prejudice'. This approach ignored the socio-economic dimensions of immigration, such as labour-market segmentation and competition in the housing market. It also ignored the political experience of many migrants in anti-colonial and labour struggles prior to migration (Sivanandan 1982). The result was a one-sided explanation of the dynamics of settlement and community formation, which was to be corrected by a new generation of sociologists and political economists in the 1970s.

A purely economic focus is just as problematic: some economists still treat migrants as individual market-players who have access to full information about their options and who make rational choices on this basis (Borjas 1989). Much work by historians, anthropologists, sociologists and geographers has been devoted to correcting this view, by showing that migrants' behaviour is strongly influenced by historical experiences as well as by family and community dynamics (Portes and Böröcz 1989). Moreover, migrants have limited and often contradictory information, and are subject to a range of constraints (especially lack of power in the face of employers and governments). Migrants compensate through developing cultural capital (collective knowledge of their situation and strategies for dealing with it) and social capital (the social networks which organize migration and community-formation processes) (see Castles and Miller 1998: ch. 2). However, economic analyses remain popular with policy-makers due to their use of quantitative data and their apparent objectivity, often leading to misconceived and unsuccessful policies.

One answer to such problems is to exhort everyone working in the field to take interdisciplinary cooperation much more seriously (see Boyle et al. 1998: 73). However, this is difficult to achieve in view of the other forms of fragmentation already mentioned. As intellectual fashions develop, new disciplines enter the field and act as if they were entering an intellectual *terra nullius* awaiting cultivation through their specific approach. The result can be a blooming of ideas which, though interesting in themselves, often ignore large bodies of existing knowledge. An example of this was the sudden interest of philosophers in issues of migration and multiculturalism, starting in Canada in the early 1990s and then spreading to the USA and Europe. Similarly, cultural studies theorists became fascinated by international migration, which provided a perfect backdrop for ideas on nomadism, diasporas and hybridity. Valuable as many of these analyses were, they often showed little knowledge of the historical and social processes involved.

Paradigmatic closure

This is very closely linked to disciplinary boundaries, but is not quite the same thing. Paradigms refer to fundamental theoretical ideas or frameworks used to conceptualize and study reality. Although these may originate in a certain discipline, they often spread to others, setting the overall frameworks in which research questions are formulated, empirical studies carried out and findings interpreted and theorized. The development of knowledge and theory can give rise to 'paradigmatic shift' or a 'scientific revolution' (Kuhn 1962): a basic change in the way in which social scientists understand and study social phenomena. Paradigmatic closure arises when schools of thought become so entrenched that their leading proponents become intellectual gate-keepers who demand strict adherence to a certain conceptual framework or methodology. This can blind researchers to actual social diversity or change. It becomes more important to safeguard the purity of theory than to understand society.

The functionalist sociologists who dominated US social theory in the mid-twentieth century had the notion of an integrated social system, in which every individual or group was supposed in some way to contribute to the functioning of the whole. Those who did not were seen as deviant or dysfunctional. For migration theory, such ideas were incorporated in the Chicago School's theory of the assimilation of immigrants in the 1920s (Park 1950). Assimilation became a paradigmatic notion: up until the 1960s it was seen as the only way in which immigrants could be successfully made part of a receiving society. They had to undergo a process of 'resocialization' through which they gave up their previous norms and cultures, and took on those of the receiving societies. Assimilation theory was highly influential in many immigration countries, and is still a widely held 'common-sense' notion. Assimilation theory ignores racism, colonial experience and the importance of culture and language in the formation of personality, yet for many years immigrants who did not assimilate were seen as deviant and threatening.

From the 1960s, many researchers turned to Marxist political economy as a model for understanding the position of the millions of migrant workers recruited by Western capitalist countries. This approach focused on the historical role of 'unfree labour' in the development of the capitalist world economy (Cohen 1987), and showed the importance of institutional factors such as recruitment by employers and control of migrant labour by the state. The import of labour from less-developed areas was a form of neo-colonialism, through which capital maintained the dependency of the Third World, while simultaneously undermining the gains of the labour movement in the industrial countries. However, political economists argued in turn that migrant workers might become the ferment for a new militant workers' movement and also play a part in undermining backward Third World tyrannies. Class position and class consciousness therefore became the key issues for research (Castles and Kosack 1973). However, from the 1970s, as migrations became more diverse, with the growth of family reunion, asylum-seeker movements and highly skilled migration, the political economy model showed its limitations. It had had the valuable effect of shifting attention away from individualistic and psychological interpretations of migration and inter-group relations, but its concentration on macro-social factors, such as the state and international capital, left little scope for seeing migrants as active agents in international mobility and community formation. Moreover, the emphasis on class tended to reduce issues of gender and racism to mere manipulations designed to create 'false consciousness' and thus divide the working class.

Neo-classical economic theory is also a paradigm which closes off understanding of important dimensions of the migratory process. Neo-classical theory is based on narrow and often unspoken assumptions about human motivations and behaviour. Its emphasis on individual 'human capital' and profit maximization has spilled over from economic theory to quantitative sociology and management theory. This approach relies heavily on the statistical analysis of quantitative data, which is problematic in less-developed countries, where the quality and scope of data are rarely adequate. But even in industrial countries the reduction of human experiences to numerical indicators often requires certain assumptions (use of 'dummy variables') which can be arbitrary and misleading. Such methodologies deny the relevance of qualitative, experiential and historical knowledge, thus making important areas of social behaviour and consciousness inaccessible to analysis.

Towards a new synthesis?

Similar criticisms can be made with regard to a range of theoretical approaches. As Massey and his collaborators have pointed out with reference to the USA:

> Social scientists do not approach the study of immigration from a shared paradigm, but from a variety of competing theoretical viewpoints fragmented across disciplines, regions, and ideologies. As a result, research on the subject tends to be narrow, inefficient and characterized by duplication, miscommunication, re-invention, and bickering about fundamentals. Only when researchers accept common theories, concepts, tools, and standards will knowledge begin to accumulate.... (Massey et al. 1994: 700–1)

The underlying reason for this fragmentation is no doubt the intensely political character of migration and multicultural societies, which undermines deep-seated national myths. The question is whether the social sciences can develop new approaches more appropriate to a situation marked by globalization and the emergence of transnational communities.

This means overcoming old boundaries – both disciplinary and national. There are some encouraging signs that this is happening. Over the past twenty years or so major international debates about theoretical explanations of migration decision-making have taken place, especially with regard to less-developed countries. The outcome seems to be a growing consensus on the need to reject the mono-causal and individualistic explanations put forward by some neo-classical economists (for example, Todaro 1976). Economic analysis based on notions of individual profit maximization do have a place in explaining migration, but need to be embedded in much broader approaches, which take account of collective behaviour, long-term goals and historical factors (for an overview of such debates, see Massey et al. 1993).

One attempt to introduce a wider range of factors into economic research was provided by the dual labour-market approach, which showed the importance of institutional factors as well as race and gender in bringing about labour-market segmentation (Piore 1980). More recently, the 'new economics of labour migration' (Stark 1991; Taylor 1987) has argued that markets rarely function in the ideal way suggested by the neo-classicists. Migration needs to be explained not only by income differences between two countries, but also by factors such as the chances of secure employment, the availability of capital for entrepreneurial activity and the need to manage risk over long periods. Similarly, the role of remittances in migration cannot be understood simply by studying the behaviour of migrants themselves. Rather, it is necessary to examine the long-term effects of remittances on investment, work and social relationships right across the community.

Such findings make obvious the need for links between economic and social research. Studies of Asian migration have shown that migration decisions are not generally made on the grounds of short-term gain by individuals, but rather to maximize the long-term survival chances and well-being of families and communities. In situations of rapid change, a family may decide to send one or more members to work elsewhere. Often, a family may prefer to send young women to the city or overseas because the labour of the young men may be less dispensable on the farm. Young women are also often seen as more reliable in sending remittances. Such motivations correspond with increasing international demand for female labour as factory workers for precision assembly or as domestic servants, contributing to a growing feminization of migration (Hugo 1994). This type of analysis points to the need to look at the whole migratory process: if families and communities organize migration with a view to past experience, social linkages and long-term goals, just looking at one moment in the process (such as migration decision-making) cannot lead to full understanding.

The growing political significance of migration has brought migration studies into the mainstream of social science, leading to growing cross-disciplinary and international discussion (Cohen 1995). A promising trend is the emergence of *migration systems theory* as an approach which seeks to integrate the contributions of a wide range of disciplines and paradigms (Kritz et al. 1992). A migration system is constituted by two or more countries which exchange migrants with each other. This approach means examining both ends of the flow and studying all the linkages between the places concerned. Migration systems theory suggests that migratory movements generally arise from the existence of prior links between sending and receiving countries based on colonization, political influence, trade, investment or cultural ties.

A migratory movement can be seen as the result of interacting macro- and micro-structures (Fawcett 1989). Macro-structures refer to large-scale institutional factors, including the political economy of the world economy, inter-state relationships and the laws, structures and practices established by the states of sending and receiving countries to control migration and settlement. The micro-structures are the informal social networks developed by the migrants themselves in order to cope with migration and settlement. These include personal relationships, family and household patterns, friendship and community ties, and mutual help in economic and social matters. Such networks are dynamic cultural responses, which encourage ethnic community formation and are conducive to the maintenance of transnational family and group ties. A more detailed account is not possible here (see Boyd 1989; Boyle et al. 1998: 76–9; Castles and Miller 1998: 23–7; Massey et al. 1993; Skeldon 1997), but it does seem possible that a broadly based formulated migration systems theory could lead to a greater degree of cross-disciplinary cooperation among migration researchers.

The major link that still has to be forged is that between migration studies and the analysis of multicultural societies. Here the social-scientific division of labour still leads to a gulf which is rarely bridged. This is not surprising, not only for all the reasons already outlined, but also because of the sheer size and scope of the two areas. A full grasp of the way in which the migratory process leads to new types of societies within the context of global change requires great theoretical knowledge and historical vision – indeed, the postulate returns to the Frankfurt School notion of the need to analyse society as a totality, or Marx's notion of one science of society, rather than a fragmentation into specialized disciplines. Such ideals are hard to achieve in practice, yet it is possible for each sectoral researcher to see the need to embed her or his work into a broader contextual understanding. Some recent trends may encourage such conceptual broadening. One, as already mentioned, is migration systems theory. Another is the growing importance of citizenship studies – one of the major intellectual trends of the post-Cold War period. The end of the bipolarity between the socialist and liberal models in world affairs has led to a need to rethink the liberal model, and to find ways of overcoming the inclusion/ exclusion dialectic inherent in the modern democratic nation-state. One of the main forms of exclusion concerns the ethnic Other, who is usually a result of migration. Thus the issue of migration and its long-term result – multicultural societies – has become a key theme in political science, as shown by a plethora of books on the topic (Bauböck and Rundell 1998; Castles and Davidson 2000; Davidson 1997; Gutmann 1994; Kymlicka 1995). Citizenship studies could become a new multidisciplinary area linking researchers in migration studies and multicultural societies.

Another significant trend is the emergence of research on transnational societies (Basch et al. 1994) and diasporas (Cohen 1997). These concepts link migration and multicultural societies by emphasizing that migration does not simply mean a transition from one society to another: rather, migrants and their descendants often maintain long-term cultural, social, economic and political links with their society of origin as well as with co-ethnics all over the world. Research on transnational communities is a growing field, which found an institutional base in the British Economic and Social Research Council's transnational communities programme in 1997. Seeing migrants as members of transnational communities is a fundamental shift away from the idea of migration as a one-off event leading to assimilation. It opens new vistas for understanding the culture and consciousness of the increasingly mobile people of a world poised uncertainly between the nation-state model and globalization. Now transnational studies need to be linked to citizenship studies. One of the key questions for the twenty-first century is how to achieve and maintain democracy in a world where nation-state boundaries are becoming increasingly porous. The nation-state still tends to exclude the migrant Other from full membership, while at the same time gradually losing its capacity to protect its citizens from globalizing forces. The result is an erosion of democratic participation and control. Notions of transnationalism point to the need for new sites for democracy, both below and above the level of the nation-state. Greater self-determination for local communities, together with mechanisms for democratic control of global market forces and transnational corporations, are necessary if democracy is to remain our ideal in a globalizing world.

Note on terminology

The use of the word 'indigenous' in this book needs some explanation. In the earlier chapters it is used in the very general sense of people born in a country, so that 'immigrant workers' can be contrasted with 'indigenous workers' in Europe. Since moving to Australia in 1986, I have changed my usage: 'indigenous people' thus refers to the original inhabitants of a colonized country, such as Australian Aborigines or New Zealand Maoris. Similarly, 'coloured' immigrants is used in early chapters, where we would use 'black and Asian' today.

PART II

WESTERN EUROPE: THE 'GUESTS' WHO STAYED

2

THE FUNCTION OF LABOUR MIGRATION IN WESTERN EUROPEAN CAPITALISM

The domination of the working masses by a small capitalist ruling class has never been based on violence alone. Capitalist rule is based on a range of mechanisms: some are objective products of the economic process; others subjective phenomena arising through manipulation of attitudes. Two such mechanisms, which received considerable attention from the founders of scientific socialism, are the industrial reserve army, which belongs to the first category, and the labour aristocracy, which belongs to the second. These two mechanisms are closely related, as are the objective and subjective factors which give rise to them.

Engels pointed out that 'English manufacture must have, at all times save the brief periods of highest prosperity, an unemployed reserve army of workers, in order to produce the masses of goods required by the market in the liveliest period' (Engels 1962a: 119). Marx showed that the industrial reserve army or surplus working population is not only the necessary product of capital accumulation and the associated increase in labour productivity, but at the same time 'the lever of capitalist accumulation', 'a condition of existence of the capitalist mode of production' (Marx 1961: 632). Only by bringing ever more workers into the production process can the capitalist accumulate capital, which is the precondition for extending production and applying new techniques. These new techniques throw out of work the very men whose labour allowed their application. They are set free to provide a labour reserve which is available to be thrown

This chapter was jointly written with Godula Kasack and was first published in *New Left Review*, 73 (1972), pp. 3–21.

into other sectors as the interests of the capitalist require. 'The whole form of the movement of modern industry depends, therefore, upon the constant transformation of a part of the labouring population into unemployed or half-employed hands' (Marx 1961: 633). The pressure of the industrial reserve army forces those workers who are employed to accept long hours and poor conditions. Above all, 'Taking them as a whole, the general movements of wages are exclusively regulated by the expansion and contraction of the industrial reserve army' (Marx 1961: 637). If employment grows and the reserve army contracts, workers are in a better position to demand higher wages. When this happens, profits and capital accumulation diminish, investment falls and men are thrown out of work, leading to a growth of the reserve army and a fall in wages. This is the basis of the capitalist economic cycle. Marx mentions the possibility of the workers seeing through the seemingly natural law of relative overpopulation, and undermining its effectiveness through trade-union activity directed towards cooperation between the employed and the unemployed (Marx 1961: 640).

The labour aristocracy is also described by Engels and Marx. By conceding privileges to certain well-organized sectors of labour, above all to craftsmen (who by virtue of their training could not be readily replaced by members of the industrial reserve army), the capitalists were able to undermine class consciousness and secure an opportunist non-revolutionary leadership for these sectors (Engels 1962b: 28). Special advantages, sometimes taking the form of symbols of higher status (different clothing, salary instead of wages and so on) rather than higher material rewards, were also conferred upon foremen and non-manual workers, with the aim of distinguishing them from other workers and causing them to identify their interests with those of the capitalists. Engels pointed out that the privileges given to some British workers were possible because of the vast profits made by the capitalists through domination of the world market and imperialist exploitation of labour in other countries (Engels 1962c: 505). Lenin emphasized the effects of imperialism on class consciousness: 'Imperialism ... makes it economically possible to bribe the upper strata of the proletariat, and thereby fosters, gives shape to, and strengthens opportunism' (Lenin 1966: 96–7). 'A section of the proletariat allows itself to be led by men bought by, or at least paid by, the bourgeoisie', and the result is a split among the workers and 'temporary decay in the working-class movement' (Lenin 1966: 99–100).

The industrial reserve army and the labour aristocracy have not lost their importance as mechanisms of domination in the current phase of organized monopoly capitalism. However, the way in which they function has undergone important changes. In particular, the maintenance of an industrial reserve army within the developed capitalist countries of Western Europe has become increasingly difficult. With the growth of the labour movement after the First World War, economic crises and unemployment began to lead to political tensions which threatened the existence of the capitalist system.

Capitalism responded by setting up fascist regimes in the areas where it was most threatened, in order to suppress social conflict through violence. The failure of this strategy, culminating in the defeat of fascism in 1945, was accompanied by the reinforcement of the non-capitalist bloc in Eastern Europe and by a further strengthening of the labour movement in Western Europe. In order to survive, the capitalist system had to aim for continuous expansion and full employment at any price. But full employment strikes at a basic principle of the capitalist economy: the use of the industrial reserve army to keep wages down and profits up. A substitute for the traditional form of reserve army had to be found, for without it capitalist accumulation is impossible. Moreover, despite Keynesian economics, it is not possible completely to avoid the cyclical development of the capitalist economy. It was therefore necessary to find a way of cushioning the effects of crises, so as to hinder the development of dangerous social tensions.

Immigrants as the new industrial reserve army

The solution to these problems adopted by Western European capitalism has been the employment of immigrant workers from under-developed areas of southern Europe or from the Third World.[1] Today, the unemployed masses of these areas form a 'latent surplus population'[2] or reserve army, which can be imported into the developed countries as the interests of the capitalist class dictate. In addition to this economic function, the employment of immigrant workers has an important sociopolitical function for capitalism: by creating a split between immigrant and indigenous workers along national and racial lines, and by offering better conditions and status to indigenous workers, it is possible to give large sections of the working class the consciousness of a labour aristocracy.

The employment of immigrant workers in the capitalist production process is not a new phenomenon. The Irish played a vital part in British industrialization. Not only did they provide a special form of labour for heavy work of a temporary nature on railways, canals and roads (see Thompson 1968: 469–85), their competition also forced down wages and conditions for other workers. Engels described Irish immigration as a 'cause of abasement to which the English worker is exposed, a cause permanently active in forcing the whole class downwards' (Engels 1962a: 123). Marx described the antagonism between British and Irish workers, artificially created by the mass media of the ruling class, as 'the secret of the impotence of the English working class, despite their organisation' (Letter to S. Meyer and A. Vogt, 9 April 1870 in Marx and Engels 1962: 552). As industrialization got under way in France, Germany and Switzerland in the latter half of the nineteenth century, these countries too brought in foreign labour: from Poland, Italy and Spain. There were 800,000 foreign workers in the German Reich in 1907. More than a third of the Ruhr miners were Poles. Switzerland had half a million foreigners in

1910 – 15 per cent of her total population. French heavy industry was highly dependent on immigrant labour right up to the Second World War. According to Lenin, one of the special features of imperialism was 'the decline in emigration from imperialist countries and the increase in immigration into these countries from the more backward countries where lower wages are paid' (Lenin 1966: 98). This was a main cause of the division of the working class. The fascist form of capitalism also developed its own specific form of exploiting immigrant workers: the use of forced labour. No less the 7.5 million deportees from occupied countries and prisoners of war were working in Germany by 1944, replacing men recruited for the army. About a quarter of German munitions production was carried out by foreign labour (Pfahlmann 1968: 232).

Compared with early patterns, immigration of workers to contemporary Western Europe has two new features. The first is its character as a permanent part of the economic structure. Previously, immigrant labour was used more or less temporarily when the domestic industrial reserve army was inadequate for some special reason, such as war or unusually fast expansion; since 1945, however, large numbers of immigrant workers have taken up key positions in the productive process, so that even in the case of recession their labour cannot be dispensed with. The second is its importance as the basis of the modern industrial reserve army. Other groups which might conceivably fulfil the same function – non-working women, the disabled and the chronic sick, members of the lumpenproletariat whose conditions prevent them from working,[3] have already been integrated into the production process to the extent to which this is profitable for the capitalist system. The use of further reserves of this type would require costly social measures (adequate kindergartens, for example). The main traditional form of the industrial reserve army – men thrown out of work by rationalization and cyclical crises – is hardly available today, for reasons already mentioned. Thus immigration is of key importance for the capitalist system.

The development of immigration since 1945

By 1970 there were around 11 million immigrants[4] living in Western Europe, making up about 5 per cent of total population. Relatively few have gone to industrially less-developed countries like Norway, Austria and Denmark, while large concentrations are to be found in highly industrialized countries like Belgium, Sweden, West Germany, France, Switzerland and Britain. Our analysis concentrates on the four last-named which have about 90 per cent of all immigrants in Western Europe between them (see Table 2.1).

Most immigrants in Germany and Switzerland come from southern Europe. The main groups in Germany are Italians (574,000 in 1970), Yugoslavs (515,000), Turks (469,000), Greeks (343,000) and Spaniards

Table 2.1   *Immigrants in Britain, France, Switzerland and West Germany*

	Immigrants (thousands)	Immigrants as % total population	Date of figures (latest available)
Britain	2,603	5.0	1966
France	3,177	6.4	December 1969
Switzerland	972	16.0	December 1969
West Germany	2,977	4.8	September 1970

Source: Castles and Kosack (1973) (see also for detailed analysis of social conditions of immigrants)

(246,000). In Switzerland, the Italians are by far the largest group (532,000 in 1969), followed by Germans (116,000) and Spaniards (98,000). France and Britain also have considerable numbers of European immigrants, but in addition large contingents from former colonies in Africa, Asia and the Caribbean. France has 617,000 Spaniards, 612,000 Italians, 480,000 Portuguese, as well as 608,000 Algerians, 143,000 Moroccans, 89,000 Tunisians, about 55,000 black Africans and an unknown number (probably about 200,000) from the remaining colonies (euphemistically referred to as overseas departments) in the West Indies and the African island of Réunion. The largest immigrant group in Britain comes from the Irish Republic (739,000 in 1966). Most of the other Europeans are displaced persons and the like who came during and after the war: Germans (142,000), Poles (118,000). Cypriots number 60,000. There is also an increasing number of southern Europeans, often allowed in on a short-term basis for work in catering and domestic service. Coloured immigrants comprise about one-third of the total, the largest groups coming from the West Indies (269,000 in 1966), India (240,000) and Pakistan (75,000).

The migratory movements and the government policies which direct them reflect the growing importance and changing function of immigrant labour in Western Europe. Immediately after the Second World War, Switzerland, Britain and France recruited foreign workers. Switzerland needed extra labour for the export boom permitted by her intact industry in the middle of war-torn Europe. The 'European voluntary workers' in Britain (initially displaced persons, later Italians) were assigned to specific jobs connected with industrial reconstruction. The reconstruction boom was not expected to last. Both Switzerland and Britain imposed severe restrictions on foreign workers, designed to stop them from settling and bringing in their families, so that they could be dismissed and deported at the least sign of recession. France was something of an exception: her immigration policy was concerned not only with labour needs for reconstruction, but also with permanent immigration to counteract the demographic effects of the low birth rate.

When West German industry got under way again after the 1949 currency reform there was at first no need for immigrants from southern Europe. An excellent industrial reserve army was provided by the 7 million expellees from the former Eastern provinces of the Reich and by the 3 million refugees from East Germany, many of whom were skilled workers. Throughout the 1950s, the presence of these reserves kept wage growth slow and hence provided the basis for the 'economic miracle'. By the mid-1950s, however, special labour shortages were appearing, first in agriculture and building. It was then that the recruitment of foreign workers (initially on a seasonal basis)[5] was started. Here, too, an extremely restrictive policy was followed with regard to family entry and long-term settlement. 'Rotation' of the foreign labour force was encouraged. In this stage, the use of immigrants in the countries mentioned followed the pre-war pattern: they were brought in to satisfy special and, it was thought, temporary labour needs in certain sectors. They were, as an official of the German employers' association put it, 'a mobile labour potential' (Gienanth 1966).

By the 1960s, the situation was changing. Despite mild cyclical tendencies, it was clear that there was not going to be a sudden return to the pre-war boom–slump pattern. The number of immigrant workers grew extremely rapidly in the late 1950s and early 1960s. Between 1956 and 1965 nearly one million new workers entered France. The number of foreign workers in West Germany increased from 279,000 in 1960 to over 1.3 million in 1966. In Switzerland there were 326,000 immigrant workers (including seasonals) in 1956, and 721,000 in 1964. This was also the period of mass immigration to Britain from the Commonwealth (see Rose et al. 1969). The change was not merely quantitative: immigrants were moving into and becoming indispensable in ever more sectors of the economy. They were no longer filling gaps in peripheral branches like agriculture and building but were becoming a vital part of the labour force in key industries like engineering and chemicals. Moreover, there was growing competition between different countries to obtain the 'most desirable' immigrants; that is, those with the best education and the least cultural distance from the receiving countries. The growing need for labour was forcing the recruiters to go further and further afield: Turkey and Yugoslavia were replacing Italy as Germany's main labour source. Portugal and North Africa were replacing Italy and Spain in the case of France.

As a result, new policies intended to attract and integrate immigrant workers, but also to control them better, were introduced. One such measure was the free labour movement policy of the EEC, designed to increase the availability of the rural proletariat of Sicily and the Mezzogiorno to Western European capital.[6] Germany and Switzerland liberalized the conditions for family entry and long-term settlement, while at the same time tightening political control through measures such as the German 1965 Foreigners Law. France tried to increase control over entries, in order to prevent the large-scale clandestine immigration which had taken place throughout the 1950s and 1960s (and still does, despite the new policy). At the same time, restrictions were made on the permanent settlement of non-Europeans – officially because of their 'greater difficulties in integrating'. In Britain, racialist campaigns led to the stopping of unrestricted Commonwealth immigration in 1962. By limiting the labour supply, this measure contradicted the economic interests of the ruling class. The new Immigration Act of 1971, which could provide the basis for organized and controlled labour recruitment on the German and French pattern, is a corrective, although its application for this purpose is not at present required, since the ruling class has created an internal industrial reserve army through unemployment.

In view of the stagnant domestic labour force potential and the long-term growth trend of the economy, immigrant labour has become a structural necessity for Western European capitalism.[7] It has a dual function today (Becker et al. 1971: 753). One section is maintained as a mobile fluctuating labour force, which can be moved from factory to factory or branch to branch as required by the development of the means of production, and which can be thrown out of work and deported as required without causing social tensions. This function was shown clearly by the West German recession of 1966–7, when the foreign labour force dropped by 400,000, although there were never more than 29,000 receiving unemployment benefit. As a United Nations study pointed out, West Germany was able to export unemployment to the home countries of the migrants (United Nations Economic Commission for Europe 1968: 49). The other section is required for permanent employment throughout the economy. They are offered better conditions and the chance of long-term settlement.[8] Despite this they still fulfil the function of an industrial reserve army, for they are given inferior jobs, have no political rights and may be used as a constant threat to the wages and conditions of the local labour force.

Occupational position

The immigrant percentage of the population given in Table 2.1 (see page 30) in no way reflects the contribution of immigrants to the economy. They are mainly young men, whose dependants are sent for later if at all. Many of them remain for only a few years, and are then replaced by others, so that there are hardly any retired immigrants. Immigrants therefore have higher than average rates of economic activity, and make contributions to health, unemployment and pension insurance far in excess of their demands on such schemes.[9] Particularly high rates of activity are to be found among recently arrived groups, or among those who for social and cultural reasons tend not to bring dependants with them: Portuguese and North Africans in France, Turks in Germany and Pakistanis in Britain. Immigrant workers are about 6.5 per cent of the labour force in Britain, 7–8 per cent in France, 10 per cent in West Germany and 30 per cent in Switzerland. Even these figures do not show adequately the structural importance of immigrant labour, which is concentrated in certain areas and types of work.

The overwhelming majority of immigrants live in highly industrialized and fast-growing urban areas like Paris, the Lyon region, the Ruhr, Baden-Wurttemberg, London and the West Midlands. For example, 31.2 per cent of all immigrants in France live in the Paris region, compared with only 19.2 per cent of the total population; 9.5 per cent of the inhabitants of the Paris region are immigrants.[10] In Britain, more than one-third of all immigrants are to be found in Greater London compared with one-sixth of the total population. Immigrants make up 12 per cent of London's population (1996 census).

More important still is the concentration in certain industries. Switzerland is the extreme case: the whole industrial sector is dominated by foreign workers who make up more than 40 per cent of the factory labour force. In many branches – for instance, textiles, clothing, building and catering – they outnumber Swiss employees. Of the nearly 2 million foreign workers in Germany in September 1970, 38.5 per cent were in the metal-producing and engineering industries, 24.2 in other manufacturing branches and 16.7 per cent in building. Foreign workers accounted for 13.7 per cent of total employment in metal-producing and engineering. The proportion was even higher in some industries with particularly bad working conditions, such as plastic, rubber and asbestos manufacture (18.4 per cent). In building, foreign workers were 17.5 per cent of the labour force. On the other hand, they made up only 3.4 per cent of all employees in the services, although their share was much higher in catering (14.8 per cent) (Bundesanstalt für Arbeit 1971). Similar concentrations were revealed by the 1968 census in France: 35.6 per cent of immigrant men were employed in building and 13.5 per cent in engineering and electrical goods. Of foreign women, 28.8 per cent were domestic servants. In Britain, the concentration of immigrants in certain industries is less marked, and different immigrant groups have varying patterns. The Irish are concentrated in construction, while Commonwealth immigrants are over-represented in metal manufacture and transport. Pakistani men are mainly to be found in the textile industry and Cypriots in clothing and footwear and in distribution. European immigrants are frequently in the service sector. Immigrant women of all nationalities tend to work in services, although some groups (Cypriots, West Indians) also often work in manufacturing (1966 census). (For a detailed analysis of immigrant employment, see Jones and Smith 1970; as well as Castles and Kosack 1973: ch. 3.)

In general, immigrants are concentrated in certain basic industries where they form a high proportion of the labour force. Together with their geographical concentration, this means that immigrant workers are of great importance in the very type of enterprise and area which used to be regarded as strongholds of the class-conscious proletariat. The real concentration is even greater than the figures show, for within each industry immigrants tend to have become predominant in certain departments and occupations. There can be hardly a foundry in Western Europe in which immigrants do not form a majority, or at least a high proportion, of the labour force. The same applies to monotonous production-line work, such as car assembly. Renault, Citroen, Volkswagen, Ford of Cologne and Opel all have mainly foreign workers on the assembly line. (The British motor industry is an exception in this respect.)

Perhaps the best indication of the occupational concentration of the immigrant labour force is given by their socio-economic distribution. For instance, a survey carried out in 1968 in Germany showed that virtually no southern Europeans are in non-manual employment. Only between 7 per cent and 16 per cent of the various nationalities were skilled workers, while between 80 per cent and 90 per cent were either semi-skilled or unskilled (Bundesanstalt für Arbeit 1970: 86). By comparison, about a third of German workers are non-manual, and among manual workers between one-third and one-half are in the skilled category in the various industries. In France, a survey carried out at Lyon in 1967 found that, where they worked in the same industry, the French were mainly in managerial non-manual or skilled occupations, while the immigrants were concentrated in manual occupations, particularly semi-skilled and unskilled ones. The relegation to unskilled jobs is particularly marked for North Africans and Portuguese (Anon. 1969: 112). In Britain, only about 26 per cent of the total labour force fall into the unskilled and semi-skilled manual categories, but the figure is 42 per cent for Irish workers, 50 per cent for Jamaicans, 65 per cent for Pakistanis and 55 per cent for Italians (1966 census).

Immigrants form the lowest stream of the working class carrying out unskilled and semi-skilled work in those industrial sectors with the worst working conditions and/or the lowest pay.[11] The entry of immigrants at the bottom of the labour market has made possible the release of many indigenous workers from such employment, and their promotion to jobs with better conditions and higher status; that is, skilled, supervisory or white-collar employment. Apart from the economic effects, this process has a profound impact on the class consciousness of the indigenous workers concerned. This will be discussed in more detail below.

Social position

The division of the working class within the production process is duplicated by a division in other spheres of society. The poor living conditions of immigrants have attracted too much liberal indignation and welfare zeal to need much description here. Immigrants get the worst types of housing: in Britain slums and run-down lodging houses; in France *bidonvilles* (shanty-towns) and over-crowded hotels; in Germany and Switzerland camps of wooden huts belonging to the employers and attics in the cities. It is rare for immigrants to get council houses. Immigrants are discriminated against by many landlords, so that those who do specialize in housing them can charge extortionate rents for inadequate facilities. In

Germany and France, official programmes have been established to provide hostel accommodation for single immigrant workers. These hostels do provide somewhat better material conditions. On the other hand, they increase the segregation of immigrant workers from the rest of the working class, deny them any private life, and above all put them under the control of the employers twenty-four hours a day.[12] In Germany, the employers have repeatedly attempted to use control over immigrants' accommodation to force them to act as strike-breakers.

Language and vocational training courses for immigrant workers are generally provided only when it is absolutely necessary for the production process, as in mines for example. Immigrant children are also at a disadvantage: they tend to live in run-down overcrowded areas where school facilities are poorest. No adequate measures are taken to deal with their special educational problems (such as language difficulties), so that their educational performance is usually below average. As a result of their bad working and living conditions, immigrants have serious health problems. For instance, they have much higher tuberculosis rates than the rest of the population virtually everywhere.[13] As there are health controls at the borders, it is clear that such illnesses have been contracted in Western Europe rather than being brought in by the immigrants.

The inferior work situation and living conditions of immigrants have caused some bourgeois sociologists to define them as a 'lumpenproletariat' or a 'marginal group'. This is clearly incorrect. A group which makes up 10, 20 or 30 per cent of the industrial labour force cannot be regarded as marginal to society. Others speak of a 'new proletariat' or a 'subproletariat'. Such terms are also wrong. The first implies that the indigenous workers have ceased to be proletarians and have been replaced by the immigrants in this social position. The second postulates that immigrant workers have a different relationship to the means of production than that traditionally characteristic of the proletariat. In reality both indigenous and immigrant workers share the same relationship to the means of production: they are excluded from ownership or control; they are forced to sell their labour power in order to survive; they work under the direction and in the interests of others. In the sphere of consumption both categories of workers are subject to the laws of the commodity market, where the supply and price of goods are determined not by their use value but by their profitability for capitalists; both are victims of landlords, retail monopolists and similar bloodsuckers and manipulators of the consumption-terror. These are the characteristics typical of the proletariat ever since the Industrial Revolution, and on this basis immigrant and indigenous workers must be regarded as members of the same class: the proletariat. But it is a divided class: the marginal privileges conceded to indigenous workers and the particularly intensive exploitation of immigrants combine to create a barrier between the two groups, which appear as distinct strata within the class. The division is deepened by certain legal, political and psychological factors, which will be discussed below.

Discrimination

Upon arrival in Western Europe, immigrants from under-developed areas have little basic education or vocational training, and are usually ignorant of the language. They know nothing of prevailing market conditions or prices. In capitalist society, these characteristics are sufficient to ensure that immigrants get poor jobs and social conditions. After a period of adaptation to industrial work and urban life, the prevailing ideology would lead one to expect that many immigrants would obtain better jobs, housing and the like. Special mechanisms ensure that this does not happen in the majority of cases. On one hand, there is institutionalized discrimination in the form of legislation which restricts immigrants' civic and labour market rights. On the other hand, there are informal discriminatory practices based on racialism or xenophobia.

In nearly all Western European countries, labour-market legislation discriminates against foreigners. They are granted labour permits for a specific job in a certain firm for a limited period. They do not have the right to move to better-paid or more highly qualified positions, at least for some years. Workers who change jobs without permission are often deported. Administrative practices in this respect have been liberalized to some extent in Germany and Switzerland in recent years, due to the need for immigrant labour in a wider range of occupations, but the basic restrictiveness of the system remains. In Britain, Commonwealth immigrants (once admitted to the country) and the Irish had equal rights with local workers until the 1971 Immigration Act. Now Commonwealth immigrants will have the same labour-market position as aliens. The threat of deportation if an immigrant loses his or her job is a very powerful weapon for the employer. Immigrants who demand better conditions can be sacked for indiscipline and the police will do the rest.[14] Regulations which restrict family entry and permanent settlement also keep immigrants in inferior positions. If a migrant may stay for only a few years, it is not worth his or her while to learn the language and take vocational training courses.

Informal discrimination is well known in Britain, where it takes the form of the colour bar. The Political and Economic Planning (PEP) study (Daniels 1968), as well as many other investigations, has shown that coloured immigrants encounter discrimination with regard to employment, housing and the provision of services such as mortgages and insurance. The more qualified a coloured person is, the more likely he or she is to encounter discrimination. This mechanism keeps immigrants in 'their place', that is, doing the dirty, unpleasant jobs. Immigrants in other European countries also encounter informal discrimination. Immigrants rarely get promotion to supervisory or non manual jobs, even when they are well qualified. Discrimination in housing is widespread. In Britain, adverts specifying 'no coloured' are forbidden, but in Germany or Switzerland one still frequently sees 'no foreigners'.

The most serious form of discrimination against immigrant workers is their deprivation of political rights. Foreigners may not vote in local or national elections. Nor may they hold public office, which in France is defined so widely as to include trade-union posts. Foreigners do not generally have the same rights as local workers with regard to eligibility for works councils and similar representative bodies. The main exception to this formal exclusion from political participation concerns Irish and Commonwealth immigrants in Britain, who do have the right to vote (the same will not apply to those who enter under the 1971 Act). But the Mangrove case shows the type of repression which may be expected by any immigrants who dare to organize themselves. Close police control over the political activities of immigrants is the rule throughout Europe, and deportations of political and trade-union militants are common. After the May Events in France, hundreds of foreign workers were deported. Foreign language newspapers of the CGT labour federation have been repeatedly forbidden. The German Foreigners Law of 1965 lays down that the political activity of foreigners can be forbidden if 'important interests of the German Federal Republic require this' – a provision so flexible that the police can prevent any activity they choose. Even this is not regarded as sufficient. When Federal Chancellor Willy Brandt visited Iran in March 1972 to do an oil deal, the Shah complained strongly about Iranian students being allowed to criticize him in Germany. The Greek and Yugoslav ambassadors have also protested about the activities of their citizens. Now the German government is working on a new law which would go so far as to make police permission necessary even for private meetings of foreigners in closed rooms (*Der Spiegel*, 7 February 1972).

Prejudice and class consciousness

Discrimination against immigrants is a reflection of widespread hostility towards them. In Britain, this is regarded as 'colour prejudice' or 'racialism', and indeed there can be no doubt that the hostility of large sections of the population is at present directed against black people. Race-relations theorists attribute the problems connected with immigration partly to the immigrants' difficulties in adapting to the prevailing norms of the 'host society', and partly to the indigenous population's inbred distrust of newcomers who can be distinguished by their skin colour. The problems are abstracted from the socio-economic structure and reduced to the level of attitudes. Solutions are to be sought not through political action, but through psychological and educational strategies.[15] But a comparison of surveys carried out in different countries shows that hostility towards immigrants is everywhere as great as in Britain, even where the immigrants are white.[16] The Italian who moves to the neighbouring country of Switzerland is as unpopular as the Asian in Britain. This indicates that hostility is based on the position of immigrants in society and not on the colour of their skin.

Racialism and xenophobia are products of the capitalist national state and of its imperialist expansion (Cox 1959: 317ff). Their principal historical function was to split the working class on the international level, and to motivate one section to help exploit another in the interests of the ruling class. Today such ideologies help to deepen the split within the working class in Western Europe. Many indigenous workers do not perceive that they share a common class position and class interests with immigrant workers. The basic fact of having the same relationship to the means of production is obscured by the local workers' marginal advantages with regard to material conditions and status. The immigrants are regarded not as class comrades, but as alien intruders who pose an economic and social threat. It is feared that they will take away the jobs of local labour, that they will be used by the employers to force down wages and to break strikes.[17] Whatever the behaviour of the immigrant workers – and in fact they almost invariably show solidarity with their indigenous colleagues – such fears are not without a basis. It is indeed the strategy of the employers to use immigration to put pressure on wages and to weaken the labour movement.[18] The very social and legal weakness of the immigrants is a weapon in the hands of the employers. Other points of competition are to be found outside work, particularly in the housing market. The presence of immigrants is often regarded as the cause of rising rents and increased overcrowding in the cities. By making immigrants the scapegoats for the insecurity and inadequate conditions which the capitalist system inevitably provides for workers, attention is diverted from the real causes.

Workers often adopt racialism as a defence mechanism against a real or apparent threat to their conditions. It is an incorrect response to a real problem. By preventing working-class unity, racialism assists the capitalists in their strategy of 'divide and rule'. The function of racialism in the capitalist system is often obscured by the fact that racialist campaigns usually have a petty-bourgeois leadership and direct their slogans against the big industrialists. The Schwarzenbach Initiative in Switzerland – which called for the deportation of a large proportion of the immigrant population – is an example,[19] as are Enoch Powell's campaigns for repatriation. Such demands are opposed by the dominant sections of the ruling class. The reason is clear: a complete acceptance of racialism would prevent the use of immigrants as an industrial reserve army. But, despite this, racialist campaigns serve the interests of the ruling class: they increase tension between indigenous and immigrant workers and weaken the labour movement. The large working-class following gained by Powell in his racialist campaigns demonstrates how dangerous they are. Paradoxically, their value for capitalism lies in their very failure to achieve their declared aims.

The presence of immigrant workers is one of the principal factors contributing to the lack of class consciousness among large sections of the working class. The existence of a new lower stratum of immigrants changes workers' perception of their own position in society. Instead of a dichotomic view of society, in which the working masses confront a small capitalist ruling class, many workers now see themselves as belonging to an intermediate stratum, superior to unskilled immigrant workers. Such a consciousness is typified by a hierarchical view of society and by orientation towards advancement through individual achievement and competition, rather than through solidarity and collective action. This is the mentality of the labour aristocracy and leads to opportunism and the temporary decay of the working-class movement.

Immigration and society

The impact of immigration on contemporary Western European society may now be summarized.

Economic effects: The new industrial reserve army of immigrant workers is a major stabilizing factor of the capitalist economy. By restraining wage increases, immigration is a vital precondition for capital accumulation and hence for growth. In the long run, wages may grow more in a country which has large-scale immigration than in one which does not because of the dynamic effect of increased capital accumulation on productivity. However, wages are a smaller share and profits a larger share of national income than would have been the case without immigration.[20] The best illustration of this effect is obtained by comparing the German and British economies since 1945. Germany has had large and continuous increases in labour force due to immigration. At first wages were held back. The resulting capital accumulation allowed fast growth and continuous rationalization. Britain has had virtually no growth in labour force due to migration (immigration has been cancelled out by emigration of British people to Australia and so on). Every phase of expansion has collapsed rapidly as wages rose due to labour shortages. The long-term effect has been stagnation. By the 1960s, German wages overtook those of Britain, while economic growth and rationalization continued at an almost undiminished rate.

Social effects: The inferior position of immigrant workers with regard to employment and social conditions has led to a division of the working class into two strata. The split is maintained by various forms of discrimination and is reinforced by racialist and xenophobic ideologies, which the ruling class can disseminate widely through its hegemony over the means of socialization and communication. Large sections of the indigenous workforce take the position of a labour aristocracy, which objectively participates in the exploitation of another group of workers.

Political effects: The decline of class consciousness weakens the working-class movement. In addition, the denial of political rights to immigrants excludes a large section of the working class from political activity, and hence weakens the class as a whole. The most exploited section of the working class is rendered voiceless and powerless. Special forms of repression are designed to keep it that way.

Working-class movement and immigrant labour

Immigrant labour has an important function for contemporary Western European capitalism. This does not mean, however, that socialists should oppose labour migration as such. To do so would be incorrect for two reasons. First, it would contradict the principle of proletarian internationalism, which rejects the maintenance of privileges for one section of the working class at the expense of another. Secondly, opposition to immigration would cause immigrants in Western Europe to regard the working-class movement as its enemy, and would therefore deepen the split in the working class – which is exactly what the capitalists are hoping for. The aim of a socialist policy on immigration must be to overcome the split in the working class by bringing immigrant workers into the labour movement and fighting against the exploitation to which they are subjected. Only by demanding full economic, social and political equality for immigrants can we prevent the employers from using them as a weapon against working-class interests.

The policies of the trade unions with regard to immigration have varied widely. The Swiss unions oppose immigration, and have since the mid-1950s campaigned for a reduction in the number of foreign workers. At the same time, they claim to represent all workers, and call upon foreigners to join – not surprisingly, with little success. The British unions opposed the recruitment of European voluntary workers after the war, and insisted upon collective agreements limiting their rights to promotion, laying down that they should be dismissed first in cases of redundancy and so on (see Hepple 1968: 50 and appendix II). The policy towards Commonwealth immigration has been totally different: the TUC has opposed immigration control, and rejected any form of discrimination. This rejection has, however, been purely verbal, and virtually nothing has been done to organize immigrants or to counter the special forms of exploitation to which they are subject. The CGT in France opposed immigration completely during the late 1940s and the 1950s, condemning it as an instrument designed to attack French workers' conditions. More recently the CGT, as well as the two other big labour federations, the CFDT and the FO, have come to regard immigration as inevitable. All have special secretariats to deal with immigrant workers' problems and do everything possible to bring them into the unions. In Germany, the DGB has accepted immigration and has set up offices to advise and help immigrants. The member unions also have advisory services, and provide foreign language bulletins and special training for immigrant shop stewards. In general, those unions which have recognized the special problems of immigration have not done so on the basis of a class analysis (here the CGT is to some extent an exception). Rather, they have seen the problems on a humanitarian level, they have failed to explain the strategy of the employers to the workers, and the measures taken have been of a welfare type, designed to integrate immigrants socially, rather than to bring them into the class struggle.

Therefore, the unions have succeeded neither in countering racialism among indigenous workers, nor in bringing the immigrant workers into the labour movement on a large scale. The participation of immigrant workers in the unions is on the whole relatively low. This is partly attributable to their rural background and lack of industrial experience, but in addition immigrants often find that the unions do not adequately represent their interests. The unions are controlled by indigenous workers, or by functionaries originating from this group. In situations where immigrant and indigenous workers do not have the same immediate interests (this happens not infrequently due to the differing occupational positions of the two groups, for instance in the question of wage differentials), the unions tend to take the side of the indigenous workers. Where immigrants have taken action against special forms of discrimination, they have often found themselves deserted by the unions (for details of such cases, see Castles and Kosack 1973: ch. 4). In such circumstances it is not surprising if immigrants do not join the unions, which they regard as organizations for local labour only. This leads to a considerable weakening of the unions. In Switzerland many unions fear for their very existence, and see the only solution in the introduction of compulsory 'solidarity contributions', to be deducted from wages by the employers. In return the unions claim to be the most effective instrument for disciplining the workers. When the employers gave way to a militant strike of Spanish workers in Geneva in 1970, the unions publicly attacked them for making concessions.

Where the unions do not adequately represent immigrant workers, it is sometimes suggested that the immigrants should form their own unions. In fact they have not done so anywhere in contemporary Western Europe. This shows a correct class position on their part: the formation of immigrant unions would deepen and institutionalize the split in the working class, and would therefore serve the interests of the employers.[21] On the other hand, all immigrant groups do have their own organizations, usually set up on the basis of nationality, and having social, cultural and political functions. These organizations do not compete with the trade unions, but rather encourage their members to join them. The aims of the political groups have so far been concerned mainly with their countries of origin. They have recruited and trained cadres to combat the reactionary regimes upon returning home. At present, as a result of greater length of stay and increasing problems in Western Europe, many immigrant political groups are turning their attention to class struggle in the countries where they work.

It is the task of the revolutionary movement in Western Europe to encourage this tendency, by making contact with immigrant groups, assisting them in coordinating with immigrants of other nationalities and with the working-class movement in general, giving help in political education and cadre-training, and carrying out joint actions. Such cooperation means surmounting many problems. First, language and culture may make communication difficult. Secondly, the risk of repression to which immigrant militants are exposed may make them reluctant to make contacts. Thirdly, the experience of discrimination may cause immigrants to distrust all local people. This leads in many cases to cultural nationalism, particularly marked for historical reasons among black people. In order to overcome these difficulties, it is essential for indigenous political groups to study the problems of immigrants and the special forms of discrimination and exploitation to which they are exposed. Concrete attempts to combat these must be made. Indigenous groups must offer cooperation and assistance to immigrants in their struggle, rather than offering themselves as a leadership.

It is not only when revolutionary groups are actively trying to cooperate with immigrant workers' organizations that they come up against the problems of immigration. The majority of immigrants are not politically organized, whether through apathy or fear of repression. Groups agitating in factories or carrying out rent campaigns are likely to come up against large numbers of unorganized immigrants in the course of their daily work. It is then essential to take special steps to communicate with the immigrants and to bring them into the general movement. Failure to do so may result in the development of petty-bourgeois chauvinism within factory or housing groups, which would correspond precisely with the political aims of the capitalists with regard to labour migration. In Germany, the large numbers of revolutionary groups at present agitating in factories almost invariably find it necessary to learn about the background and problems of immigrant workers, to develop special contacts with them, and to issue leaflets in appropriate languages. The same applies to housing groups, which frequently find that immigrants form the most under-privileged group in the urban areas where they are working.

Immigrant workers can become a class-conscious and militant section of the labour movement. This has been demonstrated repeatedly; immigrant workers have played a leading part in strike movements throughout Western Europe. They are at present in the forefront of the movement that is occupying empty houses in German cities. Immigrant workers showed complete solidarity with the rest of the working class in May 1968 in France; they were militant in strikes and demonstrations and developed spontaneous forms of organization in the struggle.

But such successes should not make us forget the capitalist strategy behind labour migration. Powerful structural factors connected with the function of immigrants as an industrial reserve army, and the tendency of part of the indigenous working class to take on the characteristics of a labour aristocracy, lead to a division between immigrant and indigenous workers. Solidarity between these two sections does not come automatically. It requires a correct understanding of the problems within the revolutionary movement and a strategy for countering ruling-class aims. It is necessary to assist immigrant workers in fighting exploitation and in defending their special interests. At the same time revolutionary groups must combat racialist and xenophobic ideologies within the working class. These are the preconditions for developing class consciousness and bringing immigrant workers into the class struggle.

Notes

1 In this chapter we examine the function of labour immigration only for the countries of immigration. Migration also plays an important stabilizing role for the reactionary regimes of the countries of origin – a role which is understood and to some extent planned by the ruling class in Western Europe. Although we are concerned only with Western Europe in this chapter, it is important to note that the use of certain special categories of workers, who can be discriminated against without arousing general solidarity from other workers, is a general feature of modern capitalism. The blacks and chicanos are the industrial reserve army of the USA, the Africans of white-dominated South Africa. Current attempts by 'liberal' capitalists to relax the colour bar to allow blacks into certain skilled and white-collar jobs, both in the USA and South Africa, however estimable in humanitarian terms, are designed mainly to weaken the unions and put pressure on wages in these sectors.

2 Marx mentions several forms taken by the industrial reserve army. One is the 'latent' surplus population of agricultural labourers, whose wages and conditions have been depressed to such an extent that they are merely waiting for a favourable opportunity to move into industry and join the urban proletariat (Marx 1961: 642). Although these workers are not yet in industry, the possibility that they may at any time join the industrial labour force increases the capitalist's ability to resist wage increases. The latent industrial reserve army has the same effect as the urban unemployed. Unemployed workers in other countries, in so far as they may be brought into the industrial labour force whenever required, clearly form a latent industrial reserve army in the same way as rural unemployed within the country.

3 For the role of the lumpenproletariat in the industrial reserve army, see Marx (1961: 643).

4 We use 'immigrants' in a broad sense to include all persons living in a Western European country which is not their country of birth. Much migration is of a temporary nature, for a period of 3–10 years. But such temporary migration has effects similar to permanent migration when the returning migrant is replaced by another with similar characteristics. Such migrants may be regarded as a permanent social group with rotating membership.

5 Many foreign workers are still employed on a seasonal basis in building, agriculture and catering in France and Switzerland. This is a special form of exploitation. The worker has no income in the off-season and is therefore forced to work very long hours for the 9–10 months when work is available. Seasonal workers cannot bring their families with them, they have even more limited civic rights than other immigrants, and they have absolutely no security, for there is no guarantee that their employment will be continued from year to year.

6 Eurocrats refer to the free-movement policy as the beginning of a 'European labour market'. But although EEC citizens have the right to choose which country to be exploited in, they lack any civic or political rights once there. Moreover, the

southern Italian labour reserves are being absorbed by the monopolies of Turin and Milan, so that intra-EEC migration is steadily declining in volume, while migration from outside the EEC increases.

7 Where formalized economic planning exists, this necessity has been publicly formulated. Prognoses on the contribution of immigrants to the labour force were included in the Fourth and Fifth Five-year Plans in France, and play an even more prominent part in the current Sixth Plan.

8 The distinction between the two sections of the immigrant labour force is formalized in the new French immigration policy introduced in 1968. There are separate regulations for southern Europeans, who are encouraged to bring in their families and settle permanently, and Africans (particularly Algerians), who are meant to come for a limited period only, without dependants.

9 It is estimated that foreign workers in Germany are at present paying about 17 per cent of all contributions to pension insurance, but that foreigners are receiving only 0.5 per cent of the total benefits (Salowsky 1972: 16–22).

10 Calculated from 'Statistiques du Ministère de l'Intérieur' (Ministère de l'Intérieur 1970).

11 Some employers – particularly small, inefficient ones – specialize in the exploitation of immigrants. For instance, they employ illegal immigrants, who can be forced to work for very low wages and cannot complain to the authorities for fear of deportation. Such cases often cause much indignation in the liberal and social-democratic press. But, in fact, it is the big, efficient firms exploiting immigrants in a legal and relatively humane way that make the biggest profits out of them. The function of immigration in Western European capitalism is created not by the malpractices of backward firms (many of whom incidentally could not survive without immigrant labour), but by the most advanced sectors of big industry which plan and utilize the position of immigrant workers to their own advantage.

12 'So far as we are concerned, hostel and works represent parts of a single whole. The hostels belong to the mines, so the foreign workers are in our charge from start to finish,' stated a representative of the German mining employers proudly (Bundesvereinigung Deutscher Arbeitgberverbände 1966: 81).

13 A group of French doctors found that the tuberculosis rate for black Africans in the Paris suburb of Montreuil was 156 times greater than that for the rest of the local population (Nicoladze et al. 1969: 8). For further examples, see Castles and Kosack (1973 ch. 8).

14 For a description of how a strike of Spanish workers in a steel-works was broken by the threat of deportation, see Gavi (1970: 225–6).

15 See Mark Abrams's study on prejudice in Rose et al. (1969: 551–604). The results of the study are very interesting, but require careful interpretation. The interpretation given by Abrams is extremely misleading. The results of the prejudice study, which was said to indicate a very low level of prejudice in Britain, attracted more public attention than all the other excellent contributions in this book. For a re-analysis of Abrams's material, see Christopher Bagley (1970).

16 We have attempted such a comparison in *Immigrant Workers and Class Structure in Western Europe* (Castles and Kosack 1973: ch. 9). Historical comparisons also tend to throw doubt on the importance of race as a cause of prejudice: white immigrants like the Irish were in the past received with the same hostility as black immigrants today.

17 Surveys carried out in Germany in 1966 show a growth of hostility towards immigrants. This was directly related to the impending recession and local labour's fear of unemployment.

18 Historically, the best example of this strategy was the use of successive waves of immigrants to break the nascent labour movement in the USA and to follow extremely rapid capital accumulation. *The Jungle* by Upton Sinclair gives an excellent account of this. Similar was the use of internal migrants (the 'Okies') in California in the 1930s; see John Steinbeck's *The Grapes of Wrath*.

19 Although the federal council, the parliament, the employers, the unions and all the major parties called for rejection of the Schwarzenbach Initiative, it was defeated only by a small majority: 46 per cent of voters supported the Initiative and 54 per cent voted against it.

20 A good study of the economic impact of immigration is Kindleberger (1967).

21 We do not wish to imply that it is always incorrect for minority groups to form new unions, if the existing ones are corrupt and racialist. It was obviously necessary for militant blacks in the USA to do this, as the existing union structure was actively assisting in their oppression. But organizations like the Detroit Revolutionary Union Movement (DRUM), though consisting initially of blacks only, were not separatist. They had the perspective of organizing class-conscious workers of all ethnic groups. Such organizations appear to be neither necessary nor possible in the present stage of struggle in Western Europe.

3

THE SOCIAL TIME BOMB: EDUCATION OF AN UNDERCLASS IN WEST GERMANY

The immigration experienced by all Western European industrial nations since 1945 is generally regarded as having two distinct forms: first, the permanent settlement of black citizens from former colonies in Britain, France and Holland; secondly, the temporary recruitment of 'guest-workers' from Mediterranean countries for a limited period of employment in West Germany, Switzerland, France, Sweden, and so on. […] But even in the 1960s there was evidence that temporary migration was going to turn into permanent settlement – even in countries like Switzerland and West Germany, which were vehemently opposed to it (Castles and Kosack 1973). […]

The 1970s indeed witnessed the expected change from temporary migration to settlement. But, parallel to this convergence in the two forms of migration, a more important change was taking place: the function of immigrant workers for capitalism was changing throughout Western Europe. The relatively labour-intensive expansion was at an end; the capital accumulation made possible by the exploitation of immigrant labour (together with other factors) now ushered in a new phase of restructuring of the world economy. The policy of the most advanced sectors of capital was now to export capital (and jobs) to low-wage countries, rather than to import labour. This meant a decline in industrial employment in Western Europe, which was intensified in the mid-1970s by the decline in growth, starting with the so-called 'oil crisis', and in the late 1970s by the rapid introduction of micro-processors (see Sivanandan 1979).

The reaction throughout Western Europe was to stop the import of labour and to start repatriation schemes. But although right-wing parties have demanded the repatriation of all immigrants, this has not been the strategy of big capital nor of the governments concerned. A reduced and stabilized immigrant population still has a vital socio-economic function for them: that of a social buffer at the lowest level of society, absorbing the worst impact of restructuring, and helping to cushion higher strata against it. But immigrants can only have this function if legal, social and

This chapter was first published in *Race and Class*, 21 (4) (1980), pp. 369–87.

economic pressures keep them collectively in an underclass position. This is the task of measures restricting entry, labour-market and civil rights. In turn, such discriminatory measures lead to responses from immigrant workers in the form of economic and political struggle. So, throughout Western Europe we see a process of class formation before our eyes.

This chapter will examine the transition from temporary migration to permanent settlement in West Germany, and then look at one aspect of class formation: the way in which the education system works to guarantee that second-generation immigrants will remain at the lowest occupational and social levels of society.[1]

How government policies turned temporary into permanent migration – while claiming the opposite

The migration of workers to West Germany started later than to most other countries, but soon developed into the most rapid and highly organized movement of labour anywhere in post-war Europe. The number of foreign workers rose from 95,000 in 1956 to 1.3 million in 1966, dipped to 900,000 during the recession of 1966–8, and then shot up to 2.5 million by the summer of 1973. Most workers were recruited in their home countries by branches of the German Federal Labour Office (see Castles and Kosack 1973: 39–43 for a description of migration). At first, migration was regarded as a transitory necessity, and government policies were designed to keep it that way, by preventing entry of dependants and severely restricting workers' rights. But by the mid-1960s labour demand was soaring throughout Western Europe. Regulations were relaxed to attract foreign workers and to increase their flexibility and mobility. It became easier for a worker to bring dependants to West Germany after a certain period. At the same time, many families found their own way of reuniting by getting the second partner recruited as a worker and bringing in children as 'tourists'. By 1971, 2 million foreign workers had about one million non-working dependants with them. Of course, population structure still showed an over-representation of young working males and the rate of activity was 66 per cent, compared with about 40 per cent for Germans. Many migrants still came for a few years only, before returning home to set up a small service enterprise, buy land or build a house. But members of this group often re-emigrated to West Germany after a while, when their businesses failed. A second time, they were more likely to bring dependants, having lost their illusions about the chances of escaping poverty in the under-developed south.

Then, in November 1973, the federal government suddenly issued the *Ausländerstopp*, an administrative order banning all further immigration of workers from non-EEC countries. The explanation given for this was the falling demand for labour due to the 'oil crisis'. The real underlying reasons (as mentioned above) were the growing trend to export labour-intensive production processes to low-wage countries in the Third World and the changes in the production process beginning to result from the introduction of micro-processors. Further factors which played a part in West Germany were the costs and tensions caused by the growing social requirements of foreign workers' families and fears of political conflict resulting from the leading part played by foreign workers in the strike wave of the summer of 1973 (Castles and Kosack 1974).

During the 1973–5 recession, the number of foreign workers fell by over half a million. Since the *Ausländerstopp* remained in force during the following period of expansion, the employment of foreign workers became stabilized at just under 2 million (1,869,000 in mid-1978). But the foreign population did not drop, for existing legislation gave more and more of the workers the right to bring in dependants. In terms of numbers, the departing workers were replaced by the wives and children (and sometimes parents) of the workers who remained. The foreign population became stabilized at just below 4 million (3,981,000 on 30 June 1978) (*Statistisches Jahrbuch für die Bundesrepublik Deutschland* 1979). The rate of activity declined to about 50 per cent, and demands for housing, education and social facilities rose accordingly. The *Ausländerstopp* had changed the whole pattern of migration to West Germany. By keeping out new single workers, it accelerated the tendency towards normalization of family structures. Moreover, many workers who would previously have remained for only a few years and then returned to the country of origin decided to remain, for the chance of a second migration in case of failure at home was now blocked. Such workers became long-term settlers and brought in dependants. Altogether, the 1973 *Ausländerstopp* can be compared with the effects of the 1962 Immigration Act in Britain, in making temporary migration permanent without intending to.

Another piece of ill-conceived and discriminatory legislation reinforced this tendency. The SPD–FDP government's tax reform, which came into force on 1 January 1975, granted considerable increases in child benefits. However, these were not to be paid to foreign workers whose children remained in the country of origin. This group was to receive only the scale of benefits they would be entitled to in those countries – which meant little or nothing. Despite protests from trade unions and foreign workers' organizations, the government remained firm, hoping to save about DM 1,000 m per year (*Handelsblatt* 13 September 1974). The predictable result was that many children who had previously been looked after by grandparents in Turkey and Yugoslavia were now brought to West Germany. Sometimes the grandparents came too.

A third measure compounded the effects of the *Ausländerstopp* and the tax reform: the *Stichtagregelung* laid down that foreign workers' dependants who entered West Germany after the 'key date' of 30 November 1974 were not subsequently to be granted a labour permit (Bundesminister für Arbeit und Sozialordnung 1977). This meant that immigrants' children entering after this date would receive compulsory education, but would not be permitted to take up employment upon completing school. The idea was obviously to force the children who had been brought in because of the tax reform to leave the country again when they became adult. But the actual effect was rather different: many of the young people concerned were unable or unwilling to return to their country of origin, and remained in Germany as 'non-persons' – entitled neither to work nor social-security benefits. The likely results of such a situation are clear: barred from any legitimate ways of earning a living, such youths have no choice but to take illegal (and highly exploitative) employment or resort to crime.

By 1976 it was evident that West Germany's policy towards foreign workers had become a contradictory shambles. What had started off as a carefully organized movement of short-term workers had turned into large-scale family immigration, of a long-term and probably permanent nature. The measures taken to control the movement had failed, often achieving the opposite of what had been intended. The West German economy, after benefiting for fifteen years from the profits made from relatively low-paid workers, whose dependants were abroad, was now faced with the social costs of integrating a large immigrant population. And there was growing fear of social and political tensions if these costs were not met. At the same time, slowing economic growth and increasing international competition made the cutting of public expenditure imperative.

In this situation the federal Labour Minister in 1976 convened a commission, representing federal and *Länder* governments, unions and employers, with the urgent task of reviewing migration policies. Its report, issued in February 1977, started by declaring 'The Federal Republic is not a country of immigration', despite the obvious fact that it had long since become one. It called for the maintaining of the *Ausländerstopp* and the *Stichtagregelung*, although the 'key date' for the latter was to be extended to 31 December 1976. Apart from this, it proposed a 'dual strategy' consisting of, on the one hand, measures designed to increase the legal, social and economic integration of immigrants and, on the other, measures designed to encourage them to go back home (Bundesminister für Arbeit und Sozialordnung 1977).

The structure of the immigrant population

Government migration policies, such as the 'dual strategy' mentioned above, are designed to maximize the profitability of foreign workers, while minimizing the social costs. Inevitably they are reflected in the composition and structure of the immigrant population, with regard to nationality, sex, age and family size. Hence, as Table 3.1 shows, the greatest proportion of immigrants come from the most disadvantaged sending countries.

Table 3.1 *Selected immigrant groups by sex on 30 September 1978
in West Germany (thousands)*

	All immigrants	Turks	Yugoslavs	Italians	Greeks	Spaniards
Male	2,320	693	348	357	163	110
Female	1,662	473	262	215	143	79
Total	3,982	1,166	610	572	306	189

Source: *Statistisches Jahrbuch für die Bundesrepublik Deutschland* 1979

The Turks form by far the largest national group among immigrants in West Germany. Moreover, this group is still increasing, both absolutely and proportionally, while the other national groups have declined slightly in recent years. The Turks now form 29 per cent of the immigrant population, compared with only 26 per cent in 1975. Table 3.1 also indicates the persisting imbalance of the sexes: 58 per cent of immigrants are male and 42 per cent female. This applies to all main groups, but is most pronounced for the Italians (62 per cent males), indicating continuing temporary labour migration for these European Community nationals.

An important indication of the trend towards permanent migration is given by statistics on length of stay, which show that more than 60 per cent of immigrants had been in West Germany for over six years in mid-1978. Twenty-six per cent had actually been resident for over ten years. This applies to all main immigrant nationalities (*Statistisches Jahrbuch für die Bundesrepublik Deutschland* 1979). Moreover, as Table 3.2 shows, the age structure of the immigrant population is a direct result of a policy of organized recruitment. Two features stand out: the predominance of 21–45-year-olds (over half the immigrant population) and the large number of 1–6-year-olds. The first feature indicates the economic benefit of recruiting foreign workers – most are in the most productive age group, and pension demands are far away. But, of course, this is also the most fertile age group, which is one reason for the large number of those under 6 years. Besides, most immigrants come from peasant societies, where, for obvious socio-economic reasons, large families are still the norm. The move to an urban industrialized society should in the long run bring the fertility level close to that of the indigenous population. However, this tendency is countered by the repatriation aspect of the 'dual strategy': by undercutting any trend towards 'integration', and hence keeping immigrants in a permanent state of insecurity, this policy reinforces existing social and cultural patterns, in particular that of regarding a large family as a form of insurance for old age. So immigrant birth rates have remained high in recent years, while German birth rates have fallen dramatically. The children of immigrants form a growing proportion of the births in inner-city areas, where the immigrants are concentrated.[2] In recent years, one-third of all births in cities such as Stuttgart, Frankfurt and Duisburg have been to foreign parents, a situation which has fed the racism and xenophobia which helped create it in the first place.

At present, as Table 3.2 shows, there are 494,000 immigrant children aged 6–15, which is the age group subject to compulsory education in

Table 3.2   *Immigrants by age on 30 September 1978 in West Germany*

	No. (thousands)	%
Under 6	393	11
6–9	248	7
10–14	246	7
15–17	121	3
18–20	151	4
21–34	1,280	34
35–44	770	21
45–54	347	9
55–64	116	3
65 +	79	2

Source: *Statistisches Jahrbuch für die Bundesrepublik Deutschland* 1979

West Germany. They make up 5.8 per cent of this age group. But, for all the reasons mentioned above, the foreign proportion of children aged under 6 is far higher – namely 10.8 per cent (my calculations based on *Statistisches Jahrbuch für die Bundesrepublik Deutschland* 1979). These are the children who will be entering compulsory education in the next few years, so that the proportion of children locked into a permanent second-class status is going to almost double.

Policies on the education of immigrant children

Education policy is the responsibility of the *Länder* governments rather than the federal government, which has merely a coordinating role. *Länder* measures have varied considerably. Since the large-scale entry of foreign children was neither anticipated nor officially desired, nothing was done to prepare for it in advance. In the early years it was not even clear whether schooling should be compulsory for them. There was also confusion as to whether the governments of the countries of origin should be permitted to set up national schools – a course much favoured by authoritarian regimes such as those of Spain, Greece and Turkey as a means of political and cultural control. By the late 1960s most of the thirteen *Länder* had made attendance at German schools compulsory, and were beginning to take special measures to tackle the problems of foreign children. But it was not until 1971 that a general policy for the whole Federal Republic was proposed in a decision of the Standing Conference of Education Ministers (a consultative body linking federal and *Länder* authorities). The policy was revised and up-dated by a new decision in 1976, although it remained unchanged in most substantial points. The 1976 decision laid down the following policy aim.

> It is a question of enabling foreign pupils to learn the German language and to obtain German school-leaving certificates, as well as allowing them to keep and improve their knowledge of their mother tongue. At the same time, educational measures should contribute to the social integration of the foreign pupils during the duration of their stay in the German Federal Republic. They also

assist in the maintenance of their linguistic and cultural identity (Beschluss der Kultusministerkonferenz, 1976).

Again, we see the 'dual strategy' already noted in the case of general policies towards immigrants. Schools are to help foreign children integrate into West German society, and yet at the same time prepare them for return to their countries of origin. Accordingly, two main types of special classes have been established:

1 *Preparatory classes* to give intensive language instruction to prepare foreign pupils to join normal school classes.
2 *Classes in the mother-tongue*, as a compulsory part of school curriculum for foreign pupils, with the aim of maintaining knowledge of the language and culture of the country of origin.

Immigrant children in education

Nurseries

Apart from language, the main problem for immigrant children on commencing school is the extreme difference in the form of socialization experienced at home and at school. Foreign children share the same difficulties as other working-class children, but have further grave problems of their own. Their background is characterized by two factors: first, pre-industrial forms of production and social organization, and the associated norms with regard to behaviour, sexual roles, family structures and religion; secondly, the crisis and incipient dissolution of these pre-industrial patterns in the face of economic, political and social change (migration itself being one element of this crisis) (Akpinar et al. 1977). The socialization conditions of immigrant children are therefore both contradictory and insecure. The gravity of this problem varies according to duration of stay in West Germany. Foreign children born there are torn between two cultures, but do at least have the chance of learning the language and getting used to the society before starting school. Children who arrive just before starting school (which is common, for parents often leave them with relatives in the country of origin until they reach school age) are faced with a sudden confrontation between two cultures. At the same time they have to learn a new language and get used to a new home situation with parents and siblings they may hardly know. Children who do not arrive until an even later age have the greatest difficulty. Whether they have attended school at home or not, they have great problems in adapting to school in Germany. They are likely to get stuck in preparatory classes with much younger children, and their chances of successfully completing school are very slim.

Nurseries could have a very important function for foreign children born in West Germany or coming at an early age, reducing their educational disadvantage by helping to prepare them for the demands of school. But, unfortunately, the proportion of immigrant children who go to nurseries is low. On average, 60–80 per cent of 3–6-year-olds attend nurseries in West Germany, but various surveys have shown that the rate of attendance for foreign children is on average only half or less than the rate for German children (Akpinar et al. 1977: 38–9).

Why do those children who would benefit most from nurseries not attend them? One reason lies in the unfamiliarity of foreign parents with this institution, which is much less widespread in their countries of origin. They mistrust the nurseries and see little use in them. Another factor is the concentration of immigrant families in inner-city areas, where nurseries are least adequate, both in quantity and quality. Moreover, many foreign workers may be unable or unwilling to pay the fees charged by nurseries. Procedures for obtaining free places may be unknown or too complicated for them. Whatever the reason, the fact remains that many immigrant children under 6 years old are left alone all day. Others are cared for by elder sisters, whose own education is hindered. Some are cared for by unqualified child-minders, usually of the same nationality.

Even where immigrant children do attend nurseries, little is done to deal with their special difficulties. There are a few special nurseries – national, bilingual or multi-lingual – which are trying out various strategies for the cultural integration of immigrant children. But the overwhelming majority of immigrant children who attend nurseries go to normal ones, designed to meet the needs of German children.[3] It is extremely rare for the staff of these nurseries to receive any special training in the problems of foreign children, and there are virtually no special educational programmes to deal with the situation. In other words, nurseries do not have much of a 'compensatory' effect in dealing with the language and socialization difficulties of immigrant children. Since the basic dispositions required for success at school are largely provided (or not provided) in pre-school socialization, most foreign children start compulsory education with a severe handicap.

Preparatory classes

Foreign children take the same tests on starting school as German children. If their knowledge of German is thought to be adequate, they start in normal classes. If not, they enter a special preparatory class (*Vorbereitungsklasse*), designed to give intensive instruction in the German language and at the same time to give instruction in the normal German curriculum. Transition to normal schooling is supposed to take place as soon as the pupil is adequately prepared for it – as officially laid down, within two years. The class teacher in preparatory classes is generally a compatriot of the children, while German language is supposed to be taught by a German.

However, the realization of this policy has met with considerable problems. The transition from preparatory to normal classes is rarely as rapid and smooth as it should be. The causes for this lie both in the cultural problems of migration and in the socio-economic position of foreign children and teachers in West Germany. As already pointed out, a quarter or more of all school beginners are foreign in many cities. There are districts of industrial towns where the proportion is as high as 80 per cent. Putting children in a one-nationality class may seem an easy solution to many authorities. Sometimes all foreign pupils in a town are collected in one school. This may involve bussing children in from outlying areas. The rationale for this course is that centralization allows the provision of specialized language and remedial facilities, but frequently this appears to be window dressing. Another explanation is that German parents fear that their children may be at a disadvantage in schools where most pupils are foreign. Inevitably, one-nationality classes and *Gastarbeiter* schools tend to become ghettos that are hard to leave.

Moreover, the language problems of immigrant children are often far more complex than is realized. Their mother-tongue is often not the main language of the country concerned – this applies, for instance, to Kurds from Turkey or Slovenians and Macedonians from Yugoslavia. Even where the language is nominally the same, a child's first medium of communication may be a dialect that is very distant from the official language: an Anatolian child may hardly understand Turkish or a Sicilian child may have great difficulty with Italian. So the immigrant child entering a preparatory class may be confronted with a teacher of the same nationality whose speech he or she cannot understand. At the same time, immigrant pupils are expected to learn High German from a German teacher (if they are lucky enough to have one). Yet communication with local children may be a much greater priority, and this involves not High German, but a very different local dialect, like Hessisch, Bayrisch or Berlinerisch. Many immigrant children have in effect to cope with four different languages (or even five in the case of Turkish children attending Koran school where they are taught in Arabic).

Difficulties in preparatory classes are further increased by the wide age range that is often found in them. This is partly because children who are not regarded as suitable for transition to a normal class may remain in the same class for several years. Moreover, pupils newly arrived from abroad are usually put in the first class whatever their age. A 6-year-old Turk born in Frankfurt may find her- or himself sitting next to a 9-year-old straight from Anatolia. An educational social worker in Frankfurt reports working in classes with children ranging from 6 to 9 years and 7 to 12 years (Fries 1975). Even the best teacher is likely to have trouble maintaining discipline and keeping all children interested in classes of such varied ages. This situation hampers learning the German language and also makes it very hard to keep pace with the normal curriculum, so that when a pupil does finally make the transition to a normal class, she or he will probably experience great difficulties. In fact, as many as 40 per cent of children end up being sent back to preparatory classes (Boos-Nünning and Hohmann 1976).

An important cause of the problems related to preparatory classes is the insecure and contradictory position of the foreign teachers who teach in them. Since the use of foreign teachers is one of the main planks of West Germany's 'dual strategy' towards immigrant children, it is worth looking at the problem in more detail. It is important to note that tens of thousands of teachers have come to West Germany from countries like Turkey, Spain and Greece, but they have come as manual workers – not teachers. They have been forced to migrate by economic need and political persecution. It might be thought that members of this group would be the best recruits for teaching their compatriots in German schools, for they are usually fluent in the language and have the knowledge and experience necessary to help in the social integration of immigrant children. But most West German education authorities have been unwilling to employ such teachers. Instead, they have left recruitment to the authorities of the countries of origin. These, in turn, have rejected the use of teachers already in Germany, whose political loyalty is suspect. They have recruited politically reliable teachers in the home country. The amount of special training they receive before coming to Germany is generally negligible, so that many foreign teachers speak little German and have little knowledge of German society upon commencing work. Nor have the West German education authorities provided training facilities to prepare foreign teachers for their specialized and difficult task.

Foreign teachers are paid neither according to their qualifications (which may vary widely), nor according to their actual work as teachers. Employed specifically to teach *Gastarbeiter* children, their contracts are inferior in both pay and conditions to those of German teachers. Unlike German teachers, who are usually granted tenure for life, immigrant teachers have no security of employment whatsoever. They appear to themselves and their pupils as 'second-class teachers for second-class pupils' (Spaeter-Bergamo 1974). This insecure status certainly hampers the success of foreign teachers in integrating their pupils into the German school system. In fact, an unwitting premium is put on failure to meet declared policy aims: a foreign teacher who successfully prepares his or her pupils for entry to normal German classes is working him- or herself out of a job. As soon as the number of pupils in a preparatory class falls below twelve, the class may be dissolved and the teacher may be dismissed. This is specifically stated in foreign teachers' contracts of employment (Fries 1975). In recent years, the insecurity of foreign teachers has grown. With rising unemployment among German teachers, there is talk of giving them special training to replace foreign teachers in preparatory classes. Whatever the educational merits of such a course, its present effect is to worsen the already difficult relations between German and foreign teachers.

Statistics on immigrant children's length of schooling in preparatory classes appear to be unobtainable, but there is considerable evidence to indicate that very few children manage the transition after just one year.

Many children stay far longer than even two years in preparatory classes. Often the term 'preparatory class' is just a euphemism for permanent one-nationality classes – ghettos within the schools – that prevent rather than facilitate integration into normal classes. As the Frankfurt branch of the teachers' union (GEW) has stated, 'From this provisory solution, in the meantime an illegitimate but firmly constituted national school system has become established. This ends for the majority of foreign pupils – namely 65 per cent – without a school-leaving certificate' (Fries 1975). Many immigrant pupils spend all of their primary schooling and even some of their secondary-school career in one-nationality classes. Their chance of integrating into normal classes and meeting the requirements of the West German curriculum after this are extremely small. The 1976 decision tacitly recognized this by legalizing permanent one-nationality classes – giving tacit acceptance to a ghetto situation for immigrant pupils.

Normal classes

Clearly, those immigrant children who start their school career in normal classes together with German children, or at least enter such classes after a relatively short period in a preparatory class, have the best chances of educational success. But such children should not be regarded as being without educational problems. They still have language problems as well as all the difficulties mentioned above with regard to contradictory patterns of socialization. Overcoming these problems requires special attention on the part of their teachers – in other words, some sort of 'positive discrimination' to compensate for their educational disadvantages. But this is all too seldom available.

Indeed, West German teachers find themselves confronted with a task for which they are ill equipped. Immigrant children tend to be concentrated in areas where schools are old and overcrowded. In such inner-city areas, foreign pupils may be more than a quarter of the total number in a class, even though there is an official norm restricting the proportion of foreign children in a class to 15 per cent. For instance, the Minister of Education of Lower Saxony stated in 1978 that this *Land* had 203 primary school classes and 96 secondary modern classes with over 20 per cent foreign children ('Ausländerkinder werden künftig doppelt gezält', in *Erziehung und Wissenschaft*, no. 1, 1978). (By contrast, there were no grammar or middle school classes with such high proportions of foreign children.) Most German teachers find it difficult to cope in a large class with several different nationalities.

The widely varying ages of the children transferred from preparatory classes does not help matters. A 10-year-old in a class of 7-year-olds presents enormous problems for the teacher. Bored by the childish subject matter, and ashamed at being put on a level with much younger pupils, the 10-year-old is likely to assert him- or herself through aggression and disruption. The whole climate in the class may be damaged by such situations, so that the most liberal teacher may begin to feel hostile towards immigrant pupils. Above all, the teacher simply does not have time to devote him- or herself to the specific problems of each immigrant pupil. There are thirty other pupils who require attention. Moreover, German parents are likely to put pressure on teachers at 'parents' evenings', insisting that the teacher should concentrate on their children and not allow them to be held back by too much concern for foreign children in the class.[4]

Very little has been done to prepare teachers for the task of teaching foreign pupils. Until very recently, teachers' training colleges did not provide any special instruction on this topic. Today, there are some courses, but they are still relatively rare. Nor has much been done to provide special teaching material and aids related to the situation of immigrant children. There also appears to be little communication between German teachers in normal classes and the foreign teachers in preparatory classes, so that coordination of methods and subject matter rarely occurs – even within one and the same school.

Classes in the mother-tongue

The evidence given above indicates that the official aim of securing integration and equality of opportunity for immigrant children in the West German education system has not been achieved. Have the authorities been more successful with their other declared aim of preparing children for return home and for reintegration into the school systems of the countries of origin? This is the task of the special classes set up to maintain fluency in the mother-tongue as well as to give basic instruction in the history, geography and culture of the home country. Such classes have been set up widely and appear to be available to most children of the main immigrant nationalities. They are financed by the West German authorities, have a duration of up to five hours per week, are compulsory and take place outside normal school hours, putting additional strain on the children, taking up the time required for homework, and so hindering further their normal schooling.

There appears to be little attempt made to coordinate the content of the mother-tongue classes with normal schooling. The foreign teachers generally use the curricula and textbooks of the country concerned, which would appear desirable from the point of view of aiding reintegration later on. On the other hand, it is questionable whether educational content that is irrelevant to a child's actual situation can lead to successful learning. There is a need for special teaching material relating, for instance, to the situation of being the child of a Turkish worker in West Germany.

It is, above all, the mother-tongue classes that form a focus for the battle for ideological control of immigrant children. Authoritarian regimes try to select the teachers and influence what they teach. Teachers who are unwilling to conform may have their passports taken away by the Consulate and then be reported to the Aliens' Police, which may lead to deportation. The Demirel government of the early 1970s forced Turkish teachers to use militarist texts. The Greek Junta employed threats and violence to compel teachers to use textbooks glorifying the fascist dictatorship. Turkish parents are frequently put under official pressure to send their children to Koran schools in addition to the normal mother-tongue classes. Such Koran schools are not only bearers of religion and culture, but also often play a reactionary political role, frequently acting as recruiting bases for the terrorist Grey Wolf organization. Altogether, it is doubtful whether mother-tongue classes may be regarded as neutral purveyors of national culture. Immigrant trade unionists and political militants may find them a place of bitter conflict, which is carried out at the expense of their children.

There appears to be little hard evidence with regard to the success of the mother-tongue classes in preparing children for reintegration in the country of origin, although there is room for doubt as to their efficacy. What is certain, however, is that they detract from school success within the German system. As more and more children seem likely to remain in West Germany permanently, the role of the mother-tongue classes needs re-examining.

The consequences

The inadequacy of official measures concerning the schooling of immigrant children leads to severe educational disadvantage. This takes three basic forms. First, there is under-attendance at school. Despite compulsory education, many foreign children go to school for only a few years or not at all. To start with, some parents bring in their children illegally as 'tourists' because they cannot get permission for them to enter as dependants. These children cannot go to school; to do so would mean deportation. For obvious reasons there are no statistics on this group, but there is no doubt of its existence. But many children and young people who are legally resident do not go to school either. If we compare the school attendance of West German and foreign children in 1978 we find that 86 per cent of West Germans aged 6–18 were at primary or secondary schools, but the figure for foreigners was only 70 per cent.[5] While this cannot be taken as an accurate measure of under-attendance, because of the different age structures of the German and foreign populations, it certainly does indicate educational under-privilege.

Secondly, there is under-representation in the upper levels of selective education. West Germany still has a tripartite system (apart from a few experimental comprehensives). In mid-1978, 4.4 per cent of all pupils at West German primary and secondary schools were foreigners. Their share was 6 per cent in primary and secondary modern schools (*Hauptschule*), but only 1.4 per cent in middle schools (*Realschule*) and 1.5 per cent in grammar schools (*Gymnasium*) (*Statistisches Jahrbuch für die Bundesrepublik Deutschland* 1979). Children of foreign workers are rarely to be found in higher education, and are also very considerably under-represented in all types of occupational training. Where they do attend occupational training establishments, it is usually the general type (*Berufsschule*), which provides general instruction not leading to a useful qualification (*Statistisches Jahrbuch für die Bundesrepublik Deutschland* 1979).

Thirdly, there is under-achievement at school. Immigrant pupils are severely hampered by socialization and language problems. The preparatory classes fail to compensate for this and do not even permit pupils to keep up with curricular requirements. Immigrant pupils are generally years behind their age-standard when (and if) they are transferred to normal classes. If they leave school at 15 they lose several years of schooling. It is possible to apply to stay on longer, but many immigrant parents do not know of this possibility or are unable to make use of it for economic reasons. So not only do most young immigrants not manage to get into grammar or middle schools (the majority do not even reach the leaving standards of the secondary modern school), but it is officially admitted that two-thirds of immigrant school leavers do not obtain the school leaving certificate of the secondary modern (equivalent to British CSE) (Akpinar et al. 1977: 51).

On the whole, it is doubtful whether West German schools provide most immigrants either with useful knowledge or with formal qualifications likely to lead to success in the occupational system. To many immigrants, this type of schooling appears to be of little value. So many children attend sporadically or not at all. Teenage girls are kept at home to look after younger siblings, and boys are sent out to work long before school-leaving age – illegally and at exploitative wages. Even those who attend regularly are unlikely to obtain a school-leaving certificate. Since this is the minimum requirement for any sort of occupational training or skilled work, most second-generation immigrants are condemned to a life of insecure unskilled labour alternating with unemployment. No wonder that schooling for immigrant workers' children has been widely characterized as 'education for bilingual illiteracy' (Akpinar et al. 1977: 45).

The social time bomb

In recent years, journalists and social workers in West Germany have started referring to second-generation immigrants as the 'social time bomb'. This term is mainly used with regard to the *Stichtagregelung* which denies a labour permit to young people who entered West Germany after 30 November 1974 as dependants. Barred from legal employment, it was obvious that this group would be compelled to resort to illegal work or crime to exist. The spectre of muggings and disorder conjured up by the press caused the government to move the *Stichtag* (key date) to 31 December 1976. At the time of writing there is much discussion in official circles of removing the *Stichtag* altogether. Will the abolition of the *Stichtag* defuse the 'social time bomb'?

The answer to this question must be 'no', for the *Stichtag* is merely one of a series of discriminatory policies which determine the position of second-generation immigrants. This chapter has concentrated on education, describing the failure of the official 'dual strategy', which claims to give immigrant pupils equality of opportunity in the West German educational system, while at the same time preparing them for repatriation. Why has this policy failed? The ostensible reason is its inherent contradiction, which puts an unbearable strain on both pupils and teachers, combined with insufficient resources of finance, person power, training and research. But to grasp the underlying reason one must ask: does the West German ruling class really want to grant equality of opportunity to second-generation immigrants? Catastrophic under-achievement in education serves the interests of employers and government because it helps keep second-generation immigrants in the lowest stratum of the working class: the stratum of unskilled and unqualified workers, who are going to bear the brunt of the restructuring of the capitalist economy in the coming decades.

The role played by the education system in the formation of a new underclass corresponds with the other main aspects of immigrant workers' socio-economic position in West Germany (which is in turn comparable with the position of immigrants in other Western European countries). To get a complete picture of the current process of class formation we would have to examine:

1   *The labour market*, which immigrant workers have entered at the lowest level. Lack of education and training, as well as discrimination have kept them there. Now that employment and training opportunities are tending to contract, immigrants find their prospects deteriorating. Low occupational status is both a cause of poor educational performance of the next generation and a result of educational disadvantage in the past.

2   *The housing and social situation of the immigrant population.* It is necessary to examine the formation of national or multinational communities in inner-city and other areas and the social and economic relationships which develop in them. This includes the question of differentiation of sub-classes and their interaction with the general class system of West Germany. One tendency appears to be the development of an immigrant petit bourgeoisie, which has the function of providing services (like the retail of national foods) but is also frequently parasitical and exploitative (landlords and labour-only sub-contractors).

3   The triple oppression implicit in the *role of the working-class woman migrant*. This is particularly pronounced in the case of Turkish women. The question of the function of traditional sex roles in the formation of immigrant communities needs consideration, as do changes in these roles through work, education and interaction with modern Western European patterns.

4   *The development of new types of culture.* A Turk in West Germany should not be regarded as someone with either a (partial) Turkish or

a (partial) German culture. New types of culture are evolving through migration, and these cannot be regarded as a mere sum of national cultures. There is talk of a general *Gastarbeiterkultur* in West Germany, but the concept of specific national-group cultures of migration seems more useful.

5 *Policies with regard to residence and nationality*. The present legal restrictions on immigrant workers are designed to guarantee maximum control and prevent any collective action against an underclass situation. This applies even to foreign workers' children born in West Germany. They have no right to West German citizenship, and are subject to all restrictions on labour-market and civil rights. It is extremely difficult for immigrants to obtain naturalization, or even permits guaranteeing long-term security of residence. Discriminatory labour-market legislation helps keep immigrants in low-status jobs, and the fear of deportation hangs over their heads, restricting militancy and causing permanent insecurity. Unemployment or a minor criminal offence are sufficient grounds for expulsion from the country – a particularly appalling threat for second-generation immigrants, who may have no links at all with their parents' country of origin.

6 The general nature of *the relationship between the industrial core areas of European capitalism and the peripheral Mediterranean areas*. German capitalists have long regarded southern and south-eastern Europe as suppliers of cheap labour and raw materials and as consumers of industrial products. The form of the relationship has changed over the past century, the import of labour being its particular characteristic in the 1960s. This particular form is now in turn being superseded by new relationships, which will have important effects both on the immigrant population in West Germany and on their countries of origin.

So education is only part, albeit an important one, of the current process of class formation in West Germany. It is the creation of a new underclass which is the real 'social time bomb'. Cosmetic operations to remove particularly blatant pieces of discrimination (like the *Stichtag*) will not change the basic position of immigrant workers in West German society. Of course, it would be easy to put a list of measures to paper which would lead to basic changes and could start to bring about real equality for immigrant workers. But this is a pointless exercise, for it ignores the fact that the import of immigrant workers in the 1960s and the creation of a new lower stratum of the working class in the 1970s correspond to the interests of powerful sections of West Germany's ruling class. In the years of rapid labour-intensive expansion of the 1960s, immigrant workers provided a relatively cheap and easily available source of flexible labour. Now that economic growth has slowed, automation has cut labour needs and capital export to low-wage countries is replacing import of labour, the immigrant population is taking on a new function: it forms a sort of social buffer, cushioning the West German population against the worst effects of the restructuring of the economy. The immigrants bear much of the brunt of change, but educational under-achievement appears to provide legitimation of this, while lack of political rights helps to contain protest. Although large-scale immigration has ceased, immigrants remain an important factor in the class structure of West Germany – and of Western Europe.

Notes

1 In addition to the sources given, this chapter is based on the author's experience in training social workers for work with immigrant children in Frankfurt am Main.

2 Unlike Britain, where children born to immigrants are automatically entitled to British citizenship, children born in West Germany to foreign parents do not gain the right to West German citizenship.

3 This applies, for instance, to 99 per cent of foreign children attending nurseries in Bavaria, according to Akpinar et al. (1977: 43).

4 I can confirm this from personal experience as a parent with a child at a West German primary school.

5 Author's calculations from *Statistisches Jahrbuch für die Bundesrepublik Deutschland* 1979.

4

THE GUEST-WORKER IN WESTERN EUROPE: AN OBITUARY

The social history of industrialization is the history of labour migration: concentration of capital requires movement of labour. Temporary labour recruitment and contract labour have been significant for centuries throughout the capitalist world: Chinese labour in Malaya and the Dutch East Indies, Indian 'coolies' in the West Indies and the migrant labour system in southern Africa are just a few examples. Such systems have often followed on from slavery, and have been seen as preferable in terms of flexibility and controllability. Nineteenth-century industrialization in Europe led to large-scale migrations, both internal rural–urban and international. Most were unorganized, but Germany, France and Switzerland did develop systems of temporary recruitment between 1870 and 1914, making considerable efforts to prevent workers from settling. The Poles who helped build the mines and steelworks of the Ruhr, for instance, were forced to leave the country for a certain period each year to prevent them gaining long-term settlement rights. None the less, settlement did take place, and later policies were aimed at compulsory assimilation through suppression of the Polish language and culture. The largest and most exploitative temporary labour system was that developed by the Nazis to fuel their war economy (see Castles and Kosack 1973 for a summary of pre-1945 European labour migration). After the Second World War, several countries rapidly introduced systems of temporary labour recruitment to speed up reconstruction and to compensate in part for wartime manpower losses. (The following account is based on Castles et al. 1984: ch. 3.)

Britain

In 1945, the British government set up the European voluntary worker (EVW) scheme to recruit about 90,000 workers from refugee camps and later from Italy as well. Only single persons were eligible. They were not regarded as permanent residents and their civil rights were severely restricted. Tied for three years to a job chosen by the Ministry of Labour, they were liable to deportation for misconduct or ill health, and single

This chapter was first published in *International Migration Review*, 20 (4) (1986), pp. 761–78.

men and women recruited were rarely allowed to bring dependants
with them. British unions took a restrictive view of these EVWs (Hepple
1968: 49). The system only operated until 1951, mainly because other
labour sources proved adequate: first, British capital's traditional labour
reserve in Ireland; and, from the 1950s onwards, the inflow of black workers from the disintegrating empire. The EVWs comprised only a relatively
small share of Britain's post-war immigrants. [...]

The EVW scheme was a typical guest-worker system, but its relatively
small size points to a question, which may be well applied to other countries as well: to what extent does a guest-worker system, which usually
entails state control of recruitment, mobility and working conditions, benefit the economy of the receiving country more than spontaneous migration?
In the latter case, the labour market itself often works efficiently to assign
migrants to the jobs that are available, and this is likely to meet the needs
of employers. However, the weakness of the newcomers in the labour
market means that they may end up with exploitative wages and conditions, which is harmful not only to them, but often also to local workers and
unions. The extreme case of this is the toleration of clandestine migration
(important in the cases of France and the USA). The rightless illegal migrant
is the dream-worker for many employers, and the nightmare of the labour
movement. Yet generalization is difficult on this issue. The restriction of
civil and labour-market rights in some guest-worker systems can also have
extremely serious implications both for the situation of the migrants and for
the unity and strength of the labour movement.

Belgium

The Belgian government started recruiting foreign workers immediately
after the Second World War, through what was called *contingentensysteem*.
Workers were recruited under bilateral agreements with southern European
countries, mainly Italy. Most of them were employed in the coal mines and
the iron and steel industry. In 1946, about 60,000 Italians were recruited.
Although this was temporary labour migration of the guest-worker type,
Belgian regulations were fairly liberal about the entry of family members,
and many of the workers stayed on permanently. After 1963, the *contingentensysteem* was abolished, but foreign work-seekers continued to come in of
their own accord – as 'tourists'. Once they had employment, they were
'regularized'; that is, granted work and residence permits. In a period of
rapid economic growth, such spontaneous labour migration responded
rapidly and flexibly to labour needs. Migrants found work in a much wider
range of industries and enterprises than before 1963. In this period, the
Italians were joined by Spaniards, and then by Moroccans and Turks.

In August 1974, the government decided to stop further entry of workers (except from countries of the European Community). The ban took
some time to become fully effective, but by the 1980s few new workers
were entering [...] (see SOPEMI 1984). Entry of dependants did continue

after 1976 due to liberal regulations concerning family reunification. The foreign population grew from 453,000 in 1961 (4.9 per cent of the total population) to 716,000 in 1970 (7.2 per cent) and then to 851,000 in 1977 (8.7 per cent). Since then, the foreign population of Belgium has fluctuated around 900,000 with a negative migration balance being compensated for by natural increase to migrant parents. As in most Western European countries, children of foreign parents born in Belgium do not automatically obtain citizenship of the host country, although there are fairly liberal naturalization provisions. In recent years, most foreigners obtaining new work permits have been spouses and children of workers, entering the labour market for the first time, rather than new immigrants.

France

The French government established an *Office National d'Immigration* (ONI) in 1945 to organize recruitment of foreign workers. Labour migration was seen as a solution to post-war labour shortages, and was expected to be mainly of a temporary character (including seasonal workers for agriculture). However, in view of low birth rates, a certain amount of family settlement was envisaged. Recruitment agreements were made with southern European countries, and French employers had to make a request to the ONI and pay a fee. The ONI organized recruitment and travel. There was continuous migration of workers to France from 1945 to 1974. Two million European migrant workers entered France from 1946 to 1970 and they were joined by 690,000 dependants. However, the appearance of a highly organized system of recruitment is misleading. The ONI's legal monopoly of recruitment of European workers became more and more of a fiction. The proportion of migrants coming as 'clandestines' (on tourist visas or without passports) increased from 26 per cent in 1948 to 82 per cent in 1968 (Office National d'Immigration 1968).

    This was in part a consequence of increasing competition for labour within Western Europe during the boom period. France started recruiting in Italy, but as the labour needs of Switzerland, Belgium, The Netherlands and the German Federal Republic increased, this source became exhausted. The ONI proved incapable of meeting employers' needs, and patterns of spontaneous migration developed, first from Spain and Portugal, later from Yugoslavia and Turkey. Workers from the Iberian countries generally had to come illegally as the dictatorships of the time were unwilling to facilitate movements. Indeed, many workers came as much for political as for economic reasons. Clandestine workers met employers' needs well. They were a flexible source of labour, and their weak legal status compelled them to accept poor wages and conditions. Once they had jobs, clandestine workers were often regularized by the authorities, which granted them work and residence permits. Unions and welfare organizations called for more control to prevent exploitation of migrants by 'slave dealers' (labour-only sub-contractors), unscrupulous employers and landlords.

The ONI was only responsible for migrants from European countries. Citizens of France's colonies and former colonies were able to enter freely until the late 1960s. By 1970, there were over 600,000 Algerians in France, as well as 140,000 Moroccans and 90,000 Tunisians. Increasing numbers of black workers were coming in from West Africa and the French West Indies. By now the problems of uncontrolled migration were becoming evident: severe housing shortages, which even led to the growth of shanty-towns (called *bidonvilles*) around French cities, strains on welfare, education and health facilities, and growing racial tensions, with attacks by French racist groups, particularly against black migrants – in 1973, thirty-two Algerians were murdered.

In July 1974, influenced by the 'oil crisis' and the ban on labour migration to the German Federal Republic (GFR) announced in November 1973, the French government took measures to stop entry of both workers and their dependants (except for those from countries of the European Community). The ban on entry of dependants proved impossible to enforce, for both legal and practical reasons. The official belief that many migrants would leave, and thus alleviate the strains of the growing recession, proved false: the migrant population of France continued to grow, becoming stabilized at around 4.5 million.[1] Only one element of the guest-worker system still remains in France: the recruitment of temporary workers for agriculture. Between 100,000 and 150,000 have been recruited each year since the 1950s. The figure for 1983 was 101,857. Ninety-seven per cent were employed in agriculture, and 83 per cent came from Spain (SOPEMI 1984: 22).

It is evident that an intended temporary labour system has become transformed into a permanent settlement situation. This development – typical for Western Europe – has taken place at a time of considerable economic and social stress, and without foresight or planning. The result is that the social and economic costs have been imposed first on the migrants themselves, who have high rates of unemployment, and suffer serious housing problems and other social disabilities; and, secondly, on the most disadvantaged groups of the French working class, who find themselves competing for jobs, housing and social services with the migrants. The powerful 'common-sense' reaction is to blame the problems on the migrants, and to call for mass repatriation. Right-wing groups have found a heaven-sent opportunity for agitation, and racism has become a central political theme. The success of Le Pen and his *Front National* is a grim warning of the consequences of a *laissez-faire* labour-market policy, motivated only by capital's short-term needs.

The Netherlands

Like Britain, The Netherlands had both colonial migrants and guest-workers. Large numbers of 'repatriates' entered from the Dutch East

Indies (Indonesia) between 1945 and the early 1960s. Then there was migration from Surinam and The Netherlands Antilles, initially of students, later of workers. Recruitment of southern European guest-workers started in response to the labour shortages of the 1960s. The government concluded bilateral recruitment agreements with Italy, Spain, Portugal, Turkey, Greece, Morocco, Yugoslavia and Tunisia between 1960 and 1970. This provided a legal framework for migration, although actual recruitment was carried out mainly by the employers.

The Mediterranean workers were regarded as temporary labour, who could be used as a buffer against economic fluctuations. The recession of 1967 demonstrated this function: the number of foreign workers fell by about 7,000, so that a proportion of unemployment was exported to the countries of origin. However, 39,000 migrant workers remained, even though unemployment of Dutch workers rose sharply. Employed in jobs rejected by the Dutch, the migrants had become economically indispensable. When the recession ended, recruitment of foreign workers increased rapidly. Recruitment ceased in 1974, but this time the number of foreign workers did not decline, even though unemployment reached much higher levels than in 1967. From the beginning of the 1970s, there had been a trend towards family immigration. Now this became more pronounced: by 1977 there were 105,000 workers from the Mediterranean countries (excluding Italy) in The Netherlands, and they were accompanied by 80,000 dependants. By 1985, it was officially estimated that there were 338,000 persons of Mediterranean ethnic origin in The Netherlands, while the total number of members of ethnic minority groups (a broad category including persons of Surinamese, Antillean, and Moluccan origin, refugees and gypsies) was 659,000 (SOPEMI – Netherlands 1985: 16).

Again we have a case of the import of temporary labour, which was expected to go away when no longer needed. Developments in the post-1974 recession showed that the migratory process could not easily be reversed. It is to the credit of the Dutch government that this fact was recognized. In 1979 The Netherlands Scientific Council for Government Policy published a well-researched report, showing that most Mediterranean workers were not likely to return home. They had become permanent settlers and should be recognized as ethnic minorities, within the framework of a general minorities policy (Netherlands Scientific Council for Government Policy 1979). The government accepted this advice and gave an outline of its new policy in 1981. The groups mentioned above were categorized as minorities, and measures were announced to secure their full participation in society, through improvements in legal status, housing, social services and labour-market situation. Legislation against racism and discrimination was introduced, and foreign residents' political rights improved. It would be wrong to think that The Netherlands has escaped the social and political tensions connected with the formation of ethnic minorities in a period of crisis. Nor have all the policies been adequately implemented. Rising unemployment and increasing inner-city problems have encouraged the growth of racism, and anti-migrant parties have gained considerable support. However, the recognition of the inevitability of a multi-ethnic society, and the introduction of appropriate policies, are certainly steps forward, especially in comparison with some of the neighbouring countries.

Switzerland

From 1945 to 1974 Switzerland followed a policy of large-scale import of labour. Foreign workers were recruited abroad (mainly in Italy) by employers, but admission and conditions of residence were controlled by the government in the framework of a guest-worker system. In the early years, policies were extremely restrictive, as there were fears of an impending economic downturn. The aim was to maintain a rapid turnover of foreign workers to prevent them from settling. The admission of dependants was kept to a minimum, and workers were granted residence permits that could be withdrawn at any time. Large-scale use was also made of seasonal workers and frontier workers (that is, workers who enter daily from neighbouring countries). However, by the 1960s, increasing international competition for labour, together with employers' desire for more stable workforces, led to some liberalization: spouses and children were admitted once a worker had been in Switzerland for more than three years. Foreign workers could be granted 'establishment permits' conferring more security and rights to labour-market mobility after ten years (five for certain nationalities). An agreement concluded with Italy in 1964 made it easier to bring in dependants, and also allowed seasonal workers to obtain annual residence permits after five consecutive seasons' work in Switzerland.

The number of foreign workers in Switzerland (including frontier and seasonal workers) rose from 90,000 in 1950 to 435,000 in 1960. Rapid growth continued until the summer of 1964, by which time there were 721,000 foreign workers. Then fears of 'overheating' of the economy led to the first measures to cut entries. The number of migrant workers declined slightly, but then increased again to 834,000 in 1970, and finally peaked at 897,000 in 1973. By that time, about a third of the total labour force and about half of all factory workers came from abroad. Foreign population rose correspondingly: from 279,000 in 1950 (6.1 per cent of total population) to 570,000 in 1960 (10.8 per cent) and 983,000 in 1970 (15.8 per cent). The peak figure was 1,065,000 in 1974 (over 16 per cent).[2]

Severe restrictions were imposed on labour migration from the beginning of the 1970s. The number of foreign workers fell to 650,000 in mid-1977, then increased again to 738,000 in August 1981 – a level which has been more or less maintained since. If we count only workers considered as residents (holders of annual and establishment permits), foreign employment dropped from 599,000 in 1973 to 500,000 in 1977. After 1980, the number started rising again to reach 530,000 in 1983. However, the number of new workers entering is relatively small (24,000 in 1983) and many are either highly qualified persons or dependants of workers already in the country. Guest-worker recruitment has virtually stopped, although the system remains intact. The use of seasonal and frontier workers – the guest-workers *par excellence* – continues, with 100,000 of the former and 105,500 of the latter in 1983 (SOPEMI 1984).

Foreign population dropped from its 1974 peak to 884,000 in 1979 and then increased to 926,000 in 1983. As in other countries, stopping labour entries led to stabilization of the immigrant population, with an increasing share of non-economically active dependants. Over three-quarters of foreign residents in Switzerland now hold establishment permits – a clear indication of the long-term nature of their stay.

Switzerland is the classic case of the guest-worker system. Migrant workers were recruited to allow rates of growth and profit which would have been unthinkable with a restricted labour market. It was never intended that they should settle permanently. Yet just because they allowed most Swiss employees to move out of the low-pay and low-status jobs, they became indispensable to the Swiss economy. When foreign labour became scarce in the 1960s, the authorities had no choice but to improve migrants' rights regarding labour-market mobility, family reunification and long-term stay. Migrants had already started turning into settlers by the time the recession started, and could not be expelled.

The government has been unwilling to face up to the fact of permanent settlement and to provide the necessary housing and social facilities. Migrants' civil and political rights remain extremely restricted. Naturalization is hard to obtain, migrants' children born in Switzerland have no right to Swiss citizenship, and deportation is possible for a variety of reasons. The migrant population is marginalized and this reflects a widespread attitude of hostility towards them on the part of many Swiss. Since 1970 there has been a series of referendums calling for enforced repatriation. These have been narrowly defeated, but have generated pressure for restriction of migrants' rights. A move to introduce a slightly more liberal Foreigners Law was defeated by a referendum in June 1982.

The German Federal Republic

West German employers began importing labour later than those of other countries, partly because post-war recovery did not start until after 1948, partly because there were large internal labour reserves, particularly refugees from the East. The GFR therefore drew on the experience of other European countries, as well as on German historical experience with migrant labour, both before 1914 and within the Nazi war economy. The result was the most highly organized state recruitment apparatus anywhere in Europe – the pinnacle of the guest-worker system.

The Federal Labour Office (*Bundesanstalt für Arbeit* – BfA) set up recruitment offices in the Mediterranean countries. Employers requiring foreign labour had to apply to the BfA and pay a fee. The BfA selected suitable workers, testing their occupational skills, giving them medical examinations and screening police records. The workers were brought in groups to Germany, where employers had to provide accommodation – usually in huts or hostels on the work site. The first bilateral recruitment agreement was made with Italy in 1955. At that time temporary seasonal employment in agriculture and building was envisaged, but soon large numbers of workers were going into industry. Further recruitment agreements were concluded with Spain, Greece, Turkey, Morocco, Portugal, Tunisia and Yugoslavia.

The number of foreign workers in the GFR rose from 95,000 in 1956 to 1.3 million in 1966. Then there was a cutback due to the recession, which lasted until 1968. After that, foreign employment shot up, reaching 2 million by 1970 and 2.6 million by the middle of 1973. With half a million new workers per year, this was the greatest labour migration anywhere in post-war Europe, and was a result of rapid industrial expansion and a simultaneous shift to methods of mass production, requiring large numbers of new unskilled and semi-skilled workers. Many of the workers recruited in Turkey and elsewhere in this period were women.

Policies were shaped by the view that migrant workers were temporary labour units, which could be recruited, utilized and sent away again as employers required. A complex legal and administrative framework was established to control foreign labour (see Castles 1985). To enter and remain in the GFR, a migrant needed a residence permit and a labour permit. These were granted for restricted periods, and were often valid only for specific jobs and areas. Entry of dependants was discouraged. A worker could lose his or her permit for a variety of reasons, which was likely to lead to deportation. This was seen and used as a means of disciplining the foreign labour force. Just as in the other countries, trends towards family reunification could not be prevented. Often spouses came in as workers and, once in the country, found ways of getting together. The establishment of families was inevitable. The competition for labour in the 1960s, and the employers' wish to reduce labour turnover, encouraged the authorities to act less restrictively towards family immigration. Foreign labour was beginning to lose its mobility, and social costs (for housing, education, and so on) were rising.

These tendencies became more marked after the sudden ban on entries of non-EC workers in November 1973. Although the number of foreign workers did initially decline – from 2.6 million in 1973 to 1.9 million in 1976 – the decline in total foreign population was far smaller – from 4.1 million to 3.9 million in the same period. Clearly, family reunification was accelerating and, in addition, large numbers of children were being born to foreign parents in the GFR. Family reunification reached new levels in the late 1960s, as the most recently arrived and largest group – the

Turks – also brought in children. The foreign population peaked at 4.7 million in 1982; one-third was Turkish. This unplanned and unexpected settlement in a period of crisis became a major political issue, with none of the major parties willing to face up to the inevitability of a multi-ethnic society. In the past few years, the migration balance has again been negative, as some migrants flee from unemployment and racism. The current level of 4.4 million foreign residents is likely to be maintained. Despite the well-organized system for temporary recruitment of guest-workers, the GFR has become a country of permanent settlement.

The migratory process

This brief summary of temporary labour systems in six European countries can hardly do justice to the complexity of international labour migrations in the post-war period, but perhaps it suffices to show certain major features. First, it should be noted that virtually all the countries concerned have had migrants of varying types: guest-workers, colonial workers, skilled personnel moving between highly developed countries, and refugees. The latter do not move in search of work, but often do enter the labour force. Particularly those from Third World countries often find themselves doing the same kind of jobs as colonial workers or guest-workers. Secondly, all the countries dealt with above have tried guest-worker systems. In the case of Britain, Belgium and France, these systems were used early in the post-war period, and then abandoned in favour of spontaneous labour migration. Switzerland used a guest-worker system throughout the post-war economic expansion, while The Netherlands and the GFR introduced such systems in the late 1950s and early 1960s.

Thirdly, all the countries examined stopped labour migration at about the same time – following the 'oil crisis' of 1973, when it became clear that a world recession was impending. The only exception is Britain, where labour migration had already been severely restricted through the Commonwealth Immigrants Act of 1962. The cause lay both in Britain's already stagnating economy and in the explosive racial tensions developing in the decaying inner cities. Fourthly, none of the countries expected or intended the guest-workers to become settlers. Employers and government of the recruiting countries had an interest in a flexible source of temporary labour. The countries of origin of the workers accepted the system of temporary migration because they saw it as a palliative for unemployment, as well as a source of foreign exchange for their own economies through workers' remittances. The workers themselves generally hoped to save enough cash through three to five years' work to be able to buy land, livestock or machinery, or to set up a business. They were becoming temporary proletarians abroad to avoid permanent proletarianization in their own countries.

So what went wrong? The answer lies in the dynamics of two simulta-neous and interacting processes: the migratory process itself, and the process of restructuring of the world economy which is at present taking place. The first phase of the migratory process was the phase of mass labour migration. The intention of temporary migration is common to the initial phase of most migratory movements – even to those seen in retro-spect as permanent, such as movement to the USA, Latin America and Australia (see Piore 1980: ch. 6, for the USA). Hence the correspondence of the migrants' aims with those of the employers and states of the receiv-ing and sending countries. As time went on, many migrant workers found that it was impossible to earn and save enough to achieve their economic aims. Moreover, the deterioration of the political and economic situation in some of the countries of origin made an early return seem less and less feasible. As the prospect of going home receded, a life of nothing but hard work, frugality and social isolation seemed less acceptable. Workers started bringing in spouses and children, or starting new fami-lies. The second phase of the migratory process, the phase of family reuni-fication, got under way. Family reunification usually did not imply a decision to settle permanently. Indeed, it was sometimes seen as a way of speeding return, for family members often came as workers rather than just dependants. Family migration had its own logic: family housing and other needs raised migrants' cost of living, reducing savings yet further. Once children were born in Western Europe and started going to school, the prospect of return receded once again.

Family reunification contradicted the aims of the guest-worker system, and was initially rejected by the authorities of several countries. We have seen how competition for labour in the 1960s, together with the employers' interest in a stable labour force, led to relaxation of regula-tions. The influence of multilateral agreements within the OECD, the European Community, the Council of Europe and the Nordic Labour Market also played a part. The main cause of family reunification was simply migrants' refusal to accept the denial of the basic human right of living with their wives, husbands and children. Dependants were brought in legally where possible, illegally where the right was refused. Once large-scale labour migration was established, family immigration became inevitable.

By the time labour migration was halted in the early 1970s, the trend to family reunification was well established. The states of Western Europe hoped that stopping labour migration would cause large-scale return of both workers and dependants. Large numbers of workers did leave, but those who stayed brought in dependants, so that the total migrant population became stabilized or even grew. Once migrant families become established, and start to build communities, once their children are born and go to school in Western European cities, it is inevitable that most will stay. Since, on the other hand, the unplanned nature of this process, in a situation of crisis and racism, leads to marginalization of the migrant populations, the third phase of the migratory process is not only the phase of permanent settlement, but also the phase of the development of new ethnic minorities. This is likely to have important and permanent consequences for Western European societies.

The political economy of the guest-worker system

What were the specific trends in the development of the world economy which made guest-worker systems an appropriate form of labour mobilization for Western Europe from 1945 to 1974, and then made them superfluous?[3] In a nutshell: the former period was one of concentration of capital and production; the latter period was one of global dispersal of industrial production, accompanied by revolutionary innovations in communications and control techniques. These new trends have transformed the role of the old industrial centres in the global division of labour, and have caused new labour migrations. The migrants of the previous phase, who are now settlers, have been left by the wayside.

The expansion from 1945 to the early 1970s saw the most rapid and sustained development of production in history, with world capitalist output doubling in the period from 1952 to 1968 alone (Glyn and Harrison 1980: 5). The causes of the long boom were complex and closely interdependent: the dominance of US capital which emerged from the war allowed a restructuring of financial and commodity markets. US corporations reorganized large sectors of industrial production in Western Europe, while their growing influence in newly independent Third World countries secured cheap raw materials and agricultural products. The advanced sectors of capital became transnational as they strove to integrate production, trade and finance on a world scale. The weakening of the labour movement through fascism and war (especially in the later 'economic miracle' countries of West Germany, Italy and Japan) kept wages relatively low in relation to productivity growth in the early post-war years, encouraging high rates of investment. Post-war reconstruction led to high demand for goods of all kinds. Re-armament, the 'Korea boom' and the Cold War revived demand when it began to show signs of flagging, and this role was later taken over by the consumer boom of the 1960s and by the opportunities for renewal of fixed capital due to the expansion of new highly mechanized industries.

On average, employment in the advanced capitalist countries grew by about 1 per cent per year during the period of expansion. This seems little compared to the rate of capital accumulation (the stock of the means of production grew by about 6 per cent per year; Glyn and Harrison 1980: 5–7). Yet growth of labour supply was an essential precondition for capital accumulation. If no new workers had been available, employers wanting to expand production would have had to offer higher wages to attract labour away from competitors. These, in turn, would have had to offer higher wages to retain labour. The resulting increased rate of inflation would have led to a stop–go economy, reducing economic growth and causing an early end to the boom (see Kindleberger 1967). An OECD study summed up the function of labour migration as follows: 'To permit the industrialized countries to fill job vacancies with reduced upward pressure on wages and profits. This added to national output in those countries and protected their competitive position in world trade' (OECD 1978: 2, 17).

Labour migration was not the only source of additional supply. It complemented the increased industrial employment of women, internal rural–urban migration, absorption of returning soldiers or colonial officials, and of refugees and displaced persons. However, labour migration, particularly of the guest-worker type, was a particularly useful source of labour: it could be readily controlled by the state and employers; it was flexible and mobile. Above all, the migrants, as newcomers lacking rights and often without much education and training, could be steered towards the unskilled, dirty, hard jobs that nobody else wanted to do. Migration prevented wages in these sectors rising as they would otherwise inevitably have done. Migrant labour was, on the whole, a special type of labour: it eased social mobility for some indigenous workers, and at the same time made possible the widespread deskilling of industrial work through Tayloristic methods of mass production (conveyor-line work, piece-work, shift-work) which was so significant in the 1960s (Castles et al. 1984: ch. 5). This role of migrant labour became particularly important in the 1960s, as indigenous labour forces began to decline through previous low birth rates, increasing length of education and (in some countries) conscription of young men for military service.

There was, of course, a conceivable alternative: increased rationalization to replace labour with machinery. Some economists argued that the import of labour was economically harmful because it reduced the incentive for this. This argument forgets that the capital for rationalization has to come from past profits. A tight labour market which kept wages up and profits down would also hinder rationalization. In the boom period there was in fact a correlation between economic growth, increase of labour supply and improvement of productivity. In the GFR and Switzerland the labour force grew fast and there were also large investments in modern plants with high productivity. In the long run, the economy grew steadily and fast, and wages increased too. In Britain, on the other hand, the labour force grew little, the profit rate remained too low to induce investment in new and more productive plants, economic growth was slow and sporadic, and wages in the long run increased less than in the GFR and Switzerland. The effect of abundant labour supply in the long run was not to keep wages down absolutely, but to keep down their relative share in national income, allowing profits and investments to remain high.

So why the sudden turn-around in the mid-1970s? The most obvious cause was the 'oil crisis' and the subsequent recession, which led to unemployment and persistent economic, social and, often, political crises in the countries of Western Europe. Underlying this were two more significant factors. The first has already been dealt with: as the migratory process matured, the economic benefits of employing migrants became eroded. Family reunification reduced the flexibility and mobility of migrant labour, and created a demand for social capital investment in housing, education, health and social amenities. Where this need was not met – and this was the rule – urban decay, social tension and political conflict were the result. The states of Western Europe were becoming concerned with the strains of the shift from labour migration to settlement, which were seen as the responsibility of the state, rather than of employers. These strains were becoming increasingly difficult to manage, in view of inflation and fiscal crisis. The emphasis of state discourse was shifting from labour-market policy to issues of public order. The question raised by labour-market authorities, employers' associations and international organizations, such as the ILO and the OECD, was increasingly: 'Is it not more rational to move the machines to the workers, rather than the workers to the machines?' And this was just what was beginning to happen anyway.

Herein lies the second factor: in the post-war boom, the dynamism of Western Europe capitalism had led to high rates of capital accumulation, caused in part by the inflow of US investments, especially in West Germany. The result, by the end of the 1960s, was an over-accumulation of capital, leading to a high demand for other factors of production. There were simply too many factories requiring labour, raw materials, transport, ancillary services, land, water and air, in a small geographical area. This meant that the cost of all these production factors was soaring (cf. Grahl 1983). A further consequence of over-industrialization was pollution and destruction of the environment, leading to emission controls, which further increased costs.

Similar strains were emerging in the USA and Japan. In the current phase of restructuring, which stems from these problems, the direction and character of capital flows have changed. US and transnational capital are now being invested more in areas of the Third World – the so-called newly industrializing countries (or NICs) – and in less-industrialized parts of Europe and the US, rather than in the traditional industrial centres. The recycling of petrodollars in the period of high oil prices following 1973 played a major part in this restructuring. Western European countries, which were major labour importers in the post-war expansion period, have now become major capital exporters. Within transnational enterprises (themselves often a product of previous US investment or of fusion between US and other national capital) a new division of labour is permitting the transfer of labour-intensive production processes to other countries in the low-wage off-shore production areas of the Third World. The industrial production processes remaining in the core areas of the world economy (Western Europe, North America, Japan) are characterized by increased automation and intensification of work.

At the same time, a further important trend affects the structure of the labour markets in these areas: the development of what has been called 'global control capability' in the major cities of the capitalist world (Sassen-Koob 1985). This refers to the concentration of functions of management, communication, research and development, as well as finance, in cities like London, New York, Frankfurt, Paris, Tokyo, Sydney and Singapore. The result is a job market of highly trained and well-paid specialists, but also of a myriad of diverse service workers to provide for their sophisticated consumer needs. Such services have to be provided where they are consumed, and cannot therefore be devolved to low-wage countries. Moreover, there is a current trend towards re-establishment of certain forms of labour-intensive production in the metropoles. Growing unemployment and marginalization of certain categories of labour (especially women, youth and ethnic minorities) provide a basis for the growth of work-forms peripheral to and dependent on large companies: for example, computer outwork, garment manufacture in sweatshops or at home (mainly by ethnic minority women), widespread employment of youth as casual labour in shops and catering. A new segmentation of the labour market is developing, which can be examined both at the global and local levels (see Mitter 1986; Phizacklea 1985; Sassen-Koob 1985).

Perspectives

In conclusion, we shall address ourselves to two questions: first, what are the consequences of the developments described in this chapter for the former guest-workers? Secondly, what developments are to be observed in international labour migrations, and what perspectives are there for the continued utilization of guest-worker systems?

The guest-worker systems of Western Europe are dead, except for the use of seasonal workers in France and Switzerland. The guest-workers are no longer with us: either they have gone or they have been transmogrified into settlers and marginalized into ethnic minorities. After two or three decades of migration, foreign workers have become an integral part of the labour force. The segmentation of the labour market – itself a product of the discriminatory guest-worker system – made it impossible to dispense with them quickly when the downturn came. Most could not easily be replaced by indigenous workers, even when unemployment reached record levels at the beginning of the 1980s. Employers have, therefore, usually not been in favour of policies of mass repatriation, fearing that it would lead to acute labour shortages in certain areas, and hence to upward pressure on wages.

States have developed two main strategies to manage the ethnic minorities in the crisis. First, workers belonging to ethnic minorities are being used as a buffer partially to cushion other workers from the economic effects of the crisis. This is particularly easy in countries where migrants still lack sociopolitical rights. National preference in hiring, and refusal or withdrawal of work permits, ensure that foreign workers are the first to go. Moreover, the structure of the labour process ensures higher unemployment for minority workers. They are generally employed in the occupations and sectors hardest hit by the process of restructuring. Members of ethnic minorities in Western Europe are extremely vulnerable to dismissal during recessions, and generally have high rates of unemployment (see Castles et al. 1984: 143–9).

Secondly, the new right in Western Europe is developing an ideological and political offensive against the minorities. In some cases (notably Britain, France and the GFR) this has had a significant impact on state policy. As working-class living standards decline, as the inner cities decay, as the destruction of the environment becomes ever more evident, as the threat of war looms larger in people's minds, as youth show less and less interest in established political institutions, the state is confronted with a crisis of legitimacy. State efforts to reassert control are leading to a concentration of power in the executive, an erosion of democratic institutions, a decline in the role of political parties and a curtailment of civil liberties. One method of gaining public support for such strategies is the construction and projection of alleged threats to society presented by the ethnic minorities. A recent British study refers to a 'racialization of state policies in all areas of social life' (Centre for Contemporary Cultural Studies 1982). The construction of the 'foreigner problem' in the GFR is another example (Castles 1985). Media and politicians present an image of ethnic minorities as taking away other workers' jobs, sponging off social security, causing the housing problem, overwhelming schools and generally swamping 'our' society and culture. Minority youth threaten public order through drugs and attacks on the police. Alien extremists create social unrest through violent demonstrations and terrorism. The Islamic minorities in France, Germany and Britain are portrayed as a threat to occidental Christian civilization.

The wind has been sown by the parliamentary right, whose assertions of national interests are generally not openly racist. The whirlwind is being reaped by the extreme right and neo-fascists like Le Pen in France, the National Front in Britain, the NPD and terroristic gangs linked with it in the GFR. This revival of extremist violence may yet prove the most significant long-term impact of temporary migrant labour systems on Western European societies.

But the cause is not the employment of migrants in itself but, rather, the attempt to treat migrants purely as economic men and women, and to distinguish between labour power and other human attributes. Because permanent immigration was not expected, and the states concerned refused to take the necessary steps to provide the housing and social amenities needed for orderly settlement, migration has exacerbated some of the underlying problems of Western European societies. It is easier now to blame the victims than to come to grips with the causes.

This brings us to our second question. The current restructuring of the world economy is giving rise to new migrations. Three main trends may be identified: first, the movement of workers to new industrial areas in Third World countries, for example, to the off-shore production areas of South-east Asia and Latin America. This is mainly internal rural–urban migration of a spontaneous kind, and the majority of migrant workers are women. The second is the migration of workers from Third World countries to oil countries carrying out industrialization programmes, for example, from Pakistan to Saudi Arabia, from Turkey to Libya. This is generally within rigid guest-worker systems, prohibiting settlement and family reunification. In some cases, transnational corporations act as intermediaries.[4] Many of these contract workers have been sent home following the recent decline in the fortunes of OPEC. Will this type of guest-worker employment shift towards settlement in time? I would argue that this is likely in the long run, although the governments concerned seem determined to prevent it and are not likely to be swayed by niceties concerning human rights. The third current trend is the migration of labour to the 'world cities' where the concentration of 'global control capability' leads to demand both for highly qualified workers, and for low-skilled industrial and service workers (see Sassen-Koob 1985). This last form is at present, for the most part, not taking place within guest-worker systems.

Notes

1 It should be noted that official figures on the foreign population of France are contradictory, with divergences of several hundred thousand between census figures and data based on the number of residence permits issued by the Ministry of the Interior. This figure, quoted from SOPEMI (1984: 100) is based on the latter. (SOPEMI is the French acronym for the OECD'S Continuous Reporting System on Migration.)

2 It is difficult to relate the foreign labour force to the foreign population statistically in Switzerland, as two categories of workers – frontier workers and seasonal workers – are not counted as belonging to the population. The figures on the foreign labour force given here are the peak August figures and include all categories of workers.

3 This chapter deals with Western Europe but the concentration of labour in the industrial metropoles in this period applied also to North America and Japan, as did the subsequent global restructuring of production.

4 The West German construction giant, Philip Holzmann, AG has contracted with the Chinese government to employ Chinese workers on building sites in NICs and OPEC countries. The workers are on fixed-term contracts, and their wages are paid to the Chinese government, which passes them on (in part) to the workers in China.

PART III

THE GLOBALIZATION OF MIGRATION

5

MIGRATION AND MINORITIES IN EUROPE: PERSPECTIVES FOR THE 1990s – ELEVEN HYPOTHESES

The aim of this chapter is to look at global patterns of migration and ethnic minority formation, and to relate these to other major political, economic and cultural trends in this post-Cold War world. The significance of these developments for migrants and minorities in Western Europe will be examined, in particular with regard to migration policies, citizenship, racism and identity. Finally, I will discuss some consequences, first for social scientists, secondly for the anti-racist movement. In view of the general and provisional nature of these considerations, I will put them in the form of eleven hypotheses, which I will try to explain and justify.

(1) *The world is entering a new phase of mass population movements, in which migration to Europe and the situation of ethnic minorities in Europe can be fully understood only in a global context.*
At the beginning of the 1980s, there was a widespread belief that mass migrations to Western Europe had, for the time being, ended, allowing a stabilization of immigrant populations. The stopping of labour migration to most countries following the 'oil shock' of 1973–4, and the gradual completion of processes of family reunion (despite attempts by some governments to prevent them), seemed to provide conditions under which the new ethnic minorities could settle and form their own communities. Stabilization facilitated gradual improvement in the socio-economic situation and the civil and political rights of immigrants. This was the context

This chapter was first published in J. Wrench and J. Solomos (eds), *Racism and Migration in Western Europe* (Oxford, Berg, 1993), pp. 17–34.

for debates on pluralism, multicultural policies and measures against discrimination and racism.

The situation changed dramatically in the late 1980s, with a rapid increase of migration to North America,[1] Australia and Western Europe. There was also growth in migration concerning the countries of the South (SOPEMI 1990), including rural–urban movements within less-developed countries (LDCs), migrations between various LDCs, from LDCs to newly industrializing countries (NICs) and between LDCs and oil countries. The 'new migrations' were new in areas of origin and destination, with more and more countries participating: for instance, southern Europe, which had experienced mass emigration until the early 1970s, now became an area of immigration from Africa and Asia. The migrations were new with regard to the characteristics of migrants: for instance, the increasing participation of women workers, and an emerging polarization of skills with both unskilled and very highly qualified personnel participating. They were new with regard to forms of migration: former 'guest-worker' countries now became the destinations of family migration and refugee movements, while new 'guest-worker systems' developed in the oil countries. The overwhelming trend was towards spontaneous movements – uncontrolled though not necessarily unwanted by governments and employers – and often taking the form of illegal or refugee movements.

At present there are estimated to be 80 million migrants (that is, people living permanently or for long periods outside their countries of origin) – the equivalent of 1.7 per cent of world population. Thirty million of these are said to be in 'irregular situations' and 15 million are refugees or asylum-seekers (International Organization for Migration 1990). The number of asylum-seekers coming to European OECD countries per year increased from 65,000 in 1983 to 289,000 in 1989 (SOPEMI 1991: 122). The main increase was at the end of the decade, mainly because of movements from Eastern Europe. However, entries of workers and of family members of previous migrants also rose sharply in the late 1980s.

(2) *Previous distinctions between types of migrations are becoming increasingly meaningless. This is undermining government policies.*

Migration policies have been premised on the belief that movements could be divided up into neat categories, such as economic migration, family reunion, refugees and illegals. Economic migrants in turn were subdivided into unskilled labour, highly skilled employees and business migrants; while refugees were separated into 'convention refugees' and asylum-seekers. Another distinction regarded as highly significant has been between temporary migrants (usually workers) and permanent settlers. Such categories have been central to a variety of migration systems, including the Australian immigration programme, the US preference system, the German 'guest-worker' programme and the United Nations High Commission for Refugees (UNHCR) framework.

Today these distinctions are collapsing. Migratory chains, once established, continue, even when the original policies on which they were based are changed or reversed. For example, when the German federal government decided in 1973 to stop labour migration and to encourage return migration, the main migratory chain – that from Turkey – continued to develop, initially in the form of family reunion, then through refugee entries (Blaschke 1990). Similarly, what appears as entrepreneurial migration may in fact be a form of permanent family movement, as in the case of some South-east Asian migration to Australia, Canada and the USA.

The classic case for the erosion of neat categories is that of asylum-seekers. The overwhelming majority of these do not fall within the category of individual persecution of the UN convention definition, even though they are forced to leave their countries through war, famine, economic pressure, ethnic persecution or ecological catastrophe (Ministry of Labour Sweden 1990). For the year 1990, the UN High Commission for Refugees estimated resettlement needs at just 150,000, and called on governments to be less generous to asylum-seekers who did not meet UNHCR criteria because giving them support might divert efforts from 'real' refugees (UNHCR 1989: 2). The huge gap between the UNHCR figure, and the world's 15 million refugees and asylum-seekers casts doubt on the viability of the convention definition, and points to the pressing need for new international policies.

The overall effect is a general breakdown in regulation of migration and settlement by governments or supranational bodies. As the OECD has pointed out, policies to contain migratory flows are becoming 'difficult to implement' and there is a growth in illegal movements to Europe as well as to other regions (SOPEMI 1990). Certainly there are no comprehensive joint European policies on migration and refugees. However, where there are moves towards such policies – such as through the Schengen and Trevi agreements – the emphasis is on restriction and exclusion rather than on rational and humane immigration policies, or on providing more effective support to refugees.

(3) *The growing disparities in economic, social and demographic conditions between South and North (and East and West) provide the context for future mass migrations.*
In the 1990s, 90–100 million people will be added to world population every year. By 2025, world population is expected almost to double to 8.5 billion people. While the industrialized regions are projected to grow relatively little from 1.2 billion people in 1990 to 1.35 billion in 2025, the LDCs will increase from 4 billion to 7.15 billion (International Organization for Migration 1990). This will lead to a vast increase in demand for jobs: the total labour force of the LDCs is projected to grow by 733 million between 1990 and 2010. This is more than the total current labour force of the industrialized countries – 586 million in 1990. The LDCs need to create 36 million new jobs each year in the 1990s – a target

which seems quite unattainable in the light of past performance (Golini et al. 1990). Population growth in the LDCs is linked with rural–urban migration and rapid urbanization. In 1970, there were only twenty cities in the world with more than 5 million inhabitants. By 2000, there are expected to be forty-four, and most of them will be in the LDCs. The largest cities will be Mexico City and São Paulo with 24 million people each. Other huge cities in the LDCs will include Calcutta (16 million), Bombay (15 million), Teheran (14 million) and Jakarta (13 million). Poor housing, lack of infrastructure and high unemployment are likely to make these cities unattractive places in which to live.

These demographic and social factors will create enormous pressures for South–North migration (Zolberg 1989). In terms of the 'push–pull' models which were used to explain migrations in the past, one could argue that 'pull' factors were the main reasons for the mass labour migrations to Western Europe between 1945 and about 1973: migrant workers came either because they were recruited or because they had a justified expectation that they would find a job (Castles and Kosack 1973: 25–8). During recessions, labour migration declined. In the 1980s, this changed: the 'push' factors became dominant and people came mainly because the conditions of life were intolerable in the area of origin. Even unemployment and a marginal existence in the North became preferable to staying in the South. Such movements are likely to continue whatever the labour-market situation and the policies of governments in the North. However, 'push–pull' theories – generally based on simplistic human capital theories – have only a limited explanatory value. It is necessary to look beyond individual movements and their immediate causes to understand the fundamental processes.

(4) *Economic, social and demographic disparities alone do not cause migration. Rather, the movements are an expression of the interdependence between sending and receiving areas within the political economy of the world market. Once movements start, they often lead to chains of migration, which continue even when the initial causes or policies have changed.*

It has long been obvious that it is not people from the very poorest countries, nor the most impoverished people within a given area, who are most likely to migrate. Migration requires resource, both of finance and of cultural capital. People do not simply decide as individuals to move to another country to maximize their life chances. Most migration is based on existing economic and social links, connected with colonialism, international trade and investment or previous migratory movements. For example, the US *bracero* programme of the 1940s started a long-term migratory movement from Mexico to the USA, just as the German 'guest-worker' programme led to a permanent chain of Turkish migration. Research by Sassen (1988) has shown the strong connections between investment, trade and migration: increasing mobility of capital in the contemporary world economy is a principal determinant of labour mobility. International migration is a collective phenomenon which arises as part of a social relationship between the less-developed and more-developed parts of a single global economic system (Portes and Böröcz 1989).

Understanding these links has important consequences. Many people believe that economic development of the countries of the South will reduce emigration. The left has long called for 'development aid instead of migration', while the neo-liberal slogan has been 'trade in place of migration'. Today we must understand that economic development, at least in the short and medium term, will lead to increased emigration from the poorer countries (see Tapinos 1990). This is because the development process – that is, bringing less-developed areas into the world economy – leads to such severe disruption of existing societal structures that previous ways of living become unviable, and migration appears as the only solution. In general terms, the process has the following stages:

- Increased links between less-developed and developed countries through colonialism, trade, aid and foreign investment.
- Rural development (the 'green revolution') leads to displacement of poorer farmers and to rural–urban migration.
- Rapid growth of large cities with poor social conditions and insufficient employment opportunities.
- Improved education but few jobs for graduates, leading to the 'brain drain'.
- Cultural influence of the developed countries through mass media.
- Tourism and commodification of cultural products.
- Better transport and communications.
- Temporary labour migrations.
- Permanent movements to developed countries.
- Establishment of links between migrant communities in immigration countries and areas of origin, strengthening the cultural influence of developed countries, and sustaining migratory chains.

A good example of the way in which this process has worked for a successful newly industrializing country is Korea, where the rapid industrialization which has made the country one of Asia's 'four tigers' has been accompanied by large-scale migration, mainly to the USA (Sassen 1988: ch. 4). However, this relationship between industrialization and emigration should hardly surprise us, when we remember that Britain's industrial revolution in the eighteenth and nineteenth centuries was marked by mass overseas emigration of proletarianized farmers and artisans.

The current upsurge in South–North migration is essentially a reflection of the economic, social and cultural crisis in many countries of Asia, Africa and Latin America, caused by the post-colonial mode of incorporation into the world capitalist economy. The end of the Cold War adds a new political dimension: as long as there was a Second World which provided an alternative development model, the concept of the Third World had a political significance as a possible non-capitalist way to modernization. The rise of OPEC and the NICs had already eroded the economic usefulness of the concept of the Third World. Now the political value has been lost too: there is no other way but the capitalist one. Since millions of people have already experienced the dislocation, destitution and injustice brought about by capitalist development, they are left with no hope of realization of human dignity and rights in their own countries. Migration to the North now appears as the only way out. At the same time the end of the Soviet empire means an enormous additional potential for migration to the rich countries of Western Europe and North America. In both economic and cultural terms, East–West migration is likely to compete with South–North movements, making the situation even more complex.

(5) *The new types of migration correspond with the restructuring of the economies and labour markets of the developed countries in the past twenty years.*
The ending of organized recruitment of manual workers by industrialized countries in the early 1970s was not a mere conjunctural phenomenon, but rather a reaction to a fundamental restructuring of the labour process. The past two decades have been marked by:

- The 'new international division of labour'; that is, increased capital export from developed countries and establishment of manufacturing industries in the South.
- The micro-electronic revolution.
- Erosion of traditional skilled manual occupations.
- Growth in the services sector, with demand for both highly skilled and low-skilled workers.
- Increased significance of informal sectors in developed countries.
- Casualization of employment, growth in part-time work, increasingly insecure conditions of employment.
- Increased differentiation of labour forces on the basis of gender, age and ethnicity, through mechanisms which push many women, young people and members of minorities into casual or informal-sector work; considerable international mobility of highly skilled workers.

Taking these tendencies together, we can speak of a new polarization of the labour forces of highly developed countries: the old blue-collar skilled working class has shrunk, while both the highly skilled workforce and the unskilled, casualized workforce have grown. Social inequality and insecurity have been exacerbated by the decline of the welfare state. The labour movement has lost much of its power and its innovative capacity, in line with the erosion of its former social basis.

Ethnic minorities and new migrants have played varying parts in these developments. Labour-market policies which give preference to nationals have contributed to very high unemployment rates for former 'guest-workers' and helped cushion the effects of restructuring for local workers. The highly exploited work of migrant women in the clothing industry has partly counteracted the trend to relocation of this type of workplace to LDCs (Phizacklea 1990). The emergence of ethnic small business as a strategy for coping with racism and unemployment has played an important part in urban renewal and in economic change (Blaschke 1990; Light and Bonacich 1988; Waldinger et al. 1990). Temporary (and often illegal) foreign workers from Poland play a significant role in the German building industry, while undocumented African workers pick the fruit and vegetables of most southern European countries. In the NICs, the labour of women rural–urban migrants is central to the development of the electronics industry, while attempts at industrialization in OPEC countries have been largely based on migrant labour, both highly skilled and manual. A new political economy of migrant and ethnic minority labour is emerging.

(6) *State policies towards migrants and minorities have become increasingly complex and contradictory, as governments have sought to address a variety of irreconcilable goals, such as*:

- Provision of labour supplies.
- Differentiation and control of migrant workers.
- Immigration control and repatriation.
- Management of urban problems.
- Reduction of welfare expenditure.
- Maintenance of public order.
- Integration of minorities into social and political institutions.
- Construction of national identity and maintenance of the nation-state.

As the migratory process has matured and new migrations have developed, policies have had to address an increasing number of areas, and to deal with ever more complicated situations. State responses have almost invariably been piecemeal and *ad hoc*, without any long-term, coherent strategies. This applies particularly where governments, for political reasons, have been unwilling to admit the reality of long-term settlement and continued immigration (for example, in Germany, which according to the main political parties is still 'not a country of immigration'). To some extent the above list of goals is chronological: the emphasis was on labour supply and control of migrant workers in the 1950s and 1960s; on immigration control and repatriation in the 1970s; on management of the urban crisis and on cutting welfare in the late 1970s and early 1980s; and on public order, the long-term position of minorities and – again – on immigration control in the late 1980s and early 1990s.

The overlap of these policy goals leads to major contradictions. Here are a few examples:

- Exclusionary policies which deny rights and citizenship prevent integration into political institutions and exacerbate public-order problems.
- Immigration control and repatriation threaten the situation of existing ethnic minorities by criminalizing later segments of migratory chains.
- Policies which lead to the employment of undocumented workers provide cheap labour for certain economic sectors, but also undermine general labour-market policies, split the labour force and help cause racism.[2]
- Crisis-management strategies based on blaming the 'enemy within' contribute to racist violence and threaten public order.
- Attempts to stabilize national identity through the strengthening of ethnic boundaries lead to increased racism and push minorities into separatism and fundamentalism.

To make matters even more complicated, it is becoming difficult clearly to identify the state, both because of the unclear division of responsibilities in the migration area between national and supranational authorities, and because of still contested and unfinished reordering of the division between public and private in social policies. Which state is responsible for migration policies: the individual states of European countries, the European Union as an embryonic all-European state, or even the superstate of the North, responsible for imposing the 'new world order' on the South? Balibar (1991a: 17) concludes that there is no 'law-governed state' in Europe and that this leads to a 'collective sense of identity panic'. This contributes to the psychological insecurity which helps to cause informal racism, as well as providing the political space for populist racist movements.

(7) *Racism in Western European societies has two sets of causes. The first concerns ideologies and practices going back to the construction of nation-states and to colonialism. The second set derives from current processes of social, economic and political change. The increased salience of racism and the shift in its targets over the past twenty years reflect the rapid pace of change in living and working conditions, the dissolution of the cultural forms and organizational structures of the working class, and the weakness and ambivalence of the state.*
Racism has been a significant factor in European societies for centuries (see, for example, Cohen and Bains 1988; Gilroy 1987; Miles 1989). Its manifold roots lie in the ideologies of white superiority which underpinned colonialism, in processes of ethnic exclusion as part of the development of nation-states, in chauvinist nationalist ideologies linked to intra-European conflict, and in attitudes and practices towards immigrant minorities. Western European countries have long-established cultures of racism, which lead to a predisposition to 'racialize' immigrants and

ethnic minorities; that is, to categorize alleged differences between them and the majority group in either biological or cultural terms, which are seen as 'natural' and hence immutable (cf. Brah 1993; Miles 1993a).

This predisposition may be seen as constant, but it is clear that racism as an empirical reality changes over time, with regard to its targets, its forms of expression and its intensity. For practical politics, it is crucial to understand and explain these variations. There is considerable evidence of increasing intensity of racism of all kinds – institutional practices, vilification, discrimination, harassment, violence – in most Western European countries since the early 1970s (Castles et al. 1984: ch. 7; European Parliament 1985). The recent outbreaks of racist violence in Germany, the strength of the extreme right in France and the emergence of new racisms in southern Europe all point to the new strength of racist ideologies. Racism appears to be taking on a new character which is threatening not only to ethnic minorities but to democratic structures in general. The background to this trend lies in:

- The end of European colonialism.
- The decline of older industrial areas, the end of full employment (both as a reality and as a policy aim) and the erosion of the welfare state.
- The social and urban crisis in many parts of Western Europe.
- The economic ascendancy of some former colonies or semi-colonies, particularly in the Middle East and Asia.
- Mass migration and the establishment of new ethnic minorities in European cities.

In the early 1970s, racism appeared to have the same character towards immigrant workers in all the labour-importing countries in Western Europe, and did not depend primarily on phenotypical factors (skin colour, features and so on) or origins (non-European as opposed to European periphery). For example, there were strong similarities in attitudes and behaviour towards Italian workers in Switzerland and black workers in Britain (Castles and Kosack 1973). By the late 1980s, there appeared to be a much higher degree of social acceptance of intra-European migrants, which contrasted with strongly exclusionary attitudes towards immigrants from the South and minorities who were phenotypically different. This change can be attributed to a number of factors: the end of migration from the European periphery; the absorption of some former European migrant groups into citizenship or secure resident status; the decline of individual European nationalisms due to European integration; and the tentative emergence of a 'European consciousness'.

The danger is that this 'European consciousness' will be constructed in exclusionary and discriminatory terms, based on the perceived threat of being swamped by the 'desperate masses' of the South. Indeed, it is possible that it might turn into a much narrower Western European nationalism, owing to fears of East–West migration. An example of the ambivalence of the situation was the reaction of Italians to the so-called 'Albanian invasion' of August 1991 (see Vasta 1993a). On the one hand, there were calls to admit the several thousand spontaneous migrants on the grounds that 'after all they are Europeans too' and desperately in need of help. On the other hand, it was pointed out that letting in one group would encourage further waves and, furthermore, that it would be hard to justify excluding equally desperate people from Africa, except on openly racist grounds. In the end, the reaction of the Italian state was uncharacteristically draconian and repressive: mass expulsion using military means.

A further differentiation is currently emerging: Muslim immigrants are becoming the main targets of racist discourse. This is partly because Muslims form the largest non-European minorities in France, Germany, Britain and Belgium. Anti-Muslim attitudes are also based on historical conflicts between Christian and Muslim peoples in the Mediterranean region. A further link is with international affairs: in the early 1970s, the recession was blamed on the 'oil sheiks', while the Islamic revolution in Iran and, more recently, the Gulf War have led to fears of a challenge to Western dominance. Public debates on the 'population explosion' of the Maghreb increase the perception of an imminent invasion. Thus Muslim minorities appear threatening partly because they are linked to strong external forces, which appear to question the hegemony of the North, and partly because they have a visible and self-confident cultural presence. The Rushdie affair took on major significance because it linked all these factors. At the same time, such discourses present an ideological opportunity for the extreme right: by playing on such fears and linking them to historical traditions, it can take on a new pan-European character, and break out of its old ultra-nationalist ghetto.

The current increase in racism, and the changes in its form and character, are closely linked to the processes of rapid economic, social and political change affecting the population of Western European countries in the past three decades. Their main impact has been felt by the urban working class, which has seen its economic and social conditions severely eroded. Immigrants and new minorities have become the visible symbol of this erosion and hence the target for resentment. Thus as Balibar (1991b) points out, racism is not so much a result of the crisis as one form of its expression. Racism should not be analysed as a working-class phenomenon, but rather as one product of the dissolution of working-class culture and political organization (Balibar 1991c). As popular cultures have been pushed aside by multinational cultural industries, the power to deal with change and to absorb new influences has been lost. As the membership of unions and working-class parties has declined, the ideological and organizational basis for an effective response to the attack on living standards has been lost. The decline of the labour movement creates the social space for racism, which is central aspect of a movement based on communal (or 'white ethnic') identity (cf. Wieviorka 1993).

(8) *The constitution of new minorities, with distinct cultures, identities and institutions, is an irreversible process, which questions existing notions of national identity and citizenship.*

The transformation of immigrant groups into new ethnic minorities[3] is not inevitable. In a non-racist society immigrants could become equal members of civil society, while maintaining their own cultures and identities as much as they wished. But the experience of discrimination and racism in Western European countries forced immigrants to constitute their own communities and to define their group boundaries in cultural terms. In turn, community formation has reinforced fears of separatism and 'ethnic enclaves' on the part of sections of the majority population, leading to reinforcement of exclusionary practices and racism. Ethnic minority cultures – even when they take on traditionalist forms – have the vital task of self-protection (in both material and psychological terms) against a hostile environment.

Today, the reversal of racist and exclusionary policies would no longer be sufficient to bring about the cultural and political integration of minorities, in the sense of eliminating the need for some degree of organizational and cultural autonomy.[4] Ethnic minorities are now firmly established so that Western European countries have no choice but to accept some form of cultural pluralism for the foreseeable future. Policies based on political and cultural assimilation (the French model) or on exclusionary definitions of nationality (the German model) (see Brubaker 1990) can no longer serve as effective forms of integration of the nation-state.

(9) *Western European countries of immigration are being forced to examine the relationship between ethnic diversity, national identity and citizenship. Multicultural models appear to offer the best solution, but there are substantial obstacles to their realization.*

The varying ways in which the 'imagined community' of the nation-state has been constructed in Western European countries in the past are losing their viability. The presence of new ethnic minorities is only one facet of the challenge. Others include:

- European integration and the emergence of a European consciousness. On the positive side this means overcoming old chauvinisms; on the negative side it means erecting boundaries towards the rest of the world: the 'fortress Europe' model.[5]
- The development of a commodified global culture, borne by transnational capital and the mass media, which challenges national cultures.
- The emergence of regional movements, often based on the rediscovered ethnic cultures of historical minorities within nation-states.
- The emergence of a right-wing, populist nationalism as a reaction to the failure of modernity to keep its promise of material prosperity to substantial sections of the population.

The only viable solution appears to lie in an approach to identity and citizenship similar to the multicultural models that have emerged in

Australia and Canada. These are countries which have consciously used immigration as part of the process of nation-building, and have in the long run been forced to revise their concepts of national identity and their institutional structures to take account of the growing cultural diversity of their populations. These models are not without their problems (see Castles et al. 1992) but they have been fairly successful in managing ethnic diversity and maintaining good community relations. Western European countries did not aim to change their demographic and cultural composition through immigration, but that has in fact happened and the current debate on national identity and citizenship must take account of this, by moving away from monocultural myths.

Certainly there is a debate on multicultural models in Europe. Sweden has gone some way to applying them, though with considerable difficulties (Ålund and Schierup 1991). The Netherlands' minorities policy has similarities, though there currently appears to be a shift away from cultural pluralism, and more emphasis on labour-market and educational measures (Rath 1993). It is important to look both at the general principles necessary to apply multiculturalism in Western Europe and at specific issues, such as the social and political rights of permanent settlers, naturalization policies, citizenship of the second generation and minority cultural rights. The main issue, however, is still that of the political will to move away from outmoded forms of nationalism and the nation-state. Major obstacles to the introduction of multicultural policies include:

- The conflict between immigration policy, as a form of differential exclusion from the territory and hence society, and citizenship as a way of including people in civil society and the nation-state.
- The gap between formal citizenship (as a system of civil and political rights) and the *de facto* restriction of economic and social rights of members of ethnic minorities, particularly due to economic restructuring and the decline of the welfare state.
- Racism and nationalism.

(10) *In view of the multifaceted links between the world economy, migratory processes, minority formation and social change, research in this area can no longer be monodisciplinary and national in focus. There is a need for a multidisciplinary and international social science of migration and multicultural societies, combining elements of political economy, sociology, political science, law, demography, anthropology and related disciplines.*

In the period of mass labour migration to industrialized countries, the focus of academic research was on the economics of migrant labour, and on the sociology and social psychology of 'immigrant–host relations'. Later, in response to the apparent ending of labour migration and the permanent settlement of immigrant groups, more critical approaches developed, which sited labour migration in the political economy of capitalism, examined the sociology of minority formation and the racialization of social relations, or looked at the politics of crisis management. It is now clear that labour migration did not end, but has merely changed its form. Indeed, migration and the use of 'unfree labour' have always been part of the capitalist system (Cohen 1987). It is also clear that minority formation and racialization are central aspects of social relations at the national and international levels.

What is new is that all these processes are taking place simultaneously and increasingly in many parts of the world. The long-term result seems likely to be the emergence of multicultural societies, leading in turn to new concepts of citizenship and the nation-state. The consequence for critical social scientists working on immigration, racism and ethnic relations should be a new awareness of the global scope of the subject of research. Monodisciplinary studies of particular facets are justifiable only within the context of an interdisciplinary framework, which provides understanding of the links between the particular and the general, the local and the global. The study of migration and multicultural societies should therefore be understood as a social science in its own right, which is strongly multidisciplinary in its theory and methodology.

(11) *The increasing volume and changing character of migration, together with the emergence of ethnically heterogeneous societies in Europe, make a re-examination of political positions essential. We need to redefine the meaning of 'international solidarity' with regard to migration policies and the North–South divide, to examine potential contradictions in anti-racist positions, and to work out political agendas which can lead to democratic, multicultural societies.*

Labour migration has often been an issue of contention within the labour movement due to the potential threat it presents to wages, conditions and organizational unity. Policies have ranged from international solidarity through to racist exclusionism. Since 1945, the Western European left has generally taken an internationalist and anti-racist line. In the current situation, it seems necessary to re-examine and redefine such positions. A number of dilemmas need to be addressed.

Immigration control is by its nature selective, exclusionary and restrictive. Should we therefore reject all control and demand 'open borders' (as has recently been debated within the German Green Party)? In the present circumstances this could lead to large and chaotic flows, resulting in conflict and racism, giving increased impetus to the extreme right, and probably – in the long run – bringing about even stricter control. On the other hand, there is a realization by governments and international agencies that immigration control, in its present form, is increasingly ineffective (Ministry of Labour Sweden 1990; Purcell 1990; SOPEMI 1990).

South–North and East–West migration can present effective individual strategies for survival and improvement in life chances, but it cannot provide general solutions to global disparities. The number of people who could conceivably migrate to the industrialized countries is a drop in the ocean compared with the number of people facing severe economic and social problems in the LDCs. There is little evidence that migration, under current arrangements, does anything to support development in the areas of origin. Indeed, individual movements can hamper development; for example, by withdrawing people with desperately needed skills. In the past, the answer to this dilemma was found in the principle 'development in place of migration'. As pointed out above, it is now clear that these are false alternatives: development and industrialization actually lead to increased migration for a substantial period.

Finally, there seems to be a potential conflict between the ethnic minorities which developed out of the labour migrations between 1950 and the early 1970s and the new immigrants. The former sometimes see the newcomers as a threat to the gains they are beginning to make and as a catalyst for increased racism. Again, the actual content of solidarity needs to be discussed in this context.

There are no easy answers to any of these dilemmas. To find solutions it is necessary to perceive migrations and the shift to multicultural societies as a central aspect of contemporary global development. For the left in industrialized countries, this would mean developing and advocating a coordinated strategy which simultaneously addresses issues of migration, multiculturalism, foreign and trade policy and development policy.

Migration

It is necessary to advocate a migration policy that balances international solidarity with social and economic interests in the receiving areas. This means that Western European governments and supranational bodies, such as the European Union and the OECD, need to accept that a certain amount of both permanent and temporary migration will take place, and that it is better to plan and administer this than to drive it underground. I have in mind something like the systems adopted in the USA, Canada and Australia, where regular decisions are made on the numbers to be admitted in the categories of economic migrants, refugees and family reunion. All long-term migrants should have the right to permanent residence and family reunion, although this does not preclude special temporary admission schemes for students and trainees as part of development policies. Entry criteria should be free of discrimination on the basis of ethnicity, country of origin, religion, culture or gender. This need not prevent selectivity on the basis of criteria such as education or training (in economic migration categories) and need (in refugee categories).

The demand for a migration policy may seem paradoxical in view of previous remarks on the breakdown of migration control and the erosion of entry categories. Nobody should have the illusion that such a policy can be easily and fully implemented. My argument is that it is better for countries to have policies based on a reasonable amount of immigration, selected according to fair criteria, even if these can only be partially effective, rather than to have unrealistic and discriminatory policies which lead to chaotic, exploitative and conflictual situations.

Multiculturalism

Demands for a fairer immigration system should be accompanied by a struggle for improved rights for immigrants and their descendants. This means working towards policies of multiculturalism. Citizenship for permanent settlers and their children is crucial. Where immigrants do not want to give up their previous nationality, dual citizenship is the answer (see Hammar 1993). An alternative is some type of quasi-citizenship, which gives essential rights but stops short of naturalization. Multiculturalism also implies the guarantee of minority cultural and linguistic rights. These include not only the right to individual and collective expression, but also the provision of necessary services, such as translation and interpreting facilities, to guarantee equal access to courts and social services. Educational measures need to be twofold: on the one hand, support services to prevent disadvantage for children of different linguistic and cultural backgrounds in the mainstream school; on the other hand, support for the maintenance of other languages and cultures. The core of multiculturalism is the demand for full political, economic and social participation of all members of society, whatever their ethnic background. Multicultural policy therefore necessarily includes a range of measures to counter discrimination, to ensure equal opportunities in all areas and, above all, to combat racism.

Foreign and trade policy

Measures to reduce the North–South divide and, in the long term, to reduce the need for migration, are as much issues of foreign and trade policy as of development policy. Stopping arms exports to LDCs could be the biggest single step towards cutting the number of asylum-seekers. Trade policies which change the conditions and terms of trade in favour of the South could make a major contribution. A drastic overhaul of the European Union's common agricultural policy is an example. New attitudes towards social development on the part of the International Monetary Fund, the World Bank and similar agencies would also be important. An emphasis on human rights in all international and trade relations is an important demand.

Development policy

As pointed out, in the short to medium term, development in the countries of the South will lead to increased emigration. None the less, economic and social development is the only long-term solution to current imbalances, and should therefore be given priority. This means supporting development policies which involve real transfer of resources from North to South. A further demand is to include principles of ecologically sustainable development into all investment projects. Measures to improve health and social security in LDCs are also significant in view of their long-term demographic consequences. Finally, development and migration policies should be linked; for instance, through training schemes for migrants to provide the skills necessary for economic development upon return, or by making investment resources available to returning migrants.

Conclusion

Such proposals sound utopian in view of the current priorities of the 'new world order'. Even if they were introduced, they would not bring about quick solutions to the increasing problems of migration and racism. Global migration is certain to go on increasing for the foreseeable future, and it will take place under very difficult conditions. None the less, it is important to be able to put forward an alternative long-term perspective because it gives credibility to the more immediate demands: those for fair and humane immigration policies, and for the recognition of the rights of immigrants and ethnic minorities within multicultural societies.

Notes

1 In the case of the USA the growth got underway following the Immigration Act of 1965, which repealed the restrictive and racist measures which virtually stopped mass immigration from the early 1920s.

2 Or, as Balibar puts it, 'The modern state ... opens the door to "clandestine" circulation of the foreign labour force, and at the same time represses it' (1991a: 16).

3 For the purposes of this chapter, ethnic minorities may be seen as social groups, which are the result of both other-definition and self-definition. On the one hand, their boundaries are defined by dominant social groups according to perceived phenotypical or cultural characteristics, which leads to the imposition of specific economic, social or legal situations. On the other hand, their members generally share a self-definition or ethnic identity based on ideas of common origins, history, culture, experience and values. The relative importance of other- and self-definition varies according to the group and its situation.

4 Anyway, it is questionable whether this can ever happen in the first few generations of a migratory process even under the best possible conditions. It is also questionable whether such cultural homogenization is desirable. These are issues which will not be pursued here.

5 An interesting expression of this is the term *extracommunitario* now widely used as a label for immigrants from outside the European Union in Italy. The term has become as pejorative as *Arab* in France or *Ausländer* in Germany. It is a way of homogenizing difference in exclusionary terms, whereby the core of difference is non-belonging to a (new) imagined European community.

6

CONTRACT LABOUR MIGRATION

Characteristics of contract labour systems

Contract labour migration may be defined as temporary international movements of workers, which are organized and regulated by governments, employers or both. Such movements have been significant since the late nineteenth century and grew in volume considerably after 1945. Areas of destination for contract labour migrants have included most Western European countries, the USA and, more recently, oil-producing countries and newly industrializing countries in Asia, Africa and Latin America. Contract labour migration is limited in duration. The period may be an agricultural season, the time it takes to carry out a construction project or a specified number of months or years.

Contract labour migration may be organized by the governments of sending or receiving countries, by employers, by special agencies or by combinations of these. However, some participation by the government of the receiving country is necessary; otherwise the movement should be seen as a spontaneous or illegal one. Often contract labour migration is regulated by bilateral agreements between sending and receiving countries, or by multilateral agreements to which several states are party. The recruitment agreements or employment contracts may specify wage levels, duration of employment, working conditions and labour-market rights of the workers. The agreements may also lay down obligations for the employers or public authorities to provide housing, family allowances, health care and social insurance. The recruitment agreements, together with the laws and regulations of the receiving country, also define the legal status of the contract migrant with regard to residence and family reunion, as well as social, civil and political rights. Generally, the situation of temporary workers is a highly restricted one which denies them many of the rights of citizens or permanent residents.

Historical antecedents

Contract labour migration may be seen as one form of 'unfree labour' (Cohen 1987) through which a group of workers is controlled by a regime

This chapter was first published in R. Cohen (ed.), *The Cambridge Survey of World Migration* (Cambridge, Cambridge University Press, 1995), pp. 510–14.

which limits their rights compared with other workers. It is related to other forms of labour mobilization with coercive elements, such as recruitment of indentured workers from England for the early American colonies and the large-scale use of indentured workers from India and China in the British and Dutch colonial empires in the nineteenth and early twentieth centuries. The South African mine labour system is a colonial type of contract labour migration which still exists today.

Contract migrant labour was important in European industrialization. In the late nineteenth century, workers of Polish ethnicity (but with German citizenship) moved west to provide labour for the new industries of the Ruhr. The East German *Junkers* (landlords) replaced them with 'foreign Poles'. Fearing that a Polish influx might weaken German control of the eastern provinces, the Prussian government introduced a rigid control system. 'Foreign Poles' were recruited as seasonal workers only, were not allowed to bring in dependants, and had to leave German territory for several months each year. At first they were allowed to work in agriculture only, but were later permitted to take industrial jobs in Silesia and Thuringia, but not in the Ruhr. The migrant workers had to accept contracts laying down rates of pay and conditions inferior to German workers. Special police sections were established to deal with indiscipline through imprisonment or deportation. Such measures were deliberately used as a method to keep wages low and to create a split labour market (Dohse 1981: 33–83).

In France, too, contract labour was recruited by farmers' associations and mines before 1914. During the First World War, recruitment systems were set up to bring in workers from southern Europe, North Africa and Indo-China. After 1918, when war losses led to serious labour shortages, a sophisticated contract labour system was established. Labour agreements were concluded with Poland, Italy and Czechoslovakia. Recruitment was organized by the *Société Générale d'Immigration* (SGI), a private body set up by farm and mining interests. Foreign workers were controlled through a system of identity cards and work contracts, and channelled into manual jobs in farming, construction and heavy industry. About 567,000 workers were recruited by the SGI in the 1920s. However, greater numbers – about 1.5 million – came spontaneously. In the Great Depression of the 1930s, many migrant workers were sacked and deported (Cross 1983).

The German and French experiences showed the value for employers of a contract labour force. It created a pool of cheap labour, which could be easily exploited and controlled, and deported if no longer required. The Nazis made extensive use of foreign labour – both forced and voluntary – to fuel their war machine. Dohse (1981) argues that the need for labour was one reason for the attack on Poland. By 1944, there were 7.5 million foreign workers in the Reich, of whom 1.8 million were prisoners of war. The Nazis took exploitation of rightless migrants to an extreme which can only be compared with slavery, yet its legal core – the sharp distinction between the status of national and foreigner – was to be found in both earlier and later contract labour systems.

The US *bracero* programme

Although the USA is seen as a country of permanent immigration, use has been made of contract labour, especially for agriculture. Labour shortages in the First World War led to the admission of 76,802 Mexican workers, and smaller numbers from the Bahamas and Canada. In the Second World War, the US government created a Mexican labour programme (known as the *bracero* programme from the Spanish word for day-labourer). This was renewed during the Korean War and continued due to pressure from farmers until 1964. The *braceros* were mainly employed in the agribusiness of the south-western states, though some found industrial jobs in other regions. At the height of the programme in the mid-1950s, nearly half a million Mexican workers per year were involved. The regulations laid down wage protection, medical care, transportation, housing and other benefits, but little was done to enforce them. *Braceros* generally had poor pay and conditions, and this had negative effects on the situation of US workers – often themselves members of ethnic minorities, such as chicanos and African-Americans (Briggs 1986: 996–9; Cohen 1987: 45–55).

The *bracero* programme was stopped in 1964, but created migratory patterns that led to large-scale illegal movements, often resulting in settlement. Undocumented workers from Mexico, other Latin American countries and the Caribbean became an important and enduring part of US labour supply. Border control and periodic crack-downs – such as Operation Wetback in 1954, in which over one million illegal immigrants were apprehended – did little to stop the movements. The US government refused to penalize the employers, who had a strong interest in Mexican labour. The 1986 Immigration Reform and Control Act provided an amnesty for undocumented workers, with over 3 million applying. It also set up a 'replenishment agricultural workers programme' to bring in legal contract workers, if a shortage of labour should develop. However, illegal migration continued.

Western European 'guest-worker' systems

In the post-war economic boom, virtually all Western European countries made use of contract labour migrants, although in some cases this played a smaller part than entries from former colonies. Early examples were the British European voluntary worker scheme and the Belgium *contingenten-systeem*, which recruited workers from refugee camps (in the British case) and from Italy (in both cases), particularly for heavy industry. France established an *Office National d'Immigration* (ONI) in 1945 to organize recruitment of foreign workers from southern Europe. This included up to 150,000 temporary agricultural workers per year, and larger numbers for manufacturing and construction. However, the government soon lost control of movements, so that by the late 1960s over 80 per cent were coming illegally, with the ONI regularizing their situation once they had found work.

Switzerland, too, followed a policy of large-scale labour import from 1945 to 1974. Workers were recruited abroad by employers, while admission and residence were controlled by the government. The basis principle was 'rotation': workers were to stay only a few years, and were forbidden to change jobs or bring in their families. By the early 1970s, foreign workers made up nearly one-third of the labour force. The need to attract and retain workers, together with diplomatic pressure from Italy, led to relaxations on family reunion and permanent stay, leading to settlement.

The key case for understanding the 'guest-worker system' was the highly developed state recruitment apparatus established by the Federal Republic of Germany (FRG). Starting in the late 1950s, the Federal Labour Office (*Bundesanstalt für Arbeit* or BfA) set up recruitment offices in the Mediterranean countries. Employers requiring foreign labour paid a fee to the BfA, which selected workers, checking their skills, health and police records. Employers had to provide initial accommodation. Recruitment, working conditions and social security were regulated by bilateral agreements between the FRG and the sending countries: first Italy, then Greece, Turkey, Morocco, Portugal, Tunisia and Yugoslavia. The number of foreign workers in the FRG rose from 95,000 in 1956 to 1.3 million in 1966 and 2.6 million in 1973. Foreign women played a major part, especially in the later years: their labour was in high demand in industries like textiles, clothing and electrical goods.

German policies conceived of migrant workers as temporary labour units, which could be recruited, utilized and sent away again as employers required. To enter and remain in the FRG, a migrant needed a residence permit and a labour permit. These were granted for limited periods, and were often valid only for specific jobs and areas. A worker could be deprived of his or her permit for a variety of reasons, leading to deportation. Entry of dependants was discouraged, but it proved impossible to prevent family reunion and settlement. Some migrants were able to get employers to request their spouses as workers. Competition with other labour-importing countries for workers led to the relaxation of restrictions on the entry of dependants in the 1960s. Families became established and children were born. Foreign labour was beginning to lose its mobility, and social costs (for housing, education, health care) could no longer be avoided. When the federal government stopped labour recruitment in November 1973 the motivation was not only the looming 'oil crisis', but also the belated realization that permanent immigration was taking place.

The case of the FRG shows both the principles and the contradictions of contract labour systems. These include the belief in temporary sojourn, the restriction of labour-market and civil rights, the recruitment of single workers, the inability to prevent family reunion, the gradual move towards longer stay and the inexorable pressures for settlement. Contract worker migration to Western Europe was virtually stopped after 1974.

However, the now-established migratory chains continued through entries of family members, illegal workers and asylum-seekers, while the former migrant workers were transformed into new ethnic minorities (Castles et al. 1984).

Labour migration to oil countries

The rapid increases in oil revenues after 1973 encouraged oil-producing countries to embark on ambitious programmes of construction and industrialization. The Arab oil countries hired expatriate experts in Europe, the USA and other Middle East countries. Low-skilled workers came from Arab countries, such as Egypt, Yemen and Jordan, as well as from Asian countries, particularly India, Pakistan, Bangladesh, Sri Lanka, the Philippines and South Korea. The total number of foreign workers in the six Gulf Cooperation Council states (Bahrain, Kuwait, Oman, Qatar, Saudi Arabia and the United Arab Emirates) rose from 685,000 in 1970 to 2.7 million in 1980, when they made up 70 per cent of the total labour force (Birks et al. 1986: 801). Libya recruited workers in Egypt, Tunisia and other parts of Africa. Non-Arab oil states like Venezuela and Nigeria also employed large numbers of migrant workers, though most came spontaneously rather than through contract labour systems.

The distinguishing feature of labour recruitment to the Arab oil countries was the high degree of regulation, designed to prevent settlement. Arrangements varied: most Arab workers came spontaneously, but were subject to strict control once in the country. As time went on, the Gulf monarchies became worried about threats to labour discipline and public order allegedly posed by Arab workers, especially Palestinians and Yemenis. They therefore increased recruitment from South and South-east Asia. The movements were organized by the governments of both sending and receiving countries, as well as employers and special recruiting agencies. The Philippines government established an overseas employment administration to encourage migration and to safeguard workers' conditions. In some cases, workers were recruited by international construction firms which were undertaking major projects in the oil states. Korean building companies made a successful business of providing their own labour – a practice encouraged by strict government control. By contrast, most workers from South Asia were recruited through private agents based in the countries concerned. This gave rise to a lucrative 'migration industry', which increased the impetus to move abroad, even when government wanted to restrict migration (Abella 1992: 150–2).

Between 1969 and 1989, nearly 12 million Asians are estimated to have worked in other countries, mainly the Middle East. At first the great majority were men, but the proportion of women migrating as domestic servants, nurses or office workers increased over time. Worker rights were highly restricted: migrants were not allowed to settle nor bring in dependants, and lacked civil or political rights. They were generally segregated in barracks. They could be deported for misconduct, and were often forced to work very long hours. Women domestic workers were subjected to exploitation and sexual abuse. The big attraction for workers were the wages: often ten times as much as could be earned at home. However, wage levels declined during the 1980s as labour demand fell, and competition between labour-sending nations increased. Many migrant workers were exploited by agents and other intermediaries, who took large fees (up to 25 per cent of their first year's pay). Agents sometimes failed to keep their promises concerning employment, transportation, wages and working conditions.

The governments of labour-sending countries saw the migrations as vital to their development programmes, partly because they hoped they would reduce unemployment and provide training and industrial experience, but mainly because of the workers' remittances. Billions of dollars were sent home by workers, making a vital contribution to the balance of payments of countries with severe trade deficits, such as Pakistan and India. Millions of families had improved living standards because of remittances. However, the money was often spent on luxury goods, dowries, housing or land, rather than on productive investments. Since the migrants generally came from the middle strata rather than the poorest groups, remittances often exacerbated social inequality and led to increased concentration of land ownership.

The vulnerability of contract workers was demonstrated in the mid-1980s when oil prices fell and labour demand declined. There were mass expulsions from Nigeria in 1983 and 1985 and from Libya in 1985. The 1990–1 Gulf crisis led to even greater disruption: some migrants were killed or injured, and many more endured hardship when forced to flee the area. An estimated 5 million people were displaced, resulting in enormous loss of remittances and income for countries from South-east Asia to North Africa. After the crisis, many workers did return to Kuwait and other Gulf countries, but at the same time new patterns of labour migration were becoming evident within Asia.

Labour migration in Asia

In recent years rapid economic growth and declining fertility have led to considerable demand for migrant labour in some Asian countries, including Japan, Hong Kong, Taiwan, Singapore and oil-rich Brunei. South Korea and Thailand are on the verge of making the transition from labour export to import.

Japan has been experiencing severe labour shortages in recent years. In the 1980s, increasing numbers of women were admitted, mainly from Pakistan, the Philippines, Bangladesh and Korea to work as waitresses and entertainers. They were followed by male compatriots, who worked – generally illegally – as factory or construction workers. The Japanese government is reluctant to introduce a contract labour system due to fears of overpopulation and concern to preserve ethnic homogeneity. In 1990, revisions to the Immigration and Refugee Recognition Law introduced severe penalties for illegal foreign workers and their employers. However, various arrangements tantamount to a 'backdoor' contract labour system were permitted. These include the recruitment of unskilled foreigners of Japanese origin (the so-called 'Japanese Brazilians'), the employment of 'trainees' from developing countries in industry, and the admission of foreigners who register as students of Japanese language schools and are allowed to work 20 hours per week. Once Japan comes out of the recession of the early 1990s an official contract labour scheme seems probable.

Singapore is heavily dependent on unskilled workers from Malaysia, Thailand, Indonesia and the Philippines: about 160,000 foreign workers make up 11 per cent of the labour force. They are strictly controlled. The government imposes a foreign worker levy (S$300 in 1990) to equalize the costs of foreign and domestic workers. Unskilled workers have to rotate every few years and are not permitted to settle or to bring in their families. Unskilled workers are forbidden to marry Singaporeans and women have to undergo regular pregnancy tests. In 1989 there was an amnesty for illegal workers, after which a mandatory punishment of 3 months' jail and three strokes of the cane was introduced. On the other hand, Singapore is eager to attract skilled and professional workers, particularly those of Chinese ethnicity from Hong Kong. They are encouraged to settle and quickly granted permanent residence status (Skeldon 1992: 44–6).

Fast-growing countries like Korea and Thailand are sending fewer workers abroad as job opportunities open up locally. In 1983, 225,000 Korean workers were abroad, of whom 42 per cent were construction workers. By 1989 only 76,000 were abroad, of whom 10 per cent were construction workers. Korea is considering recruiting unskilled workers from China (Martin 1991: 188). In Thailand, Burmese and Cambodians work on the farms of the north-east, many of which belong to migrants who are in the Middle East. Brunei has about 40,000 foreign workers, over 40 per cent of the labour force. Hong Kong has shortages of both skilled and unskilled workers. Some unskilled workers are recruited legally from China. There are also foreign workers from the Philippines and South Asia, and even from Nigeria. In all these cases, the number of illegal workers considerably exceeds the number of legal contract workers. Taiwan is one of the world's most densely populated countries, yet economic growth has led to labour shortfalls. There are thought to be up to 300,000 illegal workers, and the government has now decided to admit foreign workers on one-year visas.

Conclusions and perspectives

Contract labour migration is often portrayed as a highly organized system of labour recruitment to meet temporary needs, such as rapid economic growth, industrialization, special construction projects or reconstruction after a war. The workers are supposedly brought to the receiving country for a specific period, do not seek social integration, send their savings home, and are repatriated when the job is completed. The reality is usually different. Many receiving countries have used contract workers to meet long-term labour needs. Length of stay has increased, both because employers still needed the workers, and because the migrants did not wish to return. The US *bracero* programme and European 'guest-worker' systems demonstrate how contract labour systems can establish migratory flows, which continue in new forms even when receiving governments try to stop them. The result is permanent settlement and the formation of ethnic minorities. Such groups tend to be disadvantaged and socially iso-lated because of their legal status as non-settlers without citizenship rights. Hostile reactions from local populations are exacerbated by the fact that governments have portrayed the movements as temporary ones, which would not lead to settlement.

Many contract labour systems have been poorly organized, workers have been employed under exploitative conditions, and their special status has denied them recourse to normal legal or political remedies. Trade unions in receiving countries have been faced with the dilemma of opposing contract labour because it might damage the conditions of local workers or trying to organize the migrants to prevent abuse. The borderlines between contract labour migration, individual temporary labour migration and illegal movements are often fluid. This is especially evident in the case of contemporary labour movements in Asia. Governments may tacitly accept illegal movements because it is politi-cally inopportune to set up a contract labour system; this applies as much to Japan today, as it did to the USA after the abolition of the *bracero* pro-gramme in 1964.

In the past, contract labour migration concerned predominantly low-skilled workers going to a limited number of destinations. Today, contract labour arrangements are to be found in many parts of the world, and their scope and range are increasing. This brief survey has described only a few important cases. Other examples include the recruitment by Nigeria of skilled personnel such as teachers from the Philippines. Australia's Northern Territory trade development zone encouraged the entry of Chinese workers who produced for off-shore countries at wage rates far below official levels, until local trade unions intervened. Many highly skilled workers, such as managers, financial experts and technicians migrate on temporary employment contracts. It is hard to draw a precise line between the privileged 'professional transients' moving within inter-national labour markets and vulnerable low-skilled migrants.

These shifts, and the slippage between contract labour migration and other forms of migration, indicate that the phenomenon cannot be use-fully analysed in isolation. Contract labour migration is just one aspect of the increasing global mobility of people, which in turn is closely linked to growing movements of capital, commodities and ideas (Castles and

Miller 1998). With rapid improvements in transport and communication, and the growth of migration networks, old distinctions between labour migration, settler migration and movements of asylum-seekers are breaking down. Movements can no longer be clearly separated into permanent or temporary, and migration chains are becoming two-way streets.

7

MIGRATION IN THE ASIAN PACIFIC REGION: BEFORE AND AFTER THE CRISIS

The past two decades have been a period of massive transformation in the Asian Pacific region. This vast and populous area has experienced economic, demographic, political and social change on a pace and scale almost without historical precedent. One of the most significant aspects has been a substantial increase in international migration of all kinds. Family and community networks play a major role, and increasing numbers of both migrant workers and refugees are women. Whether temporary or permanent, international migration is likely to have long-term effects on the societies of both emigration and immigration countries. Migration is both a result of globalization and economic change, and a powerful factor helping to shape societies.

Since 1997, the Asian financial and economic crisis has brought about important changes in migratory flows. Receiving-country governments are trying to stop labour recruitment and send migrant workers home. However, many migrants seem to be staying on, while new migratory flows are emerging. Overall, the changes are complex and often take unexpected directions. This chapter provides an overview of the way in which migratory patterns have developed since the 1970s, and looks at perspectives for change, based on the data available in late 1998.

The emergence of new migrations

Asian migration is not new: westward movements from Central Asia helped shape European history in the Middle Ages, while southward movement of Chinese workers and traders to South-east Asia goes back centuries. In the colonial period millions of indentured workers were recruited (sometimes by force) within the European empires, and transported to other regions and continents. In the nineteenth century, there was considerable migration from China and Japan to the USA, Canada and Australia. By the 1880s, discriminatory legislation was enacted to prevent these movements. Such restrictions, together with economic and

---

This chapter is partly based on the article 'New migrations in the Asia-Pacific region: a force for social and political change', *International Social Science Journal*, 156 (1998), pp. 215–27.

political conditions, kept Asian migration at fairly low levels in the first half of the twentieth century.[1]

The massive growth in Asian migration from the 1970s was closely linked with the development of economic and political relationships with the industrialized countries in the post-colonial period. Western penetration through trade, aid and investment created the material means and the cultural capital necessary for migration. The dislocation of economic and social structures through industrialization and the 'green revolution' impelled people to leave the countryside in search of better conditions. Political instability, internal conflicts and wars (such as those in Vietnam and Afghanistan) led to major refugee flows. The rapid industrial take-off of some areas and the continuing stagnation of others led to massive labour movements, first to the Gulf oil countries and then to the newly industrializing economies within Asia.

There are no accurate systems for monitoring population movements within the Asian Pacific region. By the mid-1990s, there were estimated to be about 3 million Asians employed outside their own countries within the Asian region, and another 3 million employed in other continents (Martin et al. 1996: 163). In addition, there were millions of refugees and family members. The number of illegal migrants could only be guessed at, but might well exceed that of legal migrants. The situation is complicated by the emergence of a 'migration industry': large numbers of migration agents or labour recruiters, motivated by commercial or other considerations. These people organize migration through transnational networks, which are difficult for governments to control. Some agents have links with organized crime, and indulge in the trafficking of illegal migrants, the exploitation of workers and the abuse of women and children through recruitment for the sex industry.

A key development has been the increasing feminization of migration: about 1.5 million Asian women were working abroad by the mid-1990s, and in many migratory movements they outnumbered men. Most migrant women are concentrated in jobs regarded as 'typically female': domestic workers, entertainers (often a euphemism for prostitution), restaurant and hotel staff, assembly-line workers in clothing and electronics. These jobs are low in pay, conditions and status, and are associated with patriarchal stereotypes of female characteristics, such as docility, obedience and willingness to give personal service (Lim and Oishi 1996).

The migration systems of the Asian Pacific region

Many countries experience multiple migratory flows, each with its own specific causes, characteristics and effects. However, these flows can be seen as part of a number of 'migration systems', consisting of groups of countries linked by migration and other interchanges. (For a discussion of the 'migration system approach', see Chapter 1.) The major migration systems of the Asian Pacific region are:

- Migration from Asian countries to Western Europe, North America, Australia and New Zealand.
- Contract labour migration to the Middle East.
- Labour migration within Asia.
- Mobility of highly qualified personnel.
- Movements of students.
- Movements of refugees and asylum-seekers.

Often flows start with spontaneous labour migration or contract labour migration, and then continue with other types, such as family reunion, asylum-seeker movement or permanent settler migration. More and more countries are affected by multiple types of migration simultaneously. This trend towards diversification of migration reflects the fact that migration is a social process which develops its own dynamics. Each of these migration systems will be discussed briefly here, with a few examples.[2]

Asian migration to Western countries

Asian migration to Western Europe has been limited. After 1945, there were movements to the United Kingdom, France and The Netherlands from former colonies, but these virtually ceased by the 1970s. More recently, there has been some migration of both highly skilled Asian workers and of low-skilled workers, such as Filipino domestic servants to Italy. There were also refugee movements after the Vietnam War and asylum-seeker inflows in the 1980s and 1990s.

Migrations from Asia to the USA, Canada and Australia have common features: Asian immigration began after the removal of discriminatory restrictions in the 1960s and 1970s, with additional stimulus from Indo-Chinese refugee movements. Unexpectedly large movements have developed mainly through the use of family reunion provisions. The countries of origin have been largely the same, with increasing participation of China and Hong Kong in recent years. The largest single movement was to the USA, starting after the 1965 Immigration Act. The number of immigrants from Asia grew steadily, reaching an average of over 350,000 per year in the early 1990s (OECD 1995: 236). Since 1978, Asia has been the main source of immigrants to the USA, making up 40–50 per cent of total immigration. By 1990, there were 6.9 million Asian-Americans, and the number was expected to increase to over 10 million by the end of the century.

The picture for Canada and Australasia is very similar. By the 1990s, about half of new immigrants to Australia came from Asia. In 1994, the estimated Asian-born population was 826,000 (4.6 per cent of the total population) (NMAC 1995: 1–3). Asian immigration to Canada – particularly from Hong Kong, India, the Philippines, China, Sri Lanka and Vietnam – grew in the 1980s, making up about half of new entrants by the early 1990s. The 1991 census counted over one million Asian-born residents, out of a total overseas-born population of 4.3 million. New Zealand has experienced rapid changes in ethnic composition, with immigration from the Pacific Islands in the 1970s and 1980s, and from East Asia in the 1990s.

Contract labour migration to the Middle East

Large-scale migration from Asia to the Middle East developed rapidly after the oil price rise of 1973. Labour came at first mainly from India and Pakistan; in the 1980s also from the Philippines, Indonesia, Thailand and the Republic of Korea, and later from Bangladesh and Sri Lanka. By 1985, there were 3.2 million Asian workers in the Gulf states, of whom over 2 million were in Saudi Arabia. Recruitment declined after 1985 when oil prices fell sharply. However, by the beginning of the 1990s, movements had reached their former levels, with 933,000 Asian migrants to the Gulf in 1991. The Iraqi invasion of Kuwait and the Gulf War in 1990–1 led to the forced repatriation – under difficult and dangerous conditions – of some 450,000 Asians. After the war, recruitment of Asian workers increased again (Abella 1995; see Chapter 6 of this volume for more detail on contract labour migration).

Labour migration within Asia

From the mid-1980s, rapid economic growth and declining fertility led to considerable demand for migrant labour in some Asian countries, including Japan, the Republic of Korea, Hong Kong, Singapore and Brunei. Malaysia and Thailand experienced both emigration and immigration. Throughout the 'tiger economies', migrant workers took on the '3-D jobs' (dirty, dangerous and difficult) that nationals could increasingly afford to reject. For instance, in Singapore about 300,000 foreign workers made up 19 per cent of the labour force by the mid-1990s (Huguet 1995: 525–6). Foreign men worked in construction, ship-building, transport and services; women mainly in domestic service and other services.

Most Asian governments treated migrants as temporary workers, with very limited rights and no entitlement to settlement and family reunion. Receiving countries were worried about structural dependence on foreign labour and about the possible social effects of settlement. For instance, the Japanese government rejected a foreign labour policy due to the desire to maintain ethnic homogeneity. None the less, the strong demand for labour led to loopholes, such as the recruitment of Latin Americans of Japanese ethnic origin or the employment of foreign 'trainees'. The Singaporean government imposed a foreign worker levy to equalize the costs of foreign and domestic workers. There were quotas on foreign workers in each industry. Unskilled workers had to rotate every few years. Migrants were forbidden to marry Singaporeans, and women had to undergo regular pregnancy tests (Wong 1996). Singapore had policies to encourage the entry of ethnic Chinese immigrants (especially the highly skilled) from Hong Kong and elsewhere.

The Malaysian government was concerned about the effects of immigration on the country's complex ethnic balance (56 per cent Malay, 33 per cent Chinese, 10 per cent Indian and other). Malaysian officials seemed more willing to tolerate illegal Indonesian immigrants, compared with Filipinos or Burmese, because of their cultural and religious similarity to the Malay majority. By 1995, there were 533,000 registered foreign workers in Malaysia, of whom 253,000 were from Indonesia and the rest mainly from Bangladesh, the Philippines and Thailand (Huguet 1995: 525). In 1996, Malaysia began building a 500 kilometre wall along its northern border with Thailand to stop illegal entries. In 1997, the government announced plans for mass deportations of illegals, claimed to be as numerous as 2 million (although relatively few were actually expelled). They were blamed for crime, disease and immorality.

The labour for the 'tiger economies' came from areas with slower economic development such as China, South Asia, the Philippines and Indonesia. The Philippines became the labour-exporter *par excellence* of the modern age (rather like Italy a generation ago) with over 4 million of its people scattered all over the world (Battistella and Paganoni 1992). About half of these are permanent settlers in the USA, while the rest are temporary overseas contract workers (OCWs) in the Gulf states and Asia. In 1994 a total of 565,000 workers were recruited to work in other countries, and a further 154,000 took jobs as sailors on foreign-owned ships. The export of labour is crucial to the Philippines' economy. It has been estimated that unemployment levels would be 40 per cent higher without labour emigration. Official remittances from migrants in 1994 were US$2.94 billion, which financed 50 per cent of the external trade deficit (Amjad 1996).

Highly qualified migrants

Another growing movement has been that of professionals, executives, technicians and other highly skilled personnel. Increasingly, business people and professionals sought employment in international labour markets, and were willing to move in search of higher rewards. Immigration countries, such as the USA, Australia and Canada put increasing emphasis on skilled and business migrants, and offered inducements to attract them.

One form of skilled migration is the 'brain drain': university-trained people moving from under-developed to highly developed countries. This is an economic loss for the poorer countries, which have covered the costs of upbringing and education. On the other hand, many of the migrants are unable to find work in their home countries. Their remittances may be seen as a benefit, and many return eventually with additional training and experience, which can facilitate technology transfer. However, the 'brain drain' may lead to bottlenecks in the supply of skilled personnel if economic growth does get underway. Some governments have programmes to encourage permanent or temporary repatriation of the highly trained. The International Organization for Migration (IOM) runs a 'return of qualified human resources programme', which helps bring back highly trained ex-patriates, either permanently or temporarily.

Much highly qualified migration consists of executives and professionals sent by their companies to work in overseas branches or joint ventures, or experts sent by international organizations to work in aid programmes. Highly skilled migration grew rapidly in the 1980s and 1990s, and is a key element of globalization. Much of the movement is of a fairly short-term nature (a few months to one or two years) and involves interchange of personnel between the highly developed economies of Japan, the USA and Western Europe. However, some migration of highly skilled personnel is the result of capital investment by companies from industrialized countries in less-developed areas. For example, Japanese overseas investment has led to large movements of managers and technicians. The types of personnel involved include managers and professionals of all kinds, as well as entrepreneurs.

Skilled migration, even when temporary, may have important non-economic effects. Capital investment from overseas is a catalyst for socio-economic change and urbanization, while professional transients are not only agents of economic change, but also bearers of new cultural values. The links they create may encourage people from the developing country to move to the investing country in search of training or work. Many professionals take their families with them, and this gives rise to educational and social needs, as well as encouraging long-term settlement.

Students

Considerable numbers of Asians have gone to developed countries as students in recent years. There is considerable competition among developed countries to market education to Asia, with a trend towards joint ventures with Asian universities. Student movement to developed countries may be part of the 'brain drain', since many do not return (Skeldon 1992: 35–7). However, schemes to provide student scholarships as part of development aid often impose legal requirements to return home upon completing studies. Movements of students need to be examined as part of the more general linkages which include professional migrations and capital flows. In the long term, it is likely that they play a role in both technology transfer and cultural change.

Refugees and asylum-seekers

About one-third of the world's 27 million 'refugees and other persons of concern' to the United Nations High Commission for Refugees (UNHCR) in 1995 had their origins in Asia (UNHCR 1995: 247). Over 2 million people fled from Vietnam, Laos and Cambodia following the end of the Vietnam War in 1975. Over a million were resettled in the United States, with smaller numbers in Australia, Canada and Western European countries. Up to a third of Afghanistan's population of 18 million fled the country in the years following the Soviet military intervention in 1979.

The overwhelming majority found refuge in the neighbouring countries of Pakistan (3.6 million in 1989) and Iran (over 2 million). Apart from these two huge movements, there have been many exoduses smaller in number, but no less traumatic for those concerned.

The Asian experience shows the complexity of refugee situations: they are hardly ever a simple matter of individual political persecution. Economic and environmental pressures play a major part, while long-standing ethnic and religious differences exacerbate conflicts. The resolution of refugee situations is hampered by the scarcity of resources and lack of guarantees for human rights in weak and despotic states. Where refugees do find a haven and adequate food and shelter, basic education and health care, there may be little motivation for returning to devastated and impoverished homelands. Refugee movements, like labour migrations, are the result of the massive social transformations currently taking place in Asia.

How governments and societies responded before 1997

There are major gaps in the understanding of migratory phenomena on the part of policy-makers and social scientists in the Asian Pacific region. The reasons for this lie mainly in the dominant perspective on migration in the region, which may be termed 'the myth of temporariness': the belief that migration is motivated by short-term economic considerations and will not lead to long-term settlement. Both policy and research have therefore concentrated on the regulation of migration and on labour-market issues. However, trends towards the permanent settlement of migrants began emerging in many places by the 1990s.

Several states introduced policies designed to prevent settlement by restricting the length of stay and denying rights to migrants. Yet governments have often found that such policies fail or have unexpected and unwanted consequences. For instance, attempts to reduce legal labour migration may lead to illegal migration, or may encourage workers to prolong their stay and bring in dependants. The denial of rights to migrants may lead to social division and conflict. Autocratic states prepared to ignore international human rights norms – such as the Gulf oil states – may well be able to prevent family reunion and permanent settlement. But in many Asian countries public policy is increasingly based on the rule of law and recognition of international standards. This makes it hard to deny basic human rights to immigrants. Where they gradually gain rights to secure residence status and family reunion, permanent settlement is hard to prevent.

Sending-country governments try to regulate migration to protect workers and to ensure the transfer of remittances through official channels. In the Philippines, for instance, there is an Overseas Employment Administration, which controls recruitment, as well as an Overseas Workers' Welfare Administration, which protects and assists overseas contract workers (OCWs). Public concern about the consequences of emigration came to a head in 1995 when a Filipina maid, Flor Contemplacion, was hanged in Singapore, after being found guilty of murder. The case strained relations between the two countries and led to a heated debate about the situation of the estimated 700,000 Filipinos who go to work overseas each year. The Philippines government banned migration of domestic workers to Singapore (a ban that was largely circumvented) and introduced mea-sures for better information and protection. In June 1995, the Philippines parliament passed the Migrant Workers and Overseas Filipinos Act to improve monitoring of the conditions of OCWs (Lim and Oishi 1996: 106).

Such cases highlight the human cost of emigration. The problem is that the market power in international labour migration lies with the recruit-ing countries. Sending-country officials often find themselves powerless against unscrupulous agents and abusive employers, who may have the backing of the police and other authorities in the receiving countries. In any case, once a migratory flow has started, attempts at control by both sending- and receiving-country governments are often frustrated by the development of social networks linking emigration and immigra-tion areas. People move within transnational family and community networks. Migration decision-making is based on the micro-level rational-ity of family survival strategies, which may be quite different from the rationality prevailing at the macro-level of the state or economy (Hugo 1994).

By the mid-1990s, public attitudes to migration in the Asian labour-recruiting countries seemed rather similar to the situation in the Western European 'guest-worker'-recruiting countries in the 1970s: governments refused to plan for possible settlement because this was simply not sup-posed to happen. It took twenty years or more for policy-makers in some places to face up to the reality of settlement and new ethnic minorities. The key question in the Asian Pacific region was the extent to which long-term settlement was beginning to emerge or was likely to do so in future. However, this theme was something of a taboo in most Asian countries for it did not fit in with prevailing ideologies.

For emigration countries, admitting to permanent loss of substantial groups of emigrants could be seen as a 'national shame' because it meant admitting that the country of origin was incapable of providing an accept-able life for its people. This had become a major theme in the Philippines, especially with regard to settlement in the USA. Permanent emigrants may be seen as members of a diaspora, who retain links with the home-land (even after becoming US citizens), but who also betray the nation, by taking their energy and skills away from national development (Aguilar 1996). One way of dealing with the dilemma is by creating a special status for expatriates. In the Philippines, the category of *Balikbayans* was estab-lished as early as the 1970s. *Balikbayans* are literally 'people coming back home to the Philippines'. Programmes have been set up to facilitate their return, including special travel documentation, tax privileges and import concessions. *Balikbayans* may be overseas contract workers, US permanent residents or even US citizens of Filipino origin.

The aim of the *Balikbayan* concept seems to be to retain a feeling of national belonging for Filipino emigrants, which is seen as having both economic and political benefits. Recognition of diasporas in this way creates the potential for a de-territorialization of the nation: people who live abroad and may even have taken another citizenship are treated as a part of the national community (Blanc 1996). This draws attention to one of the key issues in contemporary migration studies: the emergence of international communicative networks, linking emigrants to their countries of origin through a variety of familial, economic and emotional ties. Globalizing tendencies, such as the improvement of transport and communications, and the pervasiveness of dominant culture values, give rise to new forms of transcultural belonging and identity (Basch et al. 1994). Such developments present a challenge to the nation-state model, with its inherent claim to undivided loyalties.

For immigration countries, admitting to the potential for permanent settlement would mean addressing issues connected to citizenship and national identity. Even Japan, with its official objective of an ethnically homogeneous population, is confronted by such problems. Many members of the Korean-origin minority – a result of colonial labour recruitment – are in the third or fourth generations of settlement. Yet they find it hard to obtain Japanese citizenship, and remain a segregated and disadvantaged minority (Esman 1994). Recently, there have been legal challenges to laws which exclude such long-term residents from the right to vote. The Japanese Supreme Court decided in 1995 that the Constitution did not give local voting rights to foreign residents, but that the Constitution did not preclude this, so that such rights could be granted through legislation.[3] If the rights of foreign residents are expanded through legislative processes, this is certain to affect other immigrant groups, which are currently growing despite official policies.

Asian migration at a turning point?

The financial and economic crisis, which started in mid-1997 in Thailand and quickly spread to the whole of South-east and East Asia, took the world largely by surprise. The rapidly growing economies which had powered the Asian model suddenly became areas of stagnation requiring international financial support and threatening to drag the whole world economy into recession. The initial reaction to the crisis by governments of Asian migrant-receiving countries was to try to reduce dependence on migrant labour, and even to send large numbers of migrant workers home. However, it is not yet clear whether this is just a short-term reaction, with the likelihood of past patterns of labour migration resuming once the crisis passes, or whether more fundamental long-term changes are to be expected. It seems possible that the crisis will be a turning-point in Asian migration, just as the 1973 oil crisis was a turning-point in European migration. There are several reasons for believing that the crisis is structural and that it will have significant effects on migratory patterns.

The first reason is *theoretical*: economic growth in capitalist economies has never proceeded in a steady fashion. Rather, since the eighteenth century, it has been possible to trace a recurring business cycle of 8–10 years' duration, in which the economy passes through four phases: expansion – peak – contraction – trough. The trough (or crisis) is a phase in which the conditions for a new expansion are created through the elimination of inefficient producers and outmoded technologies. Moreover, many economists believe that these short business cycles are overlaid by longer-term cycles in which major technological, organizational and structural changes are brought about in national and international economies. These longer cycles are variously known as 'long waves', 'Kuznets cycles' or 'Kondratrieff cycles', and are thought to have a duration of 30–50 years. In other words, economic crises are normal in capitalism, and have the function of disciplining market participants and increasing efficiency. As a system without central planning mechanisms, capitalism cannot bring about structural reforms through rational planning, but does so through market forces which bankrupt firms, destroy livelihoods and impoverish many people – just as we are witnessing in Asia today. Moreover, investment, production and distribution do not simply return to their pre-crisis patterns once growth resumes. Rather, new forms emerge, involving substantial change for employers, workers and consumers. Since labour migration was a significant aspect of the pre-crisis growth strategy in Asia, we should not expect it to continue in the same way as before once growth resumes.

The second reason is *historical-comparative*, and is based on the European experience following the 1973 oil crisis. This was a trigger for radical changes in investment patterns, economic structure and labour-recruitment strategies: the entry of so-called 'guest-workers' was curtailed, with an expectation that many of them would return to their homelands, thus allowing the industrialized countries to export unemployment. By the 1980s, it was clear that this prediction was false: rather than leaving, many workers had brought in their families and began a process of long-term settlement and community formation, leading to quite unexpected challenges for national culture and identity. Moreover, the migratory networks developed in this period were to pave the way for new forms of mass migration under the stimulus of the political and economic restructuring of Europe in the late 1980s and early 1990s.

The third reason is *analytical*: if we examine the causes of the rapid growth of migration within Asia since the 1970s we find that these are inextricably linked with the major economic and demographic transitions of the period. Migration was a necessary response to conditions prevailing during the period of rapid societal transformation from a regional political economy dominated by colonialism to one increasingly shaped by globalization. It seems unlikely that these processes have run their course; rather, it appears that the major causes of migration still exist, but that their character is changing over time. Again, the crisis may precipitate more rapid change.

However, all the reasons advanced so far for expecting continuing though changing patterns of migration are conceptual ones. It is necessary to move to the empirical level to find out what is actually happening. Before summarizing information on current trends, it is useful to look back at the factors which caused Asian migration up to 1997.

Causes of Asian migration from 1970 to 1997

The upsurge in migration from about 1970 resulted from a constellation of economic, demographic, social and political factors in both sending and receiving countries. The *economic background* was rapid economic growth and modernization, first in Japan, then in the 'tiger economies' (Taiwan, Hong Kong, Singapore and South Korea) and then in other South-east Asian countries (Thailand, Brunei, Malaysia and Indonesia). This created demand for labour, while at the same time the much slower economic growth of other countries (South Asia, China, the Philippines, Burma, Vietnam) during at least some parts of the period made labour reserves available. Although Indonesia experienced rapid economic growth in the latter part of the period, this was insufficient to absorb the very large labour reserves, so that Indonesia remained an emigration country. Overall, the 'economic transition' from a rural to an industrial and then in some cases a post-industrial economy took place in a very uneven way in the region. The result was the development of migration, initially from Asia to other areas, notably of overseas contract workers to the Gulf oil states and of permanent migrants to the USA, Canada and Australia. This was followed from the 1980s by mass labour movements within the Asian Pacific region.

The *demographic background* has been well summarized in a recent article by Hugo (1998). The Asian Pacific is currently home to 57 per cent of the world's population and contains three of the world's most populous nations. There has been a massive growth in population in recent decades, and this is particularly marked with regard to people of working age (15–64 years) and young adults (15–34) who are the group most likely to migrate. However, this growth has been very uneven. The countries with the fastest economic growth have also had the most rapid declines in fertility (the 'demographic transition'). The result is that certain fast-growing economies have run into labour shortages, while other countries have stagnant labour forces, fast-growing working-age populations and massive labour surpluses. If economic growth in certain economies is the chief 'pull-factor' for migration, then demographic growth in others is the major 'push-factor'.

However, migration cannot be adequately explained by the interaction of push and pull factors. For a 'migration system' linking certain countries to develop a complex social process is necessary (Kritz et al. 1992). This *social background* to migration has several aspects. A migratory flow can be initiated or stimulated in various ways: through labour recruitment, historical and cultural linkages, political or military relationships, investment flows and refugee movements. Once established, a migratory flow generates its own social networks through which migrants and their families cope with the changes involved. A 'culture of migration' may develop, in which the temporary migration of a family member and the remittances he or she sends home can be a vital part of family strategies for improving security and maximizing income. Such social networks can perpetuate flows even if the original causes cease to be relevant or if government policies change. One aspect of this is the development of a migration industry, consisting of agents and brokers of various kinds, who organize the migratory process.

A further social aspect has been the increasing participation of women in migratory flows, especially as workers rather than family members. If women migrate as workers, this helps to encourage later family formation and settlement, as the European experience has shown. On a quite different level, social processes in the population of the receiving country may facilitate migration. For instance, labour-market segmentation may lead to certain jobs being considered as migrant work, while local workers can obtain opportunities for educational and occupational advancement. In Asian migrant-receiving countries, nationals now refuse to do the so-called 3-D (dirty, difficult and dangerous) jobs, while migrants become increasingly concentrated in them.

The *political background* refers to government policies with regard to migration. Since the 1970s, the export of labour has become a vital part of economic policy for such countries as the Philippines, Indonesia, India and Sri Lanka. South Korea used labour export at an early stage of its economic development, but then quickly went through an 'economic transition' to become an industrial country accompanied by a 'migration transition' from sending to receiving country. Malaysia is going through a similar transition – or was until the onset of the crisis. Export of labour is seen as reducing the pressure of unemployment, contributing to the training of the workforce and, above all, as a source of remittances which provide vital foreign exchange and investment capital. Several of the countries concerned have set up agencies and introduced regulations conducive to labour export. In other countries, the activities of labour recruiters and migration brokers are tolerated.

Receiving countries within Asia have varying policies. Some, such as Singapore, Malaysia and Taiwan, have set up legal recruiting systems usually marked by fairly rigid systems of control. Other countries have left migration to market forces. In many cases this meant tacitly accepting undocumented migration – as long as labour was needed. Even those countries with labour recruitment systems experience undocumented migration or the movement of legally recruited workers into irregular employment. As for policies on settlement and the long-term position of migrants in receiving societies, these are almost completely absent, since the 'myth of temporariness' still reigns supreme. The overall impression is one of poor planning and of unsystematic *ad hoc* policies.

Such was the constellation of forces which led to the rapid growth in migration within the Asian Pacific region prior to the crisis. The main question now is how the forces which caused mass migrations are being reshaped by current events. Before discussing this, we need to look at the evidence on actual shifts in flows.

Changes in migratory patterns due to the crisis

It is difficult to assess changes since 1997 adequately at this stage since the availability and quality of data are so uneven. A picture of the unfolding events can be gained from the regular e-mail newsletters *Asian Migration News*[4] and *Migration News*.[5] Several attempts have been made to develop overviews and analyses of the effects on migration (see Battistella and Assis 1998; Skeldon 1998). The overall impression is of considerable complexity in reactions to the crisis. Initially, political leaders in immigrant-receiving countries spoke of sending large numbers of foreign workers home, and giving employment priority to nationals. Such policies of exporting unemployment are highly reminiscent of the rhetoric in Western Europe in the period 1973–80. In the meantime, it has become clear that it is not easy to reverse the labour market trends of the past few decades, and to replace migrant workers with nationals. A number of broad trends are emerging.

1 *Repatriation of migrant workers.* Policies have been announced to deport irregular migrant workers and to repatriate legal workers at the end of their contracts. Certain Gulf oil states have recently introduced programmes to replace illegal migrants with nationals in various job sectors. Some Asian countries have introduced amnesties to encourage irregular workers to leave voluntarily without any penalties. However, these policies have their limits. For instance, in a 4-month period in the early part of 1998, 33,000 illegals were rounded up and deported from Malaysia. The costs and logistical problems involved were considerable, and it became clear that it would be impossible to expel all illegals in this way (Kassim 1998). Similarly in Japan, the authorities have organized regular control campaigns and crackdowns on illegal foreigners, but the numbers arrested during any one campaign average only 200–300 – less than 1 per cent of illegal migrants (Komai 1998). Skeldon (1998) argues that 'show deportations' are carried out to demonstrate that governments are working in the best interests of workers, but that there are unlikely to be mass repatriations.

2 *Stricter immigration control.* Most Asian migrant-receiving countries have intensified border controls since the start of the crisis. For instance, Malaysia has deployed its navy as well as police and immigration officers. In the first quarter of 1998 more aliens were arrested trying to enter illegally than the total illegal entrants apprehended in the whole of 1997 (Kassim 1998). This increase may be due to more effective policing of borders or to greater numbers of illegal border-crossers or both, but it is clear that the authorities were unable to prevent all illegal entrants since the coastline is long and hard to patrol. Similarly, Thailand finds it impossible effectively to police its long land borders with Burma, Laos and Cambodia.

3 *Reduction or stopping of recruitment of new migrant workers.* Bans on recruitment have been a widespread response to the crisis. However, their effectiveness is questionable in situations where the number of irregular migrants is larger than that of legally recruited workers. Irregular movements are not likely to be greatly affected by recruitment bans..

4 *Redeployment of migrant workers within receiving countries.* Some governments have attempted to shift migrant workers out of sectors where employment is declining into areas where labour is still scarce. In Malaysia the shift has been from manufacturing industry to plantations. However, such efforts are often resisted by workers, due to lower wages, poorer conditions or isolation in the new area of deployment. In Japan, *Nikkei* (workers of Japanese ethnic origin from Latin America) tend to be employed in low-skilled manufacturing jobs, while irregular workers are more likely to shift to service-industry jobs, small enterprises or informal sector work (Mori 1997).

5 *Attempts to replace migrant workers with unemployed nationals.* Several governments have introduced measures to persuade unemployed nationals to substitute for displaced foreign workers in such sectors as manufacturing and domestic service. These efforts have only limited success. Despite unemployment, many local workers still resist the downward social mobility associated with 3-D jobs. In any case there is a skills mismatch as well as a locational mismatch between the attributes of redundant local workers and the positions occupied by migrant labour (Skeldon 1998).

6 *Trends towards settlement and community formation by migrants.* Such trends were already becoming apparent in some receiving countries prior to the crisis (Kassim 1998; Komai 1998; Mori 1997). It is too early to say whether the crisis is reinforcing such tendencies. Clearly, most governments want to prevent settlement, but there are reasons for expecting it to happen. As the European experience showed, if migrants believe that they will not be able to re-enter a receiving country if they return home, they are more likely to try to stay on, and this encourages family reunion. Similarly, where patterns of circulatory migration have developed, in which one family member replaces another as a migrant worker after a period in a receiving country, this

practice may now be blocked, so that there is an incentive to stay on. The main factor in community formation is the internal dynamics of social network formation: once ethnic groups begin to cluster in a certain location and establish businesses, social facilities, places of worship and cultural associations, the conditions for further growth develop in a cumulative fashion. The ethnic neighbourhood provides assistance for new arrivals, protection against xenophobia and opportunities for employment and social advancement.

7   *A growth in xenophobia in receiving countries.* This is to some extent a continuation of trends which had started before the crisis: migrant workers were being blamed for increased crime, drug trafficking and disease. Since 1997 trends towards the scapegoating of migrants for social problems have increased, often with tacit encouragement by the authorities and certain political parties. The portrayal of migrants as a threat to employment and as a social problem leads to a climate in which social protection for migrants can be ignored and violations of their human rights may easily take place.

8   *Problems for families and the economy in migrant-sending areas due to loss of employment and remittances.* Return migration and the reduction of new movements to migrant-receiving countries are likely to lead to considerable hardship in migrant-sending countries. Böhning (1998) has attempted to estimate the likely reduction of employment opportunities for Filipinos abroad from mid-1997 to the end of 1999. He concluded that the reduction may be around 105,000 jobs. However, some of the displaced workers might be able to find new jobs abroad, so that perhaps only 50,000 would return home – a fairly small proportion of the roughly half a million Filipinos who go abroad to work each year. None the less, such estimates indicate severe social consequences for quite large numbers of households. Women migrants (who work mainly as domestic servants) originate disproportionately from the poorer regions of the country, and the loss of their earnings can be disastrous for the families who depend on them (Böhning 1998).

9   *Encouraging workers in countries affected by the crisis to seek work overseas.* Governments in certain countries are trying to step up export of labour. This applies even to countries which had become labour importers before the crisis, such as Thailand. The opportunities for new migrants are likely to be constrained by the downturn in labour demand, and the increasing numbers of work-seekers. One result might be a tendency to move to areas so far not affected by the crisis, such as the USA and Western Europe. This could lead to increased irregular movements and trafficking of migrants.

10   *Sustained or increased emigration pressures in migrant-sending countries.* Although demand for labour in migrant-receiving countries has fallen, the income differential between sending and receiving areas has become greater than ever. Mass unemployment and impoverishment in countries like Indonesia may lead people to depart out of

desperation, however limited the opportunities in receiving countries like Malaysia.

11 *Increased irregular migration and employment.* The combination of increasingly restrictive entry policies and increased pressure for departure in countries of origin is likely to lead to more irregular migration, facilitated by existing migration networks, as well as agents and brokers.

12 *Delayed-action or long-term effects.* Böhning (1998) points out that the full effects of the economic crisis will take a while to become evident. The downturn in employment may start in the banking and finance sectors, then affect construction and small-scale manufacturing, and subsequently spread to services, large-scale manufacturing as well as to tourism, entertainment and so on. Moreover, repatriation of migrants may follow after some time, and the drop in remittances will be later still, as returnees are likely to repatriate all their savings at once. It is therefore possible that the most severe impacts of return migration are still to come.

Causal factors under changed conditions

It is now possible to return to the causes of migration and discuss the extent to which they have changed in response to the crisis.

Economic factors

The rapid growth which created the conditions for migration has disappeared in many economies – at least for the present. Average annual rates of increase of GNP in the order of 5–10 per cent have been replaced by declines in GDP. Unemployment is rising, even in countries where this was virtually unknown hitherto. Hong Kong now has 5 per cent unemployed according to official figures, although the real number may be much higher. In Japan and South Korea, displaced blue- and white-collar workers roam the streets and even sleep rough in parks and railway stations. On the face of it, the conditions for labour recruitment have changed radically. But in reality things are not simple. Since the income differential between sending and receiving countries remains high, economic factors may continue to constitute a 'pull-factor' – albeit a reduced one – for migrants.

The long-term perspectives are hard to assess. If economic growth resumes in a few years' time, it appears likely that labour recruitment will also recommence. However, new growth is likely to take place in the context of processes of technological change and industrial restructuring. This would not necessarily mean less demand for migrant workers, but could mean that their employment patterns might change. For instance, a shift from manufacturing employment to service jobs seems very likely. The European experience of the 1970s and 1980s seems relevant here. Some countries (for example, France) followed policies of 'renationalization' of the construction and manufacturing sectors, with the result that migrants often shifted to the services or to informal sector jobs. Such changes in employment patterns were often linked to increased irregular migration. Another European and North American experience that may be significant for Asia is the trend towards the diversification of migrant employment, with the demand for both highly skilled personnel and low-skilled manufacturing and service workers. Global cities seem to generate dualistic economies (Sassen 1988).

Demographic factors

Population size and structure is one area where forecasts are possible since future structures are an extrapolation of existing patterns. Hugo's (1998) analysis shows quite clearly that the demographic factors which led to migration are going to become even more significant in the years ahead. Falls in fertility in migrant-receiving countries like Japan and South Korea will lead to a decline in the proportion of the population of working age, while the rapid growth in the young adult population of the main Asian labour-reserve countries means that the number of people in the most active migration age (15–34 years) will be greater than ever before. Since there is little prospect of countries like Indonesia, China, India and Bangladesh being able to create the millions of jobs needed to employ these labour-market entrants, the demographic 'push-factor' will be extremely strong (Hugo 1998).

Social factors

Social factors are complex and hard to predict. The social networks which develop within the migratory process are now well established throughout the region. They will be a powerful force in sustaining migratory flows, whatever policies governments adopt. Social networks also help to reshape migratory flows as they mature, facilitating family reunion and community formation. One of the lessons from Western Europe is that migration can shift in character – for instance, from legal labour recruitment to irregular movement, asylum-seeker entries and family reunion – if governments try to stop flows. There are already signs that this is happening in Asia (see Kassim 1998; Komai 1998) but the extent is not yet clear. Another social factor which may perpetuate migration is changing attitudes towards work on the part of receiving-country populations. Unwillingness or inability to carry out 3-D jobs by people who have achieved social mobility makes the employment of migrants necessary even at times of unemployment.

However, there are two major differences between Asia and Europe. One is the relative strength of the welfare state: in Western Europe entitlements of legal migrants to benefits were strong enough to create an incentive to stay even in the event of unemployment. This is not the case in Asia today, where the lack of a social safety net has become a major problem. The other difference is the degree to which the human rights of migrant workers are recognized. In Western Europe there was much rhetoric about deporting unwanted migrant workers and giving preference to nationals in the 1970s, but the strength of the legal system and adherence to various bilateral or multilateral agreements on migrant rights put severe constraints on such policies. Mass deportation policies never materialized, although there were many cases of non-renewal of residence permits or refusal of labour-market access for migrant youth and women who entered through family reunion. Such measures proved counter-productive and were generally abandoned as they led to the growth of irregular residence and employment. Human rights regimes and legal protection for migrants are far weaker in Asian countries. On the other hand, Asian states often lack the institutional capacity to carry out mass deportation policies, as the Malaysian and Thai experiences have shown.

Cultural factors

The development of 'cultures of migration' through which work in another country becomes a normal rite of passage is well advanced in some emigration countries. An additional factor is the increase in educational levels and cultural capital in sending countries: not only are there growing numbers of people in the main migration age groups, they are also better educated and more knowledgeable about the outside world than ever before. Such trends help perpetuate migration despite political and economic changes. The emergence of multicultural societies in receiving countries also encourages migration. People with bicultural or intercultural competencies become facilitators of mobility and communication between societies, helping to erode borders. The crisis is not likely to do much to halt such trends.

Another cultural factor concerns affinity between migrants and some groups of the receiving-country populations. South-east Asia has long traditions of circulatory migration. Indonesians or Filipinos often settle among people with similar ethnic roots in Malaysia, making it hard for the authorities to locate and deport irregular entrants. Similar situations exist in Thailand and other countries. On the other hand, fears of cultural change and the erosion of national culture and identity may be a factor leading to the emergence of anti-immigrant movements and encouraging governments to adopt restrictive entry policies. Debates on assimilation, integration and pluralism, which have been important in Europe, North America and Australia for the past half-century, have hardly taken place in Asia since the assumption has always been that migrants would not stay. In view of the trends towards settlement and community formation, change is likely in this area.

Political factors

Political interests with regard to migration are also complex. Receiving-country governments have tended to see repatriation of migrants as a way of alleviating the economic and social consequences of the crisis. However, mass deportation policies have been limited by concerns about the consequences in the countries of origin. This appears to have played some part in toning down Malaysian attempts to send Indonesian workers home. Moreover, although human rights regimes are weaker in Asian countries than in Western Europe, they are not completely absent. Nongovernmental organizations (NGOs) have attempted to protect migrant rights, and have used both public opinion and the legal system to do so. This may have had a tempering affect on deportation policies, although it is hard to make an accurate assessment.

International cooperation and standards have also played some part. Many Asian countries are signatories to ILO conventions and other international instruments concerning migrant rights. This allows international agencies to have some influence on government policies, although, again, it is hard to assess the extent to which this makes a real difference. The question is whether the crisis will lead to enhanced international and regional cooperation in an attempt to overcome the crisis and to alleviate its social consequences. So far there is little sign that this is happening. Rather, the trend seems to be towards greater emphasis on national interests in labour market policies. This may be conducive to the further erosion of the rights of migrants. On the other hand, there is increasing realization that restrictive policies that go against economic and social realities are hard to enforce and may lead to unintended consequences such as increased irregular migration and employment.

Conclusion

It is too early for definitive statements on the effects of the Asian financial and economic crisis on migration. Clearly, there is no simple tendency to reduced labour migration and increased return migration. Rather, there is a situation of complexity, with many varying and sometimes contradictory tendencies. The situation in Western Europe after the 1973 oil crisis provides the closest historical analogy to the current situation in Asia, and is therefore worth using for comparative purposes. However, there are also major structural and cultural differences so that we should not expect precise parallels.

The economic, demographic, social, cultural and political factors which caused and sustained migration in the past have not lost their significance in the current situation. A changed economic situation following the crisis may lead to differing patterns of labour migration, but is unlikely to bring about a major decline in movements. The demographic causes of migration are set to become more important than ever over the coming decades. Both social change in receiving countries and the effects of social networks look likely to play an ever-increasing role in causing and shaping migration and settlement. A range of cultural factors connected with globalization, improvements in education and cultural knowledge and the emergence of transnational communities also reinforce trends towards mobility. On the political level, governments may set out to curtail migration, but there are countervailing forces at the national, regional and international levels.

All that can be said with certainty is that migration will remain a major force for social transformation in the region, and that it is likely to change in many ways. We can make informed guesses about these changes, but not predict them with any degree of confidence. Thus there is a strong need for research on the many aspects of international migration in the Asian Pacific region. There is also a need for governments and international organizations to show flexibility and realism in their policy directions. Policies based on poor understanding of the complex phenomenon are likely to fail – often with serious human consequences.

Notes

1 The history of Asian migration is well covered in various articles in Cohen (1995).

2 Research literature and statistical data on Asian migration are still quite under-developed. The best single source is the *Asian and Pacific Migration Journal* published by the Scalabrini Migration Center in Quezon City, Philippines. Cohen (1995) also has a number of useful articles.

3 This decision is considerably more liberal than one by the German Federal Constitutional Court on a similar issue in 1990.

4 Published by the Scalabrini Migration Center, Manila (e-mail address: smc@skyinet.net).

5 Published by the Department of Agricultural and Resource Economics, University of California, Davis (e-mail address: migrant@primal. ucdavis.edu).

8

GLOBALIZATION AND MIGRATION: SOME PRESSING CONTRADICTIONS

This chapter sets out to do two things. First, to draw attention to *nine fundamental contradictions* that are typical of our time. This number is, of course, arbitrary, and the problems are so closely linked that they cannot always be clearly distinguished in practice. All the same, these categories are useful in analysing globalization and the problems it creates. Secondly, one aspect of global change – the recent rapid growth in international migration – will be used to illustrate each contradiction. Why give migration such prominence? Because it plays a key part in most contemporary social transformations. Migration is both a result of global change and a powerful force for further change in migrant-sending and receiving societies. Its immediate impacts are felt on the economic level, but it also affects social relations, culture, national politics and international relations. Migration inevitably leads to greater ethno-cultural diversity within nation-states, transforming identities and blurring traditional boundaries.

1 The contradiction between inclusion and exclusion

This refers to the tendency for global linkages to embrace every geographical area and every human group, while at the same time differentiating between these human groups: some become full members in the new global order while others are marginalized. This fundamental issue of inclusion and exclusion is a central aspect of all the other contemporary contradictions.

In the new economic order, subsistence production by families and communities breaks down, and is replaced by participation in national and international markets. Individuals or groups who possess the characteristics necessary to fit into global markets, whether for labour, capital or cultural goods, are included into the global order as citizens, with civil, political and social rights. Individuals and groups who do not fit are excluded, and may be denied even the most basic rights, such as the right to work and the right to food security.

This chapter was first published in *International Social Science Journal*, 156 (1998), pp. 179–86.

International migration is closely linked to these processes of inclusion and exclusion. Since 1945, and especially from the 1970s, there has been a burgeoning of international population movements, involving every geographical region. People may move to a neighbouring country or halfway across the world. They may be migrant workers, professionals or refugees. Increasing numbers of both economic migrants and refugees are women. Although experts try to distinguish between the various categories, this is not always possible, for migrants' motivations are complex and multidimensional.

Most migration takes place within transnational social networks, which link families and communities across long distances. Migratory chains, once started, may develop in unpredictable ways. Whatever the original intentions of migrants, employers and governments, migration usually leads to family reunion, settlement and the formation of new ethnic groups in receiving countries. Well over 100 million people live outside their countries of birth today. Some 20 million of them are refugees. That is only a small proportion of the world's population, yet migration has much greater effects than such numbers suggest.

In *countries of emigration*, families and local communities experience deep and enduring changes. Emigration is one aspect of the dissolution of traditional economic and social structures resulting from globalization. Whole countries may develop 'cultures of emigration', as in Italy half a century ago or the Philippines today. Many emigrants perceive their situation in terms of economic and social exclusion: they are forced to leave their countries because there is no place for them there any more. They may even see themselves as excluded from the national community.

Similarly, in *countries of immigration* many communities are drastically changed. Immigrant settlement may reshape the national economy, transform cities and force the re-examination of social and cultural values. The immigrants may experience exclusion here too, through economic disadvantage, denial of rights or discrimination. In older receiving countries, immigration has become a key issue in debates on social relations and national identity. The same will no doubt also happen in time in the newly industrializing countries of Asia, Latin America and Africa.

2   The contradiction between market and state

This process which includes some and excludes others appears to be the result of anonymous market forces. No individual, institution or state, therefore, seems to bear the responsibility for developments which may impoverish millions. The triumph of the market, both at the national and international levels, means that many of those in power no longer see gross inequality as a problem, but rather as vital to the efficiency of the economic system.

This insistence on unfettered markets is a new trend, although it does hark back to the nineteenth century. The traumatic experiences of the first half of the twentieth century – class struggles and two world wars – led to the emergence of welfare states in the core industrial countries. Attempts to extend welfare and state intervention to the developing world were linked to the system struggle in a bipolar world. But the collapse of the communist alternative in the 1980s has made it possible to proclaim the interests of global capital as the interests of all humanity.

So although there is no central force steering the world economy, there are powerful sanctions against those who question the new market rationality. The structural adjustment programmes of the World Bank and the International Monetary Fund have been powerful forces for creating open market economies in up to eighty countries. Such programmes have forced governments to abandon measures designed to protect the living conditions of their people, resulting in the informalization of labour, the dismantling of welfare systems and increased unemployment.

The contradiction between the market and the state is very marked in the field of international migration. States of origin often oppose the emigration of highly skilled people as a 'brain drain' and a loss of educational investment. Employers in receiving countries, by contrast, are eager to welcome skilled migrants. For the unskilled the reverse applies: the governments of sending countries encourage them to leave because this will bring remittances and ease social pressures. Governments of receiving countries are increasingly unwilling to admit unskilled migrants workers, but may turn a blind eye to illegal entry if employers need labour.

If governments try to stop migration, a new market comes into play: a global migration market, organized by labour recruiters and migration agents, who can make a profit out of migration, whether legal or not. This market is linked to the informal social networks which develop within the migratory process. Together, the migration networks and the migration industry may be more powerful in shaping population flows than the policies of states. International migration is an essential part of globalization. If governments welcome the mobility of capital, commodities and ideas, yet try to stop the mobility of people, they are unlikely to succeed. Realistic policies may help shape migration in the public interest. Prohibitions, by contrast, are unlikely to stop migration, and may simply change legal movements into illegal ones.

3   The contradiction between growing wealth and impoverishment

As Robert Reich (1991: 196–207), Labour Secretary in the first Clinton Administration, pointed out, income inequality in the USA grew sharply in the 1980s: the rich got richer, there were more poor people and the middle classes were eroded. This trend applies in virtually all the older industrial countries. The decline of welfare states has exacerbated social polarization. Growing inequalities in wealth can also be found in the newly industrializing countries. Economic development under conditions of free markets and non-interventionist states seems inevitably to lead to greater inequality. Modernization theories claim that higher living standards will 'trickle-down' to disadvantaged groups, but it is far from clear that this is happening.

The most glaring inequality, however, is still that between the industrial countries (both old and new) and those areas which have not been able to achieve sustained economic development. In many areas of Africa and Asia, real incomes are falling. This means declines in educational opportunities, health standards and even in life expectancy. Whole nations are being excluded from the new global order.

The fault-lines of conflict have shifted. The old divisions were between workers and capitalists; and between the liberal-democratic and communist models. Today's patterns are more complex: within each country, there is a division between those included in mainstream economic and social relations, and those who are excluded. In the old industrial countries, sociologists speak of the replacement of class society by the 'two-thirds society', in which the majority is still included, but a growing minority is not. In less-developed countries it is still the majority who are excluded. Such internal divisions are overlaid by an international division between rich and poor countries. But this is no longer simply the North–South divide: rich centres have emerged in the South, while parts of the old communist bloc in Europe are in crisis.

All these forms of exclusion are overlaid by differentiation based on group membership: women, ethnic and racial minorities, indigenous peoples and youth experience discrimination and disadvantage. Again, migration plays a key role. Virtually every Western country now has new ethnic minorities which have arisen through the migrations of the past fifty years. In some cases, the descendants of immigrants may remain non-citizens even if born in the country of residence. Even those who are citizens may experience discrimination on the basis of race, ethnicity or religion. Newly industrializing countries which import labour are trying hard to prevent the emergence of new minorities. Yet settlement often takes place anyway, leading to situations of marginalization, impoverishment and social conflict.

4   The contradiction between the Net and the self

One of the key problems of modernity is the tension between the principle of rational economic and political organization and the infinitely varied desires of individuals and groups. As Alain Touraine (1998) has pointed out, it was above all Nietzsche and Freud who showed how human life is ruled by this tension between society and the individual or between system-rationality and identity.

In a recent work, the sociologist Manuel Castells has analysed the new character of this old contradiction. He argues that 'Our societies are increasingly structured around a bipolar opposition between the Net and the Self' (Castells 1996: 3). He emphasizes the role of new information technologies in creating global networks of wealth, power and images. These networks can 'selectively switch on and off individuals, groups, regions, and even countries' according to their relevance in fulfilling instrumental goals (1996: 3). This system is economically efficient but incapable of giving meaning to people's lives. To escape such abstract universalism, people increasingly seek meaning through particularistic identities based on ethnicity, religion, regionalism or nationalism.

This explains why many contemporary conflicts are not concerned primarily with 'rational' economic and social interests. The defence of local or sectional interests against globalizing forces may be based on cultural symbols connected with dignity and identity. Many individuals and groups have had the experience of being dispossessed or excluded on the basis of interests portrayed as rational and general. Resistance movements may appear particularistic, and even backward-looking, because the appeal to an alternative universalistic project has been blocked by the monopolization of discourses of rationality by globalizing forces.

The conflict between the Net and the self applies on two separate levels with regard to migration. First, the rise of anti-immigration movements, often of a racist character, is observable in many countries. The underlying motivation of such movements may be fear of the disruption brought about by globalization and economic restructuring. Immigrants become the target because they are the most visible symbol of these changes, while the real causes are invisible, complex and difficult to influence. Many anti-immigration groups are essentially identity movements based on myths of homogeneous and autonomous societies.

The other level is that of the new ethnic minorities themselves. Their frequently marginalized and discriminated position puts a premium on personal and group identity. This can take two quite distinct forms: one is separatism and fundamentalism, which is usually the result of the experience of isolation and racism. The other is a mobilization within democratic societies to achieve both equality of rights and recognition as a distinct cultural group. As in the case of young people of North African origin in France, this gives rise to a call for a 'new citizenship' based on participation and cultural openness.

5   The contradiction between the global and the local

The contradiction between the global and the local is one of the key issues addressed by UNESCO's Management of Social Transformations (MOST) programme. What appears rational at the global level can have devastating effects on local communities. If global integration and economic growth is to benefit people, ways have to be found to give local communities a powerful voice in decisions which affect them. Market mechanisms are inherently incapable of doing this, while states – even democratic ones – often neglect the local in favour of overriding 'national interests'.

International migration is generally analysed at the national level, yet its strongest effects are felt locally. In communities of origin, the departure of large numbers of working-age people may disrupt agricultural and handicraft production. Gender relations and family structures undergo dramatic change. In receiving countries, there is frequently a conflict between the central state, which controls immigration policy with an eye to macro-economic consequences, and regional or local authorities, who are generally more aware of possible social costs and tensions. Local dimensions of migration need to be treated as central issues in research and political action.

Indeed, a major contemporary trend is the emergence of new levels of decision-making. The dominant role of the nation-state is being eroded not only by globalization, but also by regional bodies such as the European Union, the North American Free Trade Area, and MERCOSUR in Latin America. On the other hand, within many countries, the growing emphasis on local identities – often with long-standing ethnic, cultural and historical roots – leads to pressure for decentralization. The supra-national linkages have generally begun in economic relations, but then spread to the political and legal spheres. The infra-national identities usually constitute themselves in the cultural sphere, but have conse-quences for national politics too. Sometimes the local links with the supra-national: for instance, it may be easier for groups that want local autonomy to accept belonging to the nation-state if its power is tempered by membership of a regional association like the European Union. The nation-state still remains the most important level of power, but political action is increasingly oriented to multiple levels.

6   The contradiction between the economy and the environment

This too has become a central issue of our age. Continual economic growth means ever-greater stress on natural resources and ecological systems. Market forces cannot prevent environmental degradation because deci-sions of individual market players do not take account of long-term aggre-gate effects. National regulation is inadequate, too, because deforestation, air pollution and resource depletion are not constrained by borders. There can be no doubt of the need for supranational regulation, but the world has been slow in developing the necessary institutions.

In certain areas migration flows are a direct result of environmental degradation. Deforestation, desertification, declining soil fertility, droughts and floods all force people to move. Less directly, pressure on resources and eco-systems may lead to economic competition, political conflict and warfare, destroying productive assets and causing mass flights. The classic political refugee is being joined by the new 'environmental refugee'.

Immigration can also cause environmental strains by encouraging uncontrolled urban growth, or putting pressure on overused resources. It is not only long-term movements which cause concern: tourism is an often neglected threat to the natural environment and to cultural heritage. Again there is a need for global cooperation in understanding and managing population mobility.

7 The contradiction between modernity and post-modernity

Some contemporary theorists interpret the current situation in terms of the painful transition from modernity to post-modernity. The project of modernity was based on the Enlightenment notion of history as a grand narrative of progress towards a good society. In contrast, post-modernity is based on the notion of the fragmentation of politics, cultures and identities. Post-modernism rejects the grand narratives: there is no common human pathway towards a better life. Pessimism and relativism rule.

Yet this view of the current situation seems problematic. It can be argued that the grand narrative is stronger than ever. The globalization of markets is an all-embracing if one-sided realization of the Enlightenment project. The technologies of production, control and communication are universalistic. Moreover, economic and technological changes are linked to the global diffusion of values based on Western notions of rationality. Globalization – as both a cultural and an economic phenomenon – is a true product of modernity. What is missing – and here some post-modernists are right – is the political and social project of modernity: the idea that a strong democratic state should intervene in the social realm to achieve equal rights and a good life for all. Here the fragmentation is really taking place – in the name of free markets. Thus globalization means a modern integrated economy, but a post-modern fragmented political sphere.

This contradiction is clearly visible with regard to international migration. Neo-classical economists argue that the free circulation of labour maximizes the utility of human capital and leads to an equalization of wage rates across countries. But such positive consequences do not take place in the absence of political frameworks to ensure that the human rights and social needs of migrants are respected. Highly skilled migrants may have enough market power to secure economic and social rights, but unskilled migrant workers and refugees do not. Far from an equalization of wages, migration leads to new forms of inequality between and within countries.

However rational and efficient they may be, markets do not bring about equality and social balance. Nor can transnational problems be effectively regulated by nation-states. Even where supranational forms of regulation are emerging, the result is the creation of new lines of inclusion and exclusion. The European Union, for instance, has done much to improve the rights of the roughly 5 million people who have moved from one member country to another, but has done little for the 10 million or more residents originating outside the European Union.

8   The contradiction between the national citizen and the global citizen

The great historical achievement of the nation-state model was the democratic citizen: the individual member of society who was not only a bearer of rights, but also an active participant in the process of law-making and governing. Democratic citizenship has only been achieved in a minority of countries, and then generally only with limitations. Yet it is an aspiration shared by most of the world's people. However, there is an ambiguity in democratic citizenship: as membership in a nation-state, it denotes both civic belonging in a political community and cultural belonging in a national community. In the political community, all citizens are seen as equal, and their personal characteristics (such as gender, ethnicity and religion) are irrelevant. The national community, by contrast, is based on shared possession of supposedly unique cultural characteristics. Yet the process of nation-formation has generally involved the conquest and incorporation of other ethnic groups. These had to be assimilated into the nation, either through obliteration of their cultures or by a long process of forgetting difference, as the French historian Ernest Renan put it (1992).

The goal of cultural homogenization has always been problematic because minority cultures have proved much more resilient than expected. However, the difficulty becomes much greater in today's 'age of migration'. Porous borders and the growth in ethno-cultural diversity make cultural homogenization impossible. Today, many people commute between countries, and maintain family, social and economic links across borders. Such people have multiple identities and transcultural competencies. Many hold two or more citizenships, even if governments try to prevent this. Cultural interchange and cross-cultural marriages add to the hybridity of consciousness. There is no longer enough time to 'forget difference' – even if people wanted to!

Such experiences still only apply to a minority of people, but are an essential aspect of globalization and will continue to proliferate. The principle that each person should belong politically and culturally to just one nation-state is becoming unworkable. We need a new model of global citizenship, which will break the nexus between belonging and territoriality: people need rights as human beings, not as nationals. This model must be multicultural in the sense that it should recognize ethnic diversity and multiple identities. But multiculturalism also means protecting local diversity against the flattening effect of global cultural industries.

It is not just migration that makes global citizenship necessary. The autonomy of the nation-state and its ability to protect its citizens against outside influences are declining. The powerful economic and cultural logic of globalization cannot be controlled by individual states. Supranational institutions have to be strengthened so that they can curb the excesses of markets, and deal with social exclusion, impoverishment and environmental degradation. Supranational institutions must be made accessible and democratic to reflect the needs and aspirations of the world's people. In the long run, a world society needs a global polity.

Such developments are a long way off, and there is no point in peddling utopias. However, it is clear that the current state of affairs is dangerous and unstable. The main ray of hope is the activity of millions of people all over the world, who are seeking ways of counteracting the harmful effects of globalization, while maximizing its positive aspects. The voices of local communities are making themselves heard through 'civil society organizations' in many places. These include citizens' initiatives against environmental degradation, rural development movements, women's groups, labour unions, indigenous peoples' movements, immigrants' associations and many others.

What is new about many of these civil society organizations is that they are developing a global consciousness, even if they act locally. Moreover, they are learning to use the information technologies which are part of globalization as a tool of resistance. New forms of communication have often been an instrument of control and homogenization, but their character as decentralized networks makes them suitable for quite different purposes. For example, 'electronic democracy' based on the Internet could be used to include a broad public in complex decision-making processes. This leads on to a final contradiction.

9   The contradiction between globalization from above and globalization from below

Globalization has so far mainly meant the imposition of drastic changes on local communities by powerful forces from above. The development of countervailing forces of 'globalization from below' is the main hope for a more equal world, in which economic and social change does not mean exclusion and impoverishment for so many people. From the activity of thousands of local movements and civil society organizations is emerging a new notion of citizenship. It is based on multi-level action for a global dream of sustainable development (Dacanay 1997). If the UNESCO-MOST programme can help to facilitate the work of such groups, and to link them into the work of national and supranational organizations, then it will have carried out a very worthwhile task.

PART IV

MULTICULTURAL SOCIETIES AS A CHALLENGE TO THE NATION-STATE

9

MULTICULTURAL CITIZENSHIP: THE AUSTRALIAN EXPERIENCE

Globalization has profound effects on culture and society, partly due to the internationalization of communication and the mass media, but also because of the growing international mobility of population. The populations of many countries are becoming more diverse, leading to shifts in national cultures and identities. This is likely to have major impacts on political institutions. Such issues are of key importance for Australia, where large-scale immigration since 1945 has led to profound demographic and cultural changes. As a relatively new nation, made up of settlers from all over the world as well as indigenous people, Australia has special problems in defining its culture and identity, and in devising appropriate political institutions. Its polity is based on the model of the nation-state as it emerged in Western Europe and North America from the eighteenth century, but does this really fit the situation on the eve of the twenty-first century?

The concept of the nation-state implies a close link between ethnicity and political identity. The *nation* is usually seen as a group of people who have a feeling of belonging together on the basis of shared language, culture, traditions and history – in other words an ethnic community. The *state* is seen as a structure with territorial boundaries that should coincide with ethnic ones, and which represents the political values of the nation (Gellner 1983). Such a concept of the nation-state implies ethno-cultural

This chapter is taken from V. Bader (ed.), *Citizenship and Exclusion* (London, Macmillan, 1997), pp. 113–38. An earlier and longer version was published by the Parliamentary Research Service, Canberra, in 1996.

homogenization of the population. This can be achieved positively through institutions (such as schools, administration, church, national service) which transmit a common language and culture; or negatively through persecution of minorities and even 'ethnic cleansing'. This model of the nation-state finds it hard to cope with the increasing migration and cultural diversity linked to globalization.

A central category for analysing the link between nation and state in a democracy is *citizenship*. The central idea of this chapter is that the transformation of our society requires a new notion of *multicultural citizenship*. This may be characterized as *a system of rights and obligations which protects the integrity of the individual while recognizing that individuality is formed in a variety of social and cultural contexts*.

Growing ethno-cultural diversity sharpens a basic dilemma of liberal-democratic principles. These stipulate that all citizens are equal individuals and should be treated equally. State policies and services should therefore be based on the idea of universalism. However, the population actually consists of people belonging to a variety of social and cultural groups, with specific needs, interests and values. This makes equal treatment questionable because it may maintain or cause unequal outcomes. How is a liberal-democratic political system to resolve this dilemma?

In fact, modern states deal with this ambiguity through a range of economic, social and cultural policies. In Australia, it can be argued that recent policies on social justice and multiculturalism actually imply an underlying concept of citizenship much broader than the traditional liberal-democratic one. However, the policies have been based on restricted and short-term policy objectives, concerned with facilitating migrant settlement and avoiding community relations problems. It is now important to move more consciously towards a new notion of citizenship.

In this chapter we will start by looking at the ways in which various immigration countries have responded to the challenge of growing ethno-cultural diversity. Then we will survey current political science debates on the dilemma of universalism and difference. Finally, we will examine multicultural policies in Australia, and some of the problems connected with them.

Models for managing diversity

Mass labour migration and refugee movements have been significant in virtually all highly developed countries since 1945. Since the late 1980s, migration flows have accelerated and become more complex. Existing immigration areas (Western Europe, North America and Australia) have been joined by newcomers (southern Europe, Japan and the newly industrializing countries of Asia and Latin America). Current major international issues include immigration control, and how to respond to the presence of new minorities within society. Multiculturalism and citizenship have become hotly debated themes in many countries.

By 1993, there were 19 million foreign residents in European OECD countries, and 1.3 million in Japan. Foreign residents made up 8.5 per cent of the population in Germany, 18 per cent in Switzerland, 6.3 per cent in France and 1.1 per cent in Japan. The USA had 20 million foreign-born residents in 1991 (7.9 per cent of the total population), Canada had 4.3 million (15.6 per cent) and Australia had 4.1 million (22.7 per cent).

Such statistics give only a partial indication of ethnic diversity. Figures on foreign residents leave out illegal entrants, as well as people who have become naturalized. The data also leave out members of ethnic minorities who are not immigrants or foreigners. For instance, the United Kingdom had 2 million foreign residents in 1993 (3.5 per cent of the population) but there were a further 2.6 million ethnic minority members (4.7 per cent of the population), most of whom had been born in the UK. In the USA, the 1990 census showed an ethnic composition of 80 per cent white, 12 per cent black, 1 per cent American Indian, 3 per cent Asian and 4 per cent 'other race'. Distributed across these groups, were 9 per cent Hispanics, who could be 'of any race'. In Canada 'ethno-cultural origin' cuts across classification by immigrant or non-immigrant: 34 per cent of the population are of British origin, 24 per cent French, 5 per cent British-French combined and 38 per cent 'other' (mainly immigrant) origin (Castles and Miller 1998). Finally, most European countries have older ethnic minorities, including Jews, gypsies and regional groups (such as Basques in Spain, Corsicans in France).

Each country has developed its own responses to issues of ethnic diversity (Castles 1995). However, for the purposes of cross-national comparison, it is possible to make out three basic models:

- differential exclusion
- assimilation
- pluralism

No country fits these ideal types exactly. In some countries there has been an evolution, starting with differential exclusion, progressing to attempts at complete and rapid assimilation, moving on to ideas of gradual integration and finally leading to pluralist models (Australia is a case in point). Other countries, such as the United Kingdom and The Netherlands, are much more ambivalent, with strong elements of both assimilationism and pluralism. Policies of assimilation in specific areas (such as economic or social policy) may coexist with pluralism in other areas (such as citizenship or cultural policy).

Differential exclusion

Differential exclusion may be characterized as a situation in which immigrants are incorporated into certain areas of society (above all the labour market) but denied access to others (such as welfare systems, citizenship and political participation). Membership of civil society (as workers, tax-payers, parents and so on) does not confer a right to membership of the nation-state (as citizens). Exclusion may be effected through legal mechanisms (refusal of naturalization and sharp distinctions between the rights of citizens and non-citizens) or through informal practices (racism and discrimination). Immigrants become ethnic minorities, which are excluded from full participation in society. These minorities are usually socio-economically disadvantaged, implying a strong link between class and ethnic background. Patriarchal constructions of gender in both countries of origin and immigration lead to special forms of exclusion for migrant women. Gender is therefore linked to ethnic background and class as a factor of differentiation.

Differential exclusion is mainly to be found in countries where belonging to the nation is based on membership of a specific ethnic group. This 'ethnic' or 'folk' model is typical of Central and Eastern European countries where historical difficulties in forming nation-states led to an aggressive and exclusionary form of nationalism. A variant is found in countries like Switzerland and Belgium which have developed as nations with more than one 'founding group'. The historical arrangements developed to deal with this have led to delicate balances, which make it hard to incorporate new groups. Several newer immigration countries fit the ethnic model.

In Japan, historical isolation led to a high degree of cultural homogeneity (although with both indigenous and immigrant minorities). The move to a modern nation-state has been based on a notion of ethnic belonging, which finds it hard to accommodate new groups. Other Asian immigration countries are often recently emerged nations which have sought to build nation-states out of diverse groups in post-colonial situations. They find it hard to accept new forms of ethno-cultural difference.

Nations based on ethnic belonging are unwilling to accept immigrants and their children as members. Acceptance of new linguistic and cultural diversity is seen as a threat to national culture. This approach results in restrictive immigration policies, an ideology of not being a country of immigration even when mass immigration has taken place, the denial of civil and political rights to immigrants, and highly restrictive policies on citizenship for immigrants and their descendants. Immigration policies are based on the notion that admission of migrants is only a temporary expedient. Immigrants are kept mobile through restrictions on residence rights and the prevention of family reunion.

The contradiction of the differential exclusion model is that denial of settlement has not prevented it from taking place. Countries such as Germany, Austria and Switzerland now have large ethnic minority populations, which are politically excluded and socially marginalized. This contradicts the basic liberal-democratic principle that all members of civil society should also be members of the political community. Exclusion of minorities leads to a split society, serious social problems, growing levels of racist violence and a threat to democracy from the extreme right.

In Germany, the position of immigrants and their descendants has become a major political issue since reunification in 1990. Despite official policies, a form of *'de facto* multiculturalism' is developing in education, social work and local politics. A major debate on citizenship for minorities is taking place in all political parties. The central theme is how to reconcile national identity and culture with the reality of a diverse population. Multiculturalism has become a major issue, which would have been unthinkable even ten years ago.

Assimilation

Assimilation is usually defined as the policy of incorporating migrants into society through a one-sided process of adaptation: immigrants are expected to give up their distinctive linguistic, cultural or social characteristics and become indistinguishable from the majority population. Immigrants can become citizens only if they give up their group identity. In some cases, the notion of assimilation has been replaced with that of integration, according to which adaptation is a more gradual process. None the less, the final goal remains absorption into the dominant culture.

Assimilationist approaches are to be found in nations which base their sense of belonging both on membership of the political community and on sharing a common culture. Examples are France, Britain and The Netherlands, which combine (in varying ways) two sets of historical factors: first, ideas on racial superiority resulting from a colonial history; secondly, ideas on citizenship, civil rights and political participation which result from the democratic-nationalist movements of the eighteenth and nineteenth centuries. These three countries conferred citizenship status on their colonial subjects to bolster ideological control and cultural domination. This had the effect of facilitating migration from the former colonies as the empires crumbled after 1945. At first, migrants were welcomed by governments as useful labour, but attitudes began to change as labour needs declined and urban conflicts emerged. From the 1960s, citizenship rules have gradually been altered to eliminate the special rights of colonized peoples.

The assimilationist model was the prevailing approach in the USA in the early part of the twentieth century at a time of massive immigration and urbanization. It was also the policy of several post-1945 immigration countries, including Canada and Australia. In some cases, assimilation policies have been abandoned over time and replaced with pluralist policies. This happened in response to the recognition that recent immigrants were not assimilating, but were becoming concentrated into particular occupations and residential areas. This helped bring about the emergence of ethnic communities, which maintained their mother-tongues and established social, cultural and political associations.

Today, of all the highly developed immigration countries, metropolitan France probably comes closest to assimilationism. According to the

French 'Republican model', it is easy for immigrants and their children to become citizens, who are supposed to enjoy full rights. Although the 'Republican model' is meant to be concerned purely with individual equality, it is tacitly based on certain assumptions about language use, social behaviour, dress, secularism and political behaviour, summed up in the notion of *civisme* or civic virtues. The contradiction of this approach is that it appears to be purely political, yet it brings culture in through the back door. There is no room for cultural diversity or for the formation of ethnic communities.

Two factors negate the 'Republican model'. The first is socio-economic marginalization: people of non-European origin are concentrated in the lower segments of the labour market, and experience high unemployment rates, especially among the youth. Many are segregated in huge housing projects on the fringes of cities, which have become ghettos of disadvantage. The second factor is racism. Racist violence has increased sharply, and the attraction of racist ideologies is shown by the success of the extreme-right *Front National*, which commands up to 16 per cent of the vote in elections.

The result is a politicization of the situation of minorities, as shown by continuing debates on immigration and nationality law. There is something of a moral panic about the rise of Islam – now France's second religion. Recent events in Algeria have heightened fears of fundamentalism. Various forms of ethnic mobilization have become important, including strike movements by immigrant workers and riots by minority youth against exclusion and police repression. In recent years anti-racist movements like *SOS-Racisme* and *France Plus* have become the focus for political involvement by the *beurs* (youth of North African origin).

France is at a crossroads: the assimilationist model of turning immigrants into citizens at the price of cultural conformity no longer works adequately. Many immigrants are no longer willing to accept assimilation when it brings neither social equality nor protection from racism. Organizations based on cultural identity are increasingly seen as the only way of combating racism and achieving a political voice. The answer for the right is to shift immigration and nationality policies towards a differential exclusion model. The left argues for maintenance of the status quo. For them, multiculturalism is unthinkable for France, for it would question the prevailing ideas on secularity and equality.

Pluralism

Ethno-cultural pluralism may be characterized as the acceptance of immigrant populations as ethnic communities which remain distinguishable from the majority population with regard to language, culture and social organization over several generations. Pluralism implies that immigrants should be granted equal rights in all spheres of society, without being expected to give up their diversity, although usually with an expectation of conformity to certain key values. Here, membership of civil society, initiated through permission to immigrate, leads to full participation in the nation-state.

This model is to be found today in the 'classical immigration countries': the USA, Canada and Australia. The process of building new nations has led to the inclusionary principle that anyone allowed to be permanently resident in the territory should be offered citizenship. This goes together with encouragement of family reunion, naturalization and access to civil and political rights. For these countries pluralism appears as the best way of incorporating large groups of immigrants with diverse backgrounds. Moreover, the imperative of making immigrants into citizens reinforces the pressure for pluralist policies: when immigrants are voters, ethnic groups can gain political clout.

However, it should be noted that ethno-cultural pluralism is a fairly new approach, going back to the early part of the twentieth century in the USA, but only to the 1970s in Australia and Canada, and originating as a reaction to the failure of earlier policies of assimilation. Moreover, other forms of closure are to be found in these countries: until the 1960s, they all had racist immigration policies, which openly discriminated against non-Europeans. Today, there is still selectivity on the basis of economic, social and humanitarian criteria (which may contain hidden bias against people with certain backgrounds). The real decision on who is to become a citizen falls at the time of deciding who to admit as a permanent resident.

Pluralism has two main variants. In the *laissez-faire* approach, typical of the USA, difference is tolerated, but it is not seen as the role of the state to assist with settlement or to support the maintenance of ethnic cultures. The second variant of pluralism is explicit multicultural policies, which imply the willingness of the majority group to accept cultural difference, and to adapt national identity and institutional structures. Such policies exist in Canada, Australia and Sweden, while multicultural policies exist in specific sectors, such as education, in several other countries. The crucial factor is the role of the welfare state: cultural pluralism needs to be combined with policies designed to secure minimum economic and social standards for all if it is to lead to a reasonably equitable and peaceful society.

US society presents the paradox of a democratic political system which incorporates immigrants and other minorities as citizens, and yet is marked by extreme divisions based on class, race and ethnicity. The constitutional safeguards designed to ensure formal equality of rights for all citizens have not been sufficient to prevent the formation of ghettos and underclasses based on race and ethnicity. Three major factors explain this paradox: the extreme racism deriving from the enslavement of African-Americans up to 1865; the culture of violence resulting from the traditions of frontier society; and the tradition of individualism with its corollary of a minimalist social policy.

Canada has many similarities with Australia as a new nation with a strong tradition of state intervention in social affairs (Adelman et al. 1993; Breton et al. 1990). Sweden seems to be something of an anomaly as a society which had a high degree of ethnic and cultural homogeneity until recently. Yet it has had large-scale settlement since 1945, and adopted multicultural policies very close to those of Australia and Canada. The reason lies in the state interventionist model of Swedish social democracy, which has used the same approaches to integrating immigrants into civil society and the state as were used earlier to integrate the working class (Hammar 1985). The Swedish model is an important indicator of the relevance of multicultural approaches in the European context.

The international debate on multiculturalism

This brief account of international responses to ethnic diversity indicates how important the issue has become. The differential exclusion model, as applied in former 'guest-worker'-recruiting countries like Germany, seems highly problematic, for it attempts to deny the permanence of settlement and thus leads to the socio-economic and political marginalization of immigrants and their descendants. The assimilationist model has been gradually abandoned or modified in most countries. Where it is still applied, as in France, it is running into serious difficulties due to the contradiction between the promise of individual equality and the reality of continued socio-economic exclusion and racism.

Pluralist models have their difficulties too. In the mid-1990s, new governments in Canada and Australia moved away from multicultural policies. Swedish multiculturalism was also under strain: refugee entries were drastically cut in response to growing public hostility; generous policies on education, training, welfare and community funding for immigrants were squeezed by the fiscal crisis of the Swedish welfare state; and many immigrants began to criticize the paternalism inherent in the official notion of ethnicity (Ålund and Schierup 1991).

Multiculturalism has become a major topic of debate even in countries which used to shun such ideas. However, the term is used in very different ways. In Europe, multiculturalism is generally seen as a model based on the long-term persistence within society of groups with different values and cultures. Multiculturalism is rejected by many because it is seen as a legitimation of separatism and fundamentalism, and therefore as a threat to modernity, secularism and gender equality. In the USA, on the other hand, multiculturalism focuses on the reinterpretation of US history and culture to recognize the contribution of groups traditionally excluded from the 'dominant canon': women, African-Americans and Native Americans (Goldberg 1994). In Australia, by contrast, multiculturalism is understood as a public policy designed to ensure the full socio-economic and political participation of all members of an increasingly diverse population.

Democracy and difference

As the above discussion indicates, the relationship between immigration, citizenship and democracy is highly problematic. There appear to be four main issues. First, the *dilemma of formal inclusion* concerns access to citizenship. Failure to make immigrants into citizens undermines a basic principle of parliamentary democracy – that all members of civil society should have rights of political participation – but making them into citizens questions concepts of the nation based on ethnic belonging or cultural homogeneity. This remains a central issue in many European countries, but is not very important in Australia, where immigrants can obtain naturalization after two years' residence and where children born in the country to legally resident parents are automatically citizens.

The second dilemma concerns *substantial citizenship*; that is, the rights and obligations connected with being a member of a national political community. Where immigrants are socio-economically marginalized and targets for racist violence, granting formal citizenship does not guarantee the full civil, political and social rights which constitute modern citizenship. Achieving full participation requires a range of policies and institutions concerned with combating racism and discrimination, and improving labour-market status, access to welfare, education and housing. This issue is significant in all immigration countries, including Australia, and is a major focus of multicultural policies.

The third dilemma is that of *recognition of collective cultural rights*. This arises because it often proves impossible to incorporate immigrants into society as individuals. In many cases, immigrants and their descendants cluster together, share a common socio-economic position, develop their own community structures, and seek to maintain their languages and cultures. Culture and ethnicity are vital resources in the settlement process. Immigrants cannot become full citizens unless the state and society are willing to accept the right to cultural difference not only for individuals but also for groups. Collective cultural rights are therefore a central part of multiculturalism. However, they are only meaningful if they are linked to social justice strategies. If cultural difference leads to social disadvantage (such as high unemployment, low incomes or poor housing) then we cannot speak of equality of respect for all cultural groups.

This leads on to the fourth dilemma, that of *the appropriateness of our political institutions*. As Canadian philosopher Charles Taylor (1994) has argued, political ideas and institutions are the expression of a certain range of cultures, and may be incompatible with other ranges. Even a doctrine like liberalism cannot claim complete neutrality. For instance, its notion of the division between the public and the private is unacceptable to feminists. A multicultural society cannot expect the culturally bound principles of the group dominant in earlier phases of its history to remain appropriate when new groups are included in the political process. For Australia this implies that it may be necessary to overhaul institutional structures which claim to be universalistic, but which are in fact based on British legal and constitutional traditions of the founding fathers of the Federation.

Liberal theories of citizenship have difficulty in dealing with collective difference (Bauböck 1994). Attempts to increase democracy have generally involved making citizenship rights available to ever-wider circles of the population. Suffrage in Western countries applied initially only to male property-owners, but was later extended to the working class and then to women. In recent times, citizenship for indigenous and immigrant minorities has been seen as the key to greater equality. However, liberal citizenship tends to homogenize political identity: all citizens are supposed to have equal rights as citizens, whatever their actual economic and social positions (Pateman 1985). As women, indigenous people and immigrants have found, formal political equality may not overcome racism, economic disadvantage or social exclusion. Equality as citizens is not in itself sufficient to achieve real empowerment and change.

There are a number of solutions to this problem. The American feminist philosopher Iris Marion Young (1989) argues that full citizenship can only be achieved through recognition that people's primary social identity may not be as individual members of society but as members of a specific community. This implies the right for groups to remain different. Young therefore advocates a concept of *differentiated citizenship* with two main aspects. First, democracy must mean not only enfranchisement of all, but also mechanisms to secure participation of usually excluded social groups in decision-making. This argument would legitimate special representative bodies for certain groups – a principle already embodied in Australia in the Aboriginal and Torres Strait Islander Commission. It could also justify veto rights on certain decisions by groups directly affected.

Secondly, universality implies that laws and policies should be blind to race, gender, ethnicity and so on. The principle of equal treatment is based on the idea of generally applicable norms of behaviour and performance. But there are in fact no objective general norms: they are based on the experience of the groups who have the power to set them. Thus seemingly fair and objective standards may discriminate against those who are excluded – and indeed can serve as an ideological legitimation for that exclusion (Young 1989: 269–70). As Laksiri Jayasuriya (1993) has written: 'in a plural society, we discover that people's needs are unequal but equity policy dictates that we assume that needs are equal. Hence the paradox in a plural society ... that we cannot be egalitarian and equitable at the same time.' Differential treatment is sometimes needed to achieve equity. The obvious examples here are affirmative action measures to improve the educational or occupational level of disadvantaged groups, or special services for groups with special needs.

Young's notion of *differentiated citizenship* is both useful and problematic. It does point the way to measures for increasing equity, but it could lead to a new type of fixation and homogenization of identity. If group rights are institutionalized, this must imply some mechanism for determining and registering group membership. But many people assigned to a group may not accept this as their principal source of political identity. Fixed group membership may be experienced as repressive, especially if it means binding people to groups with rigid values on gender, religion or social behaviour.

A second approach is that of Charles Taylor (1994), who takes as his starting-point the need for *recognition*. He argues that our identity is shaped through recognition or its absence on the part of others. He sees liberal ideas on the equal worth of individuals as central to securing recognition in modern society. However, increasing cultural diversity and the emergence of multiculturalism lead to potentially contradictory discourses on two levels. On the one hand, the *politics of universalism* mean emphasizing the equal dignity of individuals through the equalization of rights and entitlements. On the other hand, the modern notion of identity has given rise to a *politics of difference*, based on recognition of the unique identity of individuals or groups, and their distinctness from everyone else. The politics of universalism require norms of non-discrimination which are blind to difference, while the politics of difference require special rights and treatment for certain groups, such as Aboriginal people.

The claims for individual rights and the protection of collective identities seem irreconcilable, but Taylor sets out to bridge the gulf, using the example of Quebec's claims for special rights for the French language and culture. He argues that one can distinguish fundamental rights (like *habeas corpus*), which should never be infringed, from rights that are important but can be revoked or restricted for reasons of public policy. On this basis, Quebeckers are justified in demanding special measures (such as priority for the French language in schools and public life) to secure the survival of their collective cultural identity, as long as they maintain fundamental liberal rights and provide protection for minorities. This approach may well be applicable in the case of Quebec, where a Francophone majority, which holds power at the level of the province, is confronted by an Anglophone majority, which holds power at the federal level. But it is not clear how Taylor's approach would work in situations in which a powerful majority is faced by a range of minorities which lack political power. Taylor does not show us general mechanisms which would secure protection and equal rights for minorities, and empower them.

A third approach is that proposed by Jürgen Habermas (1994), who argues that Taylor is wrong in postulating a basic contradiction between individual rights and the protection of collective identities. Rather, he says, there is an inherent connection between democracy and the constitutional state, in the sense that citizens can only be autonomous by collectively exercising their political rights within the law-making process. On this basis, the system of rights cannot be blind to unequal social conditions or cultural differences because bearers of individual rights develop their individuality within varying social and cultural contexts. 'A correctly understood theory of rights requires a politics of recognition that protects the integrity of the individual in the life contexts in which his or her identity is formed' (Habermas 1994: 113). Democracy in a multicultural society therefore means guaranteeing social and cultural rights for everyone, rather than just for members of specific groups. However, as Habermas points out, this does not happen by itself, but rather as the result of social movements and political struggles. The virtue of Habermas's formulation is that it removes the false contradiction between individual rights and group identities by stressing that everyone is both an individual and a bearer of a collective identity. A democratic state must therefore guarantee rights at both levels. Combined with Habermas's emphasis on the legitimate role of political action in achieving change, and his notion that no political system can remain static in a changing world, this provides a valuable philosophical framework for a new notion of citizenship.

Principles of multicultural citizenship

On the basis of this discussion, it is possible to suggest some principles for *multicultural citizenship*. The aim must be to achieve full citizenship for everybody – not only for people of migrant origin, but also for members of hitherto disempowered groups: women, indigenous peoples, people with disabilities, gays and lesbians and so on. Recognition of group difference implies departing from the idea of all citizens as simply *equal individuals* and instead seeing them simultaneously as having *equal rights as individuals and different needs and wants as members of groups with specific characteristics and social situations*.

This gives rise to the following principles for multicultural citizenship:

1 *Taking equality of citizenship rights as a starting-point.* It is essential to ensure that all members of society are formally included as citizens, and enjoy equal rights and equality before the law.
2 *Recognizing that formal equality of rights does not necessarily lead to equality of respect, resources, opportunities or welfare.* Formal equality can indeed mask and legitimize disadvantage and discrimination. Multicultural citizenship must be based on accepting group differences as legitimate, and not as disabilities or deviance.
3 *Establishing mechanisms for group representation and participation.* Despite formal equality as citizens, members of disadvantaged groups are often excluded from decision-making processes. Such groups need special institutional arrangements to secure full political participation. This means devising mechanisms to secure more democracy in more places (Davidson 1993: 8).
4 *Differential treatment for people with different characteristics, needs and wants.* Treating people equally, despite the fact that past conditions, laws, policies and practices have made them unequal in various ways,

can only perpetuate inequality. Governments should provide laws, programmes and services to combat barriers based on gender, disability, origins, ethnicity and so on.

Australian multiculturalism

To what extent do multicultural policies in Australia correspond with this notion of multicultural citizenship? Multiculturalism was originally devised in the 1970s as a model to respond to the needs of a growing immigrant population after the failure of previous policies of assimilation. It does not provide an explicit model of citizenship and democracy but, under the Australian Labor Party (ALP) government from 1983 to 1996, it developed into a set of policies that made a powerful implicit statement on these matters.

Multicultural principles and Australian citizenship

Multiculturalism was first officially embraced as a policy in Canada in 1971. In Australia, explicit multicultural policies were first introduced in 1973 by the ALP government led by Gough Whitlam. In this early phase, it was based on the rejection of assimilationism and policies for improving welfare and educational provision for mainly working-class migrants of European origin. The Liberal and Country Party coalition, which governed from 1975 to 1982, continued multicultural policies, but modified them to emphasize cultural pluralism, the role of ethnic organizations in the provision of welfare services and the value of multiculturalism for achieving social cohesion in an ethnically diverse society.

The central principle of this type of multiculturalism was the key role of the ethnic group, which was seen as having a relatively fixed and homogeneous cultural identity. Australian society appeared as a collection of ethnic communities united around a set of 'core values'. Critics of this 'ethnic group model' of multiculturalism argued that state-funding policies might actually create the communities and leaderships that government wanted to work with, while ignoring diversity and tendencies to change within each group. None the less, multiculturalism made an important new statement on substantial citizenship: that it was no longer necessary to be culturally assimilated to be an Australian citizen. You could be an Australian, even if you spoke another language and followed different cultural practices and lifestyles (as long as these did not conflict with Australian law).

The ALP government of 1983–96 again redefined multiculturalism to fit in with other key policy goals such as economic deregulation, more efficient use of human resources, maintaining the social safety net and integrating Australia into the Asian Pacific region. This move was influenced by developments such as the shift from Europe to Asia as the main source of immigration, increased emphasis on high skill levels as an entry criterion, and the labour-market entry of second-generation immigrants with much better education levels than their parents. The government moved away from the 'ethnic group approach' and developed what may be called 'a citizenship model of multiculturalism'. The new model was laid down in the *National Agenda for a Multicultural Australia* (Office of Multicultural Affairs 1989). Multiculturalism was defined as a system of rights and freedoms, combined with such obligations as commitment to the nation, a duty to accept the constitution and the rule of law, and the acceptance of basic principles such as tolerance and equality, English as the national language and equality of the sexes.

The document implicitly embodied an innovative concept of citizenship: it took for granted the three types of rights – civil, political and social rights – suggested in T.H. Marshall's classic analysis of citizenship in post-war Britain (Marshall 1964). It went on to add a new component: cultural rights. The *National Agenda* implied some of the principles of multicultural citizenship discussed above. Multiculturalism was not defined as cultural pluralism or minority rights, but in terms of the rights of *all citizens* in a democratic state. The *National Agenda* emphasized the recognition of *difference* as part of the state's task in securing *universality* in resource allocation. The programme was based on the recognition that some groups are disadvantaged by lack of language proficiency and education, together with discrimination based on race, ethnicity and gender. It was seen as the duty of the state to combat such disadvantage. There was an underlying understanding that cultural rights could not be fully realized unless they were linked to policies of social justice. The new policy document issued by the National Multicultural Advisory Council (NMAC) towards the end of the period of ALP government, *Multicultural Australia: the Next Steps – Towards and Beyond 2000* (NMAC 1995) reiterated the 1989 statement, spelling out the principles in more detail and assessing the extent to which the policy initiatives had been successfully implemented.

A wealth of government policy documents up to 1996 could be cited as evidence that the principles and rhetoric of multiculturalism did, in many respects, correspond to the principles of multicultural citizenship suggested in the previous section of this chapter. But did this official rhetoric reflect fundamental changes? Some observers argue that multiculturalism has been only a peripheral theme in the debate on Australian identity and institutions. For instance, Alastair Davidson (1993) has shown that the current debate on whether Australia should become a republic has hardly addressed the need for constitutional change to reflect the diversity of the Australian population.[...]

The move to a republic is seen by many as simply concerned with the appointment of an Australian head of state, while all else remains unchanged. This one-sidedness is a continuation of 'the long silence about citizenship' (Davidson 1993: 3) which has prevailed since Federation. The lack of debate was originally based on the fact that Australians were British citizens until 1948; since then on the notion prevailed that there was no need for change and therefore little to discuss. In the past few years, citizenship has again become a public topic, with calls for better understanding of what it means to be a citizen through programmes of civic education. At the same time, citizenship campaigns have been carried out to persuade immigrants to become naturalized. But there has been little debate about the need for redefining citizenship itself.

This is linked to the fact that Australia – like Britain, but unlike the USA, Canada and most European democracies – has no Bill of Rights to stipulate clearly what it means to be a citizen. In Canada, multicultural-ism and equality rights were integrated into the definition of citizenship through the 1982 Canadian Charter of Rights and Freedoms. This recog-nized the collective identities and collective rights of specific groups as part of citizenship. In contrast, the Australian approach was much more on the level of social policy: the special needs of ethnic groups were rec-ognized, but the measures taken to deal with them were essentially con-cerned with welfare, education or services for individuals (Jayasuriya 1993: 2). The Australian approach was based on the administration of social issues by the state, rather than active citizenship through collective participation in decision-making processes.[...] Even on the level of polit-ical principles, multiculturalism therefore still seemed far from being an effective model for Australian citizenship. However, the problems became even more marked if rhetoric was contrasted with actual social change.

Indigenous people and multiculturalism

A major problem is that multiculturalism has always been seen mainly as a strategy concerned with immigrants and their descendants. It is seldom linked to the needs of indigenous Australians. The *National Agenda* did refer to the situation of Aborigines and Torres Strait Islanders, yet the policy initiatives which flowed from the document related mainly to immigrants. Indigenous people were only included in certain general pro-grammes, such as those concerning 'access and equity' (see below) and community relations.

This near absence of Aborigines and Torres Strait Islanders in multicul-tural policies reflects a dilemma: many indigenous people reject inclusion as they feel it would make them seem like one ethnic group among others. Aboriginal spokespersons assert their special status as the original inhabi-tants of the continent. In the late 1980s and early 1990s it became increas-ingly clear that Australia could never develop a coherent national identity unless it recognized the special position of indigenous people and the historical wrongs done to them. This realization found its expression in the Mabo decision of 1992 and the Native Title Act of 1993, which overthrew the long-standing colonial legal doctrine of *terra nullius*, according to which indigenous peoples had never really possessed the land.

It is in this context that, in its last few years of office, the ALP government made attempts to broaden multicultural policies to include indigenous people.[...] Yet there were still few concrete measures which could actually make multiculturalism relevant to Aboriginal people. The only way of overcoming this might be through much more vigorous anti-racist policies, as well as effective measures to overcome the disadvantage and exclusion of Aboriginal communities. Until such steps are taken, multiculturalism will be weakened by its lack of support from indigenous Australians.

Social justice and economic rationalism

There is a strong link between cultural rights and social justice. If members of certain ethnic groups can only maintain their culture at the price of social disadvantage (for example, high unemployment and low socio-economic status) then we cannot speak of equal rights. This issue was clearly recognized in the *National Agenda*, and other ALP government policy statements, which laid down strategies to combat social disadvantage and remove labour-market barriers. Several government departments introduced social justice strategies which targeted non-English speaking background immigrants, indigenous people, women and people with disabilities. Social justice in the *National Agenda* was concerned with fair distribution of economic resources; equal access to essential services such as housing, health care and education; equal rights in civil, legal and industrial affairs; and equal opportunity for participation by all in personal development, community life and decision-making (Office of Multicultural Affairs 1989: 19).

However, there was an unresolved tension between the principles of social justice and economic efficiency. The ALP government pursued policies of deregulation and privatization of the economy based on neoclassical theories of economic rationality. Such policies reduced the ability of the government to intervene in economic matters to ensure social justice. The *National Agenda* tried to resolve the problem through the principle of 'economic efficiency', defined as 'the need to maintain, develop and utilize effectively the skills and talents of all Australians, regardless of background' (Office of Multicultural Affairs 1989: vi). This principle underpinned policies designed to make efficient use of human resources through education, training and recognition of overseas qualifications. The government also stressed 'productive diversity': the notion that it was in the general interest to make efficient use of the skills and cultural capabilities of the country's diverse population.

The objectives laid down in government social justice policies suggest indicators by which to judge their success.[...] One important area is participation in government. In 1991, only 6.7 per cent of legislators and government-appointed officials at the three levels of government were of first- or second-generation non-English speaking background (NESB), compared with their share in the population of about 25 per cent. The under-representation had actually got worse since 1986. The participation rate of indigenous Australians in government was 0.6 per cent, compared with a 1.6 per cent share in the population. NESB people were also under-represented in the public service and particularly in the senior executive service, although the situation showed some improvement since 1989. Participation by NESB and indigenous people was low in many other important public positions, such as judges, magistrates, mediators and police officers. An examination of membership of government consultative bodies showed that NESB and indigenous people were well represented on bodies concerned with social and cultural issues, but significantly under-represented on other councils, such as those concerned with economic decision-making (NMAC 1995, vol. 2: 13–15).

Participation in senior management and union leadership is another important indicator. NMAC found that NESB people made up only 6 per cent of directors and executives listed in major company handbooks. However, NESB people were over-represented among owners and operators of small businesses. A study of Victorian unions found that only 10 per cent of officials were NESB people, compared with 24 per cent of union members. Under-representation particularly affected more recent Asian immigrant groups (NMAC 1995, vol. 2: 15–16).

Another measure of social justice is unemployment levels. Indigenous people have chronically high unemployment. A major survey by the Australian Bureau of Statistics (ABS) noted an overall unemployment rate of 38 per cent in 1994. Moreover, many Aboriginal people were classified as not in the labour force because they had given up looking for a job: the ABS survey found that 32 per cent of those not in the labour force wanted a job (Australian Bureau of Statistics 1995: 45–7). Unemployment rates tend to rise faster than average for NESB people in recessions, and their overall unemployment rates are higher. In June 1995, the unemployment rate for NESB people was 12.2 per cent, compared with 8.1 per cent for the total labour force. The rate for some groups was far higher: 25.1 per cent for Lebanese; 26.8 per cent for Vietnamese (BIMPR 1995: 48).These are not recently arrived groups; their unemployment rates have been high for many years, and labour-market measures seem to have done little to improve the situation. Another government report has noted above-average unemployment rates for overseas-born youth from non-English speaking countries (HREOC 1993: 223).

Recognition of overseas skills and qualifications has long been seen as a crucial issue by ethnic communities. Despite some improvements in accreditation procedures, Australia is still far from a situation of equal opportunities for overseas-trained professionals and tradespeople in all occupations. Employers' reservations about overseas skills, and discrimination against people from particular countries, influence employment chances for engineers (Hawthorne 1994). In 1991, the Human Rights and Equal Opportunities Commission (HREOC) concluded that there was compelling evidence that the medical registration system was discriminatory under the terms of the Racial Discrimination Act of 1975. A 1995 working party recommended a broad range of reform measures to secure equal opportunities for people trained overseas (NMAC 1995, vol. 2: 36–7), although there was little sign that these would be implemented.

The HREOC's 1994 *State of the Nation* report was concerned mainly with housing issues. It reported frequent racial harassment of public-housing tenants in some areas, and also noted that housing authorities lacked effective strategies to deal with this. Perhaps as a result of the latter, over 80 per cent of tenants who had experienced harassment said they had not reported it. The report also noted 'the disjointed and haphazard approach to access and equity provision within the State Housing authorities' (HREOC 1994: 38).

Multiculturalism has given rise to many measures designed to improve social justice for ethnic minorities in Australia. Some real progress has been achieved, and the picture is certainly much better than that in countries which cling to exclusionary or assimilationist policies. However, in many key areas, progress has been painfully slow, and real socio-economic disadvantage persists for certain groups. Indigenous and NESB people are still far from equal with regard to participation in political and economic power.

Multiculturalism as bureaucratic practice

From the mid-1980s, both state and federal governments were concerned to move away from multicultural policies delivered by special agencies to special target groups. Multicultural policies were to become part of the mainstream of government service delivery. The key instrument for achieving this at the federal level was the 'access and equity strategy' known as 'A&E'. From 1989 to 1994 all Commonwealth departments and agencies were required to prepare A&E plans, and to report on their implementation annually. In 1992 a major evaluation of the A&E strategy reported improvements in language and information services, but also noted many problems and deficiencies (Office of Multicultural Affairs 1992). In 1994, NMAC noted further improvements, but also found areas with severe problems, including delivery of services to indigenous Australians; consultation and participation policies, mechanisms and processes; services to small and remote area communities; and the collection and use of ethnicity data (NMAC 1995, vol. 2: 27–8). Despite such concerns the general requirement for A&E plans was abolished in 1994. The preparation of triennial plans and of reports on their implementation were left to the discretion of individual agencies. Similarly, 1994 was the last year that federal government departments were required to report publicly on their equal opportunity programmes. This requirement was abolished, although only 9 per cent of appointments to the public service were NESB people at the time (Australian Council of Trade Unions 1995).

The bureaucratic response to racism reveals similar problems. The 1991 National Inquiry into Racist Violence showed a high incidence of racism, especially against indigenous people and Asian immigrants (HREOC 1991). Australia has no systematic monitoring of incidents of racist violence or discrimination, unlike the USA or Britain, which have established special reporting systems. Federal and state agencies set up to combat racial discrimination and vilification do not provide comprehensive information on the incidence of such practices – they merely respond to complaints.

The HREOC received 458 complaints under the federal Racial Discrimination Act in 1993–4 but there is strong evidence that only a small percentage of such cases are actually reported (Australian Council of Trade Unions 1995: 5, 10, 15). This is partly because of the complex and lengthy procedures faced by those who do complain, and partly because existing laws are weak and rarely provide effective remedies. For example, the New South Wales Anti-discrimination Board received 448 complaints on the grounds of vilification over a five-year period; of these, three cases were eventually recommended for prosecution, but not in fact proceeded with (Australian Council of Trade Unions 1995: 10). In the light of this, people may feel that complaints are a waste of time.

The decline of ethnic politics

An important reason for stagnation in the development of multicultural-ism is the relatively low level of political mobilization of ethnic communities. The higher level of activism among indigenous people may help explain why their situation has been much more on the political agenda in recent years.

One reason for the emergence of multiculturalism in the 1970s was the realization by political parties that immigrants were making up increasing proportions of the electorate. The introduction of social policies aimed specifically at immigrants, first by the ALP and then by the coalition government, put a premium on ethnic mobilization and the formation of associations to speak in the name of immigrants. This caused some observers to imply that there was some sort of sinister 'ethnic lobby' which was having an illegitimate influence on politics. Most political scientists, on the other hand, argue that there is no monolithic 'ethnic vote' which can be controlled by ethnic leaders to secure specific political outcomes. Immigrants have not constituted a united political force, mainly because the differences among them in terms of social position, interests and values are as great as among the Anglo-Australian population.

From the 1970s, leaders of ethnic associations were increasingly drawn into government consultative bodies of various kinds. The state Ethnic Community Councils and the Federation of Ethnic Communities Councils of Australia came to be predominantly funded by government. Smaller associations representing specific ethnic groups also became dependent on government grants. Links between government and ethnic communities were further encouraged by the fact that many second-generation immigrants made their careers in the public service: they often had the ambiguous role of being both government officials and ethnic lobbyists. These tendencies are contradictory. On the one hand, the closeness between ethnic communities and the government agencies was beneficial in improving communication and sensitivity to needs. But it also led to a process of creeping co-option, through which the ethnic associations became closely oriented towards bureaucratic goals and methods.

The overall result of this institutionalization of ethnic politics seems to have been a depoliticization of ethnic associations and a reduction of their political influence in the late 1980s and early 1990s. Old-style mobilization of ethnic groups still takes place around issues connected with homeland politics. But major political actions connected with multicultural issues hardly occur any more. When a conservative government came to power in 1996, ethnic organizations lacked the ability to fight effectively against cuts in social rights for immigrants.

A shift away from multicultural citizenship?

On 2 March 1996 a Liberal–National Party coalition was elected with a large majority. Prior to the election, the coalition parties had promised to retain the social safety-net, but also to cut government expenditure and deregulate the labour market. Upon taking office, the new government claimed that there was an unexpected A$8 billion deficit, which made considerable reductions in expenditure vital. The August 1996 budget contained cuts to many government services, including measures for the unemployed, health services, aged care and tertiary education.

During the March election, racism played an unexpected role, with several conservative candidates criticizing the provision of special services for minorities. In one Queensland electorate, the Liberal Party candidate, Pauline Hanson, attacked services for Aboriginal people in such an extreme way that she was disendorsed as a candidate by her own party. Despite this, she won the seat, with one of the biggest anti-Labour swings in the country. This was widely taken as a signal that anti-minority discourses were now seen as acceptable by a large share of the population.

After the election, government leaders and media commentators started to attack Aboriginal and migrant rights in a way that had not been seen in Australia for many years. Senator Herron, the Minister for Aboriginal Affairs, publicly criticized the Aboriginal and Torres Strait Islander Commission (ATSIC) for alleged poor management and corruption, and introduced strict measures to control this previously independent body. In August 1996 the government announced cuts of A$400 million to ATSIC's budget, which meant severe restrictions in the services provided to Aboriginal people in fields such as health, employment, legal aid, culture and sport.

Major cuts were quickly introduced in the immigration and multicultural area. The immigration intake for 1996–7 was cut by 11 per cent. Fees for visas were increased drastically; for instance, a family residence visa went up from A$415 to A$1,500. Costs for English language courses for new immigrants were more than doubled to A$5,000. At the same time, many occupational English courses were abolished. The largest cut was to be achieved by increasing the waiting period for eligibility for social-security benefits like unemployment support from six months to two years for new entrants, which was expected to save A$663 million. The Bureau of Immigration, Multicultural and Population Research was abolished, reducing Australia's policy-oriented research capability in this area. Perhaps the most important change in political terms was the abolition of the Office of Multicultural Affairs, which had previously been able to influence core government policies substantially from its location in the Department of Prime Minister and Cabinet. Some remnants of the office were integrated into a (re-named) Department of Immigration and Multicultural Affairs (DIMA), but with very limited resources, and no political weight.[...]

The election of a conservative government with a neo-liberal agenda of small government, privatization and deregulation heralded a major shift away from the multicultural principles of its predecessor. The government's social philosophy was based on backward-looking and monocultural ideals, reminiscent of Australia in the 1950s. However, Australia in the 1990s is a very different society, marked by great cultural diversity and the existence of many organizations representing the various ethnic communities. It remains to be seen whether current developments will lead to a re-emergence of ethnic politics and to new demands for political and economic participation by minorities.

Conclusion

Is Australia on the way to a new form of multicultural citizenship, which could be a model for other democratic countries confronted by the dilemmas arising from globalization and growing ethnic diversity? Or has the model become stalled due to a failure to tackle structural inequalities, loss of reform impetus in the treadmill of bureaucratic practice and depoliticization of protest potential?

Certainly Australia has come a long way since its racist worldview began to be questioned in the 1960s. Assimilationism, for all its problems, did create a basis for change by providing formal access to citizenship for immigrants – something that has still not been achieved in many immigration countries. The 'ethnic group model' of multiculturalism in the 1970s did begin a process of rethinking identity which moved Australia's self-image away from the myth of ethno-cultural homogeneity – again, a step still to be taken in many places. The shift in the late 1980s towards a 'citizenship model' of multiculturalism made the vital link between cultural pluralism and social justice. This raised the fundamental dilemma of how to achieve the recognition of collective cultural rights within a universalistic democracy.

However, the development of multiculturalism was not part of a conscious strategy for rethinking citizenship to make it appropriate for a culturally diverse nation on the eve of the twenty-first century. Rather, policies concerned with ethno-cultural diversity have essentially been top-down social policies. Multiculturalism has developed in an *ad hoc* way as a strategy for integrating immigrant communities into a basically unchanged society.

It is important to realize that cultural diversity is likely to bring about major changes in society. The impetus for change is unlikely to come from those in power – it must be a result of social movements and political action. Active citizenship means constant participation by citizens in decision-making at all levels. The challenge is to bring about changes in representative mechanisms and bureaucratic structures to permit more democracy in more places, for both groups and individuals. This may lead to major shifts in political identity and institutions.

10

EXPLAINING RACISM IN THE NEW GERMANY

The racist outrages of the two years since German reunification are too well known to need detailed description. The mob attacks on refugee hostels, the violence against foreigners on the streets and in their homes have been constantly in the headlines. From mid-1990 to mid-1991 about thirty foreigners died as a result of racist violence in Germany (Nirumand 1992: 7), and the situation got even worse in 1992. These acts of violence reflect a general climate of aggression and discrimination against minorities. Particularly disturbing is the success of neo-Nazi organizations in mobilizing youth sub-cultures such as skinheads. What lies behind this outburst of racist violence? In this chapter I will examine some of the explanations given by German social scientists, and link these to the responses of the state and the parties.[1]

The shock of reunification

A common approach is to attribute racism to the socio-economic effects of reunification on the East German population.[2] Reunification led to high hopes of freedom and prosperity but, within months, these were dashed. The East German economy collapsed, and West German firms were reluctant to invest. The old regime had guaranteed jobs and training. Now many people found themselves on the street. Those who went to the West in search of work often returned disappointed, finding that lack of skills gave them no chance.

At the same time, the social institutions that had given structure to life in the drab, polluted wasteland disappeared. Children had been members of the Young Pioneers, while young people were in the Free German Youth. Many rejected the political indoctrination and regimentation, yet these organizations had provided low-cost meeting places, as well as sporting and hobby activities. Their disappearance left a vacuum. The federal government did little to provide youth clubs and job-creation schemes, believing that this should be left to the private sector. Churches and welfare organizations did their best, but it was the neo-Nazis who were

This chapter was first published in Social Alternatives, 12 (1993), pp. 9–12.

quickest to start youth groups, providing meeting places, comradeship and an ideology. The strategy for combating extreme-right tendencies among youth which arises from this *socio-economic explanation* consists of a combination of job-creation schemes and intensive youth work (cf. Korfes 1992).

A second approach emphasizes psychological factors. The inefficient economy and corrupt bureaucracy of the German Democratic Republic (GDR) had left a legacy of cynicism. After the fall of the Berlin Wall, many people believed that values of democracy and free enterprise imported from the West would provide a new orientation. However, this belief disappeared as the economy collapsed and it became apparent that many West Germans saw the *Ossis* (East Germans) as comical, inferior and something of a nuisance.

The situation was complicated by the feelings of East Germans about their role in the GDR. Those who had believed the official ideology and worked hard to build 'socialism' were now told that their life's work had been misguided. Thousands had spied on their neighbours, friends and even families for the *Stasi* (secret police). Others had taught the official doctrine at schools, or had joined the ruling party as a ticket to success. Very few people had had the courage to fight the regime. Since 1989, the collective guilt and denial of the parent generation has made it difficult for them to provide moral authority and guidance to the youth. A bestseller by an East German psychotherapist explained the growth of violence through the removal of repressive control which allows the blocked inner feelings (*Gefühlsstau*) to surface through aggression (Maaz 1992). The consequence of this *psychological explanation* would be therapeutic measures to deal with the collective trauma of the East German people.

But there are problems in explaining racism simply through the crisis in the ex-GDR. The frequency of racist attacks was higher in the East than in the West (Fahin and Seidel-Pielen 1992: 42–3), but violence escalated in the West as well. According to the Federal Criminal Office, 66 per cent of the 2,380 offences against foreigners in 1991 were committed in the old *Länder*. Racist violence is a problem affecting the whole of German society.

Immigration, refugees and the state response

A *political explanation* for racism – frequently put forward by politicians – was that it was an 'understandable reaction' to mass immigration. Since 1945, Germany has had several waves of immigrants. The first consisted of about 8 million 'expellees' of German ethnic origin from Eastern Europe immediately after the war. Then came the 'guest-workers' recruited from southern Europe and Turkey to fuel the 'economic miracle' between 1955 and 1973. When recruitment ceased, many settled, and by 1989 there were over 5 million foreign residents. The third wave comprised asylum-seekers from non-European countries and Eastern Europe, especially after 1989. Simultaneously, there was a new inflow of 'ethnic Germans' from Russia and Romania.

Altogether about 2 million people entered Germany between 1989 and 1992. The government and the ruling parties claimed that many of the asylum-seekers were not victims of persecution, but would-be economic migrants. They therefore wanted to change the Basic Law (the constitution) to restrict the right of political asylum. In November 1992, the SPD agreed to support the change, despite strong opposition within the party. This is a classic 'blame the victim strategy': stop racism by keeping out its objects! This merely encourages the popular idea that it is the foreigners who are the problem, rather than German racism.

In periods of economic growth, Germany has not found it difficult to incorporate millions of immigrants. Since the mid-1970s, economic growth has slowed while immigrant families have become highly visible in the cities, competing with Germans for housing and social amenities. But successive governments have told the people that 'the German Federal Republic is not a country of immigration'. Foreigners are denied citizenship and basic rights. Misleading people about the reality of settlement, and failure to grant citizenship and basic rights to a large section of the population, are recipes for conflict and a divided society. Thus the real *political explanation* for racism lies in the discriminatory policies of the state, and its failure to introduce realistic immigration and settlement policies.

The historical culture of racism

Explanations of racism must include not only current factors but also historical constants. Germany is not unique: racism in its various guises (anti-semitism, repression of gypsies and other ethnic minorities, oppression of colonized peoples, discrimination against migrant workers) is part of European history and culture. Racism is closely linked to the struggles surrounding the building of nation-states and their colonial expansion (see Miles 1989 for a useful brief history and analysis). German racism does seem particularly threatening because of its historical antecedents, but there are big differences between 1933 and 1992: Hitler was supported by important elements in the ruling class because they saw the Nazis as a tool for destroying the labour movement and reasserting the interests of national capital. Today, the labour movement is part of the ruling bloc, and German capital is too international to support chauvinism. The neo-Nazis have no chance of gaining power, but they are a substantial threat to democracy.

Unfortunately, German social science has largely ignored *historical explanations* until recently. The general line has been to equate racism with anti-semitism, and to claim that this is no longer a major issue. Discrimination and attacks against immigrants have been labelled not as racism, but as *Ausländerfeindlichkeit* (hostility towards foreigners). It is only very recently that German scholars have begun to raise the issue of racism and to link up with some of the debates in British and French sociology (Bielefeld 1990; Butterwegge and Jäger 1992; Kalpaka and Räthzel 1990).

Some of the best analyses of German racism are still to be found in the work of the Frankfurt School, which set out (in exile in the 1930s) to explain how such a civilized people could behave so barbarically. Adorno, Horkheimer, Marcuse and Fromm put forward a combination of economic, historical and psychological explanations. Germany was a 'late nation', which was unable to form a nation-state until 1871. Industrialization was not preceded by a democratic revolution, so it took place under an absolutist state and a monopolistic bourgeoisie. Because Germany was late in the struggle for markets and colonies, its imperial expansion took on a specially aggressive form. Prussian traditions of discipline in family and school helped to form an 'authoritarian character', marked by obedience to the strong, aggression towards the weak, and lack of critical abilities.

Some sociologists are now beginning to take up this theme of historical continuity. Fahin and Seidel-Pielen (1992) studied Protestant enclaves in mainly Catholic Bavaria, showing how areas which in 1932 voted over 90 per cent for the Nazi Party today demonstrate high levels of support for the extreme-right *Republikaner*. Protestant racism can be traced back to Luther's anti-semitic tirades, and to the state church's blind support for the Prussian monarchy (Fahin and Seidel-Pielen 1992: 2–3). These links were also demonstrated by some US researchers of the 1940s and 1950s. Another issue is the concept of citizenship, which defines membership of the nation-state on the basis of German ethnicity and language. It is exclusionary towards immigrants, and makes any ethnic minority appear as a threatening 'alien body' (Hoffmann 1990). This model is not conducive to the successful incorporation of immigrants, and blocks any move towards multicultural policies.

There is also debate on the failure to combat the deep-seated effects of Nazi ideologies after 1945. 'De-Nazification' was a superficial process, in which members of the Nazi Party, the SS and the *Gestapo* were temporarily removed from official positions. With the onset of the Cold War, former Nazis (the majority of industrialists, bureaucrats and judges) were quickly rehabilitated. In the GDR the official line was that the ruling party was socialist and internationalist and had no links with Germany's past. Racism and fascism were seen as the results of capitalism and imperialism, and therefore no longer an issue. Yet many of the old bureaucrats, teachers and officers could not be dispensed with in the new state, despite the ideology.

National identity since Auschwitz

The Nazi dictatorship, defeat in the Second World War and the division of the country by the allies combined to undermine the legitimacy of

German identity. The division into two Germanies seemed appropriate not only to their European neighbours, but to many Germans too. Few people expected reunification ever to come, and little thought had been given to the character of a new all-German nation-state. Discussions of the links between insecure national identity and racism combine *psychological, political and historical explanations.*

The debate often hinges on the meaning of the Auschwitz extermination camp as a symbol of the bankruptcy of nationalism. Adorno asked whether there could be German culture after Auschwitz, while author Günter Grass said as late as 1989: 'The German people has lost its right to unity through Auschwitz' (quoted from Fahin and Seidel-Pielen 1992: 11). Bodo Mörshäuser (1992) has shown how the meaning of 'being German' has shifted across the three post-war generations. The first generation were 'the survivors' – those who had lived through the Nazi period by conforming. Afterwards they kept silent to hide their complicity. The second generation were those who came of age in the 1960s, and asked what their parents had done in the Hitler period. They broke the silence, expressed their shame at being German, and were against nationalism. The third generation are those who are in their twenties today. They question the orthodoxy of many of their parents and teachers, and want to reassert a German nationalism based on ideas of achievement and ability, even if this means a reinterpretation of the past.

> The *first generation* wanted to be silent about Auschwitz, because Auschwitz had hurt their pride. The *second generation* wanted to talk about Auschwitz, because it explained their shame at being Germans. The *third generation* does not accept Auschwitz as the centre of a moral code, and insists that they are proud to be Germans. Each new generation has a clear instinct about the taboos of the preceding ones – and digs them out. (Mörshäuser 1992: 114)

It is above all young people who lack strong emotional ties or good economic chances who accept extreme-right ideologies. They cling to 'being German' because it is their only claim to identity or even superiority. They find models among older leaders. Former Bavarian Prime Minister Strauss said in 1969: 'A people which has brought about such economic achievements has a right not to want to hear any more about Auschwitz.' Alfred Dregger, Chairman of the CDU parliamentary party declared in 1982: 'I call upon all Germans to step out of Hitler's shadow – we must become normal' (quoted from Mörshäuser, 1992: 129).

Herein lies the German dilemma: being 'normal' means either suppressing the past or reinterpreting it as something no longer shameful. Under Wilhelm II, the 'late nation' was told that it had to fight for 'a place in the sun'. Between the wars, the Germans were the losers who had to pay reparations to the victors. Reassertion of national pride took the extreme form of Nazism. After 1945, the mood was one of shame and self-denial. Today, economic achievements are seen as a source of pride, and reunification has reinforced the desire for national identity. Yet the only successful models for German nationhood – Bismarck's Second Reich and Hitler's Third Reich – are authoritarian, racist and chauvinistic.

The problem is thus to find a new model for national identity which takes account of the reality that Germany has become a multi-ethnic society. Until recently, it was widely believed that European integration would resolve matters by providing a supranational identity which left room for regional loyalties. Today, that hope looks shaky. European identity has itself taken on an exclusionary character directed against the Turkish, North African and other non-European minorities. Moreover, the beggar-your-neighbour monetary policy pursued by Germany in an attempt to finance reunification makes European solidarity dubious.

Sub-cultures and the extreme right

Authoritarian and racist attitudes are widespread and pre-date reunification. The influential 'Sinus-study', published in 1980, found that 13 per cent of voters supported extreme-right ideologies, while a further 37 per cent showed partial support for them (Fahin and Seidel-Pielen, 1992: 15). In 1992 a survey found that German voters saw the 'foreigner problem' as the number-one political issue. Foreigners were blamed for social ills such as abuse of the welfare system, unemployment, the housing problem and street crime (*Der Spiegel*, no. 44, 1992).

Some analyses suggest that the links between such widespread popular attitudes and actual racist violence are provided by youth sub-cultures – we might speak of a *sub-cultural explanation for racism*. The sub-cultures of the 1990s are often nationalistic, racist and violent. The most prominent stylistic form is that of the skinhead, but heavy metal music fans and football hooligans also play a part. Curiously, the stylistic labels are mainly imported: Germans speak of *skinheads* rather than *Glatzköpfe*; football hooligans are known as *Hools*. Even nationalists cannot escape the pervasiveness of global culture!

The youth cliques are often a product of the dissolution of the family through unemployment, alcohol abuse and domestic violence. They find their identity in opposition to the styles and norms of their parents and teachers. Toughness and readiness for violence are part of this identity. Immigrants, as marginalized, low-status groups, appear as 'natural targets' for aggression, but attacks on gays and people with disabilities are also common. The transition from violent sub-culture to racist mob is partly a result of systematic agitation by neo-Nazi groups. These have existed for many years, but the real growth has come since 1989: official membership estimates are now about 6,000 (*Frankfurter Allgemeine Zeitung*, 27 August 1992). Increasingly, anti-foreigner actions are planned and coordinated by trained groups. The 'success' achieved by racist attacks, such as the expulsion of asylum-seekers from Hoyerswerda or the burning-down of the Rostock hostel, leads to increased recruitment.

Youth sub-cultures function as loose-knit *scenes*, rather than as parties or organizations. This makes it very difficult to combat racist violence. Banning groups and arresting leaders has little effect: the groups are re-formed under new names, and the leaders become heroes. Determined police action to arrest those involved in violence, and high sentences for those convicted, might have a more deterrent effect on hangers-on, but it is doubtful whether police measures can achieve long-term solutions.

Explanations and strategies

Germany is like most other highly developed countries in that the current crisis of modernization has brought about a deep malaise, which is partly expressed through racism and racist violence. But Germany also has unique features which have led to more extreme violence: the sudden and poorly planned reunification has led to severe strains, particularly in the East; immigration policy has been unrealistic and deceptive, so that the population has not been prepared for the reality of a multi-ethnic society; and German history has left the country without an acceptable model for national identity.

Most of the explanations discussed above have some truth in them. The only one to be rejected is that which blames racist violence on mass immigration, and propagates immigration control as the solution. Germany, like most other highly developed countries, has become a multi-ethnic society, and will remain so. The debate on changing the Basic Law to keep out asylum-seekers is simply a diversion from the real problems. Blaming immigrants for racism can only deepen existing divisions in society. The real political issue here is the government policies which refuse to face reality and which deny rights to residents of migrant background. The introduction of a fair and liberal immigration policy, as well as measures to grant citizenship and rights to existing immigrants would be the first steps towards combating racist violence. Anti-discrimination legislation and laws against racial incitement are also part of the necessary political response.

The socio-economic, psychological, political, historical and sub-cultural explanations all have important lessons. But mono-causal explanations will lead to mistaken strategies. Job creation alone, or more youth work, or therapeutic models, cannot solve the problem. There is a need for an integrated approach which addresses all the causes of racism at once. Such a strategy would include rapid action by the state to combat unemployment and improve education and training, especially in East Germany. There is also a need for the provision of youth centres with appropriately trained social workers. Intensive educational and therapeutic work with members of the violent sub-cultures is particularly important. Another necessary response would be efforts by opinion-formers, such as politicians, the media, academics and educationalists, to understand German history and to work through the psychological consequences of the current transition. Suppression and denial are sure to lead to future problems, as post-1945 experience has shown; such mistakes should not be repeated. Finally, the issue of German national identity can no longer be ignored. To do so means leaving it to the extreme right and allowing them to pose as the bearers of national interests. The answer for the left could be to concentrate on a republican model of citizenship based on membership of a democratic political community.

There is little sign that such strategies are likely to be adopted. As the recession grows more severe in Germany, big companies like Mercedes, Krupp and Volkswagen are cutting back investment in the East, causing yet more bitterness (see *Guardian Weekly*, 22 November 1992). The federal government is more concerned with cutting government expenditure than with providing the resources and leadership needed to combat the crisis. By blaming racism on the 'floods of asylum-seekers' and calling for a change in the Basic Law to keep them out, political leaders are playing with fire. German history shows all too clearly that racism is a dangerous instrument of politics.

Notes

1 Apart from the sources cited, this chapter is based on newspaper and journal articles collected by the Berlin Institute for Comparative Social Research. I acknowledge the support of the Institute, and the helpful discussions with its staff in October 1992.

2 In this chapter I refer to the population of the former German Democratic Republic (GDR) as East Germans and to the population of the pre-1990 area of the Federal Republic of Germany (FRG) as West Germans.

11

THE RACISMS OF GLOBALIZATION

What are the images of racism in the mid-1990s? Amongst the most dramatic are the massacres of Rwanda, 'ethnic cleansing' in Bosnia, urban riots in the USA, skinhead attacks on asylum-seekers in Germany, and the heated debates on the Native Title Act of 1993 in Australia. Less visible, but no less important, are the countless expressions of everyday racism, which reduce the life-chances of ethnic minorities in many countries. On the level of international relations, too, racism has not lost its importance: the North–South divide is often a euphemism for the domination of the peoples of formerly colonized countries by Europe and North America – joined now by Japan and a small circle of 'newly industrializing countries'.

Yet the images have changed: in the 1960s, racism usually meant overt segregation (for example, in the US Deep South or in South Africa) or explicit racial exclusion (like the White Australia policy). Racism was often linked to colonialism or neo-colonialism (the political and economic control of former colonies without direct rule). The Vietnam War was a site of racist confrontation: the use of weapons of mass destruction by the USA against a rural people struggling for independence appeared as a continuation of the 'civilizing mission' of the West, which had justified centuries of barbarity. The labour migrations of the 1960s gave rise to a 'colour bar' in Britain, which kept black immigrants out of dance halls, rented rooms and jobs. Western European countries like Germany and France also used discriminatory practices to exploit migrant workers, although here people were reluctant to speak of racism, using instead the euphemisms 'xenophobia' or 'hostility to foreigners'.

The late 1960s and the 1970s appeared to be a 'liberal hour' as overt racism declined under the pressure of anti-colonial struggles and civil rights movements. The concept of the Third World emerged as a global symbol of the movement against white domination. The international campaign against apartheid – which was to take so long to bear fruit – was emblematic of the new climate. Desegregation and affirmative action set a new political agenda in the USA. Racial selectivity in immigration systems was abolished in Australia, Canada and other countries (though not everywhere). Indigenous peoples fought for and obtained political

This chapter was first published in E. Vasta and S. Castles (eds), *The Teeth are Smiling: the Persistence of Racism in Multicultural Australia* (Sydney, Allen and Unwin, 1996), pp. 17–45.

rights – only to find that this did not mean the end of discrimination and marginalization.

Today, no mainstream politician speaks openly of white racial superiority. The few academics who still put forward the tenets of 'scientific racism' – the conventional wisdom of the biological and social sciences up to the 1940s – are considered eccentric. Many countries now have anti-discrimination laws and equal opportunity measures. Yet racism persists. Some of its targets are the same as before (indigenous peoples, migrant workers, ethnic minorities in developed countries) but there are new ones, including minority ethnic groups[1] in former colonies, and national minorities in the emerging states of Eastern Europe. These do not easily fit into the traditional white/black schema of racism. The dividing line between racism and nationalism has become less clear. There are new types of discrimination and exclusion, as well as new ideologies to justify them. As many authors have argued (for instance, Balibar 1991d; Cohen and Bains 1988; Gilroy 1992; Miles 1993b), it is no longer useful (if indeed it ever was) to speak of racism as if it were a homogeneous phenomenon. We need to examine specific *racisms*, as they affect particular groups in various locations and times.

In this chapter, my aim is to discuss current international patterns of racism, and some of the theoretical and political debates that arise from them. In the first section, I will examine some of the problems that arise in defining racism in a rapidly changing context. The second section briefly examines the various types of racism to be found in the contemporary world. The third section attempts a theoretical explanation which links racism with the crises caused by global restructuring.

My main argument is that trends towards the globalization of politics, economic relations and culture are central to understanding the changing nature of racism. *Globalization* designates the latest stage of a process – often referred to as *modernization* – which began with European colonial expansion in the fifteenth century. Modernity implies increasingly integrated capitalist production and distribution systems, linked to secular cultures based on the principle of rationality. Modernity has meant colonization of the rest of the world, not only in the direct sense of political control, but also through the diffusion of Western cultural values. Racism – as an ideology which justified European domination – has always been part of modernity.

The concept of globalization has been used since the 1970s to refer to an acceleration of international integration based on rapid changes in political and economic relations, technology and communications (see Featherstone 1990; King 1991; Robertson 1992). Racism is an integral part of the politics and culture of this new stage: we may refer to this tendency as the *globalization of racism*. But current developments also involve new types of racism, taking on differing and shifting forms with regard to various target groups and locations. These I refer to as the *racisms of globalization* – the central theme of the chapter.[...]

Defining racism

There is a confusing plethora of literature on race and racism. For instance, Rex and Mason's (1986) useful collection of *Theories of Race and Ethnic Relations* includes Weberian, Marxist, anthropological, pluralist, rational choice, sociobiological, symbolic interactionist and identity theory approaches. These are mainly sociological theories, but one can find other works by philosophers, historians, economists, jurists, psychologists, discourse analysts and cultural theorists. Any study of racism is necessarily interdisciplinary for a full understanding can only be achieved through examination of all the factors – historical, economic, political, social, cultural and so on – which make up a given situation of racism.

If racism is a global phenomenon with a multiplicity of shifting forms, any theory of racism needs to be broad enough to take account of their diversity, without losing sight of their essential unity. This is a tall order, which has led some observers to argue that 'rather than talking about racism in the singular, analysts should ... be talking about racisms in the plural' (Gilroy 1987: 38). But this point of view ignores the obvious existence of common patterns and trends in racist ideologies and practices, which imply some commonality of character and causality. We need both the singular and the plural. Goldberg (1993: 41) argues for:

> a general but open-ended theory concerning race and racism. The theory would have to account for historical alterations and discontinuities in the modes of racial formation, in the disparate phenomena commonly addressed in racialized terms, as well as in those expressions properly considered racist. It must also enable and encourage opposition to racist expression, for ultimately the efficacy of a theory about race and racism is to be assessed in terms of the ways in which it renders possible resistance to racisms.

To be a useful guide to understanding and action, a theory of racism should therefore:

1 Explain why racism exists in many different societies, both in the past and the present.
2 Explain the varying forms of racism within any one society, as well as in different societies.
3 Explain why racism becomes more or less severe at certain times.
4 Provide ideas for strategies to combat racism.

Traditions of racism

The concept of racism is comparatively new. According to Miles (1993b: 81), it was first used in connection with Nazi ideas on race in the 1930s. However, discourses and practices of hierarchization based on the notion of race are much older (see Miles 1989: ch. 1). Since ancient times, groups of people have come into contact with each other through trade, migration or warfare. This has given rise to notions of group boundaries, marked by area of origin, language, culture, physical appearance or other characteristics. Non-belonging to a specific group was frequently used as a criterion for discrimination or hostility. Practices akin to modern racism played a part in processes of territorial expansion, in which one ethnic group subjugated others, occupying their land and exploiting their labour.

However, systematic ideas of racial hierarchy appear to be connected to European colonialism: from the fifteenth century onwards, religiously inspired views on the barbarity and inferiority of the indigenous peoples of Africa, Asia and America were used to legitimate invasion, genocide, slavery and exploitation (Cohen 1987; Potts 1990). In the eighteenth and nineteenth centuries, attempts were made to justify racism on the basis of scientific theory. Races were seen as biologically distinct entities, made up of people with different phenotypical characteristics. They were thought to form an unchanging hierarchy, in which the capacities and achievements of the members of each race were fixed by natural determinants. Domination by the 'superior race' was inevitable and desirable because it was thought to lead to human progress (Husband 1982; Miles 1989). Goldberg (1993: 41–3) argues that racism is itself a discourse which 'emerges with modernity and comes to colonize modernity's continually reinvented common sense' (Goldberg 1993: 43).

Within Europe, racial categorization was crucial in the rise of nationalism from the eighteenth century. The attempt to base membership of a nation-state on belonging to a specific race or ethnic group required the creation of national myths, since all peoples were in fact the result of historical processes of migration and intermingling. Taken to a logical conclusion, this ideology requires policies to exclude members of other races or to deprive them of rights. The Nazis went to this extreme, defining Jews and gypsies, who had been part of German society for centuries, as aliens, and physically destroying them. It is important to remember that this most extreme form of racism was carried out by one white group against others, showing that skin colour is not always a crucial marker.

Economic exploitation also played a part in the emergence of racism. Mercantile capitalists accumulated wealth through slavery and indentured labour – systems of labour mobilization based on ideas of racial hierarchy. During the Industrial Revolution, racism against white immigrant workers (such as the Irish in Britain or the Poles in Germany) was widespread, foreshadowing racism against migrant workers after 1945.

After the defeat of fascism in 1945, UNESCO convened a series of symposia to debate the legitimacy of the concept of race. Their statements demonstrated the invalidity of racial classifications in the terms of both the natural and social sciences (Montagu 1974). A *race*, therefore, is not a biologically defined group, but a social construction arising out of *racism*. Action against racism became a declared aim of the United Nations and other international bodies, laid down in a multitude of resolutions and conventions. However, at the same time, racist policies and practices continued unabated in many areas.

Social scientists are faced with a dilemma. The term 'race' has no scientific basis, yet racial categorization is a crucial factor in social structure and action. Many people believe that they belong to a specific race, and that this is important for their social identity: in other words racism helps to define both the *Self* and the *Other*. This can include discourses of hierarchy, in which members of dominant groups assert their superiority, but also discourses of solidarity, in which oppressed groups (such as black Americans or indigenous peoples) assert their unity and equality. Race may not be a biological fact, but it certainly is a social reality. So should social scientists speak of race? Some scholars have decided that the term is unacceptable yet indispensable, so that it should be used, but only in quotation marks. Others continue to use the concept of race without reflection, especially in the context of research on *race relations*. I will use the term race here because of its significance in social discourses, but in a critical sense based on the postulates: (a) that race is not a biological reality; and (b) that race is constructed through racism: a set of ideologies and practices imposed by dominant groups on less powerful groups.

Racism, sexism and class

Racism, like sexism, is a social phenomenon embracing both discourse and practices, which involves making predictions of social behaviour on the basis of allegedly fixed biological or cultural characteristics. The imposition of such categories leads to the 'inferiorization' of certain groups. This takes specific forms: 'racialization' of phenotypically or culturally defined groups and gender oppression against women. Indeed, racism and sexism are closely linked: dominant ethnic groups attribute subordinate groups with characteristics seen in patriarchal terms as feminine – weakness, dependence, emotionality, unreliability. Similarly, patriarchy classifies women in the same terms as inferior races – as exotic, passionate, savage and unpredictable. However, racism is even more arbitrary than sexism in the sense that sex *is* a biological reality, even though ideas on gender, based on this substratum, are social constructions. For race there is no such reality; it is whatever racists have the social power to define it as. Here lies perhaps the most crucial point: racism always implies the power (which can be political, economic, social or cultural) to impose a definition of the Other on the subordinate group.

Racism is also linked to sexism in the more direct sense that black, immigrant and ethnic minority women experience racial and gender oppression simultaneously. Here the question arises as to which of these forms of oppression has primacy – an issue of considerable importance for strategic discussions in the women's movement. Minority women's groups have often argued that race has been the primary source of oppression. Mainstream feminist groups have, on the other hand, often argued for the primacy of gender, and tended to ignore the experience of black and immigrant women (Martin 1986: 246). The emergence of organizations such as the Immigrant Women's Speakout Association of New South Wales and the Association of Non-English Speaking Women of Australia (ANESBWA) is one reaction to the neglect of issues of racism by mainstream feminism (Vasta 1993b: 10).

According to Essed (1991: 31), racism and sexism 'narrowly intertwine and combine under certain conditions into one, hybrid phenomenon. Therefore it is useful to speak of *gendered racism* to refer to the racist oppression of Black women as structured by racist and ethnicist perceptions of gender roles.' Balibar (1991e: 49) argues that 'racism always presupposes sexism.' They are not simply analogous forms of oppression of weaker groups by dominant groups, but rather 'a historical system of complementary exclusions and dominations which are mutually interconnected'. To put it more simply, the type of social order which subordinates women is also likely to racialize ethnic minorities.

It is tempting, then, to portray both forms of domination as mechanisms designed to sustain male ruling-class power in capitalist society. Wallerstein (1991: 33), for instance, sees racism as 'a magic formula' which makes it possible simultaneously to minimize the costs of labour power and to minimize the protests of the labour force. By 'ethnicizing' the workforce – dividing it up on racial and ethnic criteria – capitalists can pay workers differently and at the same time gain mass support for this hierarchy. According to Wallerstein (1991: 34–5), just as 'ethnicization' permits very low wages for some segments of the workforce, sexism reinforces exploitation by forcing women to do unpaid work in the household or to take low wages outside it.

There is certainly a sound historical basis for the argument that racism, sexism and class domination are linked, but Wallerstein's interpretation here seems problematic. It comes close to the classical Marxist argument that class domination had primacy over other forms of domination and that class struggle was therefore more important than gender or racial emancipation. This led to the concept of 'false consciousness': the idea that all workers 'really' had the same interests, but were duped by the capitalists into accepting divisions based on race, gender, skill level and nationality (see, for instance, Cox 1959). This approach has been criticized by feminist and ethnic minority scholars (see Anthias and Yuval-Davis 1983; Barrett 1980; Brah 1991; Hartmann 1979). They see the idea of the primacy of class as a form of functionalism, which reduces both racial and gender oppression to mere mechanisms of ruling-class manipulation. However, the total unity of the working class has never existed: racism and sexism have always played a part within labour movements, as well as in the wider society. There is thus no justification for according primacy to class domination over racism and sexism. All three are forms of 'social normalisation and exclusion' (Balibar 1991e: 49) which are intrinsic to capitalism and modernity and which have developed in close relationship to each other.

Nationalism and democracy

Racism and sexism provide legitimations for hierarchy and differential treatment in liberal-democratic societies ostensibly based on ideologies of universalism and equality (Wallerstein 1991). Here we see the link to another important constituting factor of modernity: the nation-state and the accompanying ideology of nationalism. Recent debates have raised the issue of whether nationalism automatically leads to racism; that is, that racism is a sort of supernationalism (see Anderson 1983; Goldberg 1993: 79; Nairn 1980). Against this may be put the idea of 'good and bad nationalism' (Balibar 1991e: 47). 'Good nationalism' is one that helps construct a nation-state or provides the focus for a struggle for emancipation of an oppressed group (like African-Americans). 'Bad nationalism' is one that subjugates other nations and oppresses internal minorities. But does a good nationalism turn bad once it has gained power? Is there an automatic link between the encouragement of national feeling as a way of building identity and community, and the development of hatred and contempt for members of other national groups?

These are questions that cannot be discussed fully here, but it is vital to grasp that the nexus between racism and nationalism is central to modern nation-states. This is obvious in the case of authoritarian regimes: there is no better way to legitimate an undemocratic regime than to claim that it represents national feelings and interests against other nations or against internal minorities which are conspiring against it. A national community is based on the fundamental equality of being a member of the nation (portrayed as superior and sacred) against all the rest of the world, who are excluded from membership. This equality masks and legitimates political domination and economic exploitation. The nation is worth dying for even if one is at the bottom of the social order. Thus, replacing the politics of class with the politics of race stabilizes ruling-class domination.

But what of democracies? Why do they too generate racism? A democratic nation-state also has a strong need to define its boundaries. If being a citizen confers rights, then it is essential to define who is not a citizen and therefore should not enjoy the rights. Being a citizen implies equality and political community – enshrined in ideals such as the French Declaration of the Rights of Man or the US Bill of Rights – but it also implies exclusion and domination of non-citizens. And this is not simply a conceptual issue. The whole history of democratic nation-states is full of this ambiguity: colonialism, treatment of internal ethnic minorities (such as Jews or gypsies), exploitation of immigrant workers. Ivo Andric (1994: 265) draws out the fatal essence of the nexus between democracy and nationalism in his famous novel about Bosnia, pointing out that in 1914 'the rulers of human destinies drew European humanity from the playing fields of universal suffrage to the already prepared arena of universal military service.' The right to vote, in the nationalist model, is linked to the duty to die for your country, and this in turn requires racism towards members of other nations.

Nationalism required the construction of myths of common origins, traditions and culture – that is, of ethnicity – in order to achieve the integration of the 'imagined community' of the nation (Anderson 1983). Within this basic scheme, there are many variations. At one extreme, the 'German model' defines membership of the nation almost exclusively in terms of myths of descent. To this day the principle of *ius sanguinis* (law of the blood) restricts naturalization of foreign immigrants, leading to the marginalization of 7 million permanent inhabitants of the country. At the other extreme is the French 'Republican model', which claims to base national belonging simply on membership of the political community. This model was used to assimilate the peoples of colonies into French culture, just as it is used today to assimilate immigrants. However, there is a catch: political assimilation requires possession of the necessary civic virtues, which in effect means assimilation into French culture (see Schnapper 1991; Weil 1991). Assimilation is racist in the sense that it hierarchizes cultures, and legitimates their destruction as a precondition for equality.

It is hard to imagine a nationalism without an ideology to legitimate the exclusionary boundaries of the nation-state. Some nationalists deny the link to racism by claiming to see all nations as equally sacred. But that only applies as long as the other people stay 'at home', and as long as there are no existing internal minorities. These conditions are never realized in practice, particularly in an increasingly mobile world. Thus the link between nationalism and racism is very strong.

Exclusion and exploitation

Racism does not always seek to exclude or exterminate the Other. It is equally common for racists to seek to inferiorize and exploit minorities (see Balibar 1991e: 39–40). Indeed, the racism of inferiorization comes first historically: colonialism subjugated the peoples of occupied areas in order to exploit their labour. However, the racism of exclusion and extermination was applied if the colonized group stood in the way of the colonizers' economic aims, as with Australia's indigenous peoples. The racism of inferiorization applies equally to modern situations of migrant labour: denial of rights forced Western Europe's 'guest-workers' of the 1960s to take the jobs no one else wanted. Similar practices apply in Middle Eastern labour-recruiting countries today. The racism of exclusion and extermination is used against ethnic minorities which are seen either by the state or by certain sections of the majority population as a threat. Nazi anti-semitism is the classic example, and 'ethnic cleansing' in former Yugoslavia is similar in character.

Sometimes the two types of racism exist side by side and are linked to class interests. The ruling class is more likely to be interested in the racism of exploitation, while workers may favour exclusion. For instance, German employers today see a need for labour from the East, partly because it is easily exploitable; German workers call for its exclusion just because they fear the competition. The racism of exclusion may lead to inferiorization: in Japan, official policies exclude unskilled workers, leading to large-scale entry of illegal migrants, who can be easily exploited by employers (Esman 1992; Sekine 1990). US agricultural employers have done the same with undocumented Mexican workers for many years.

In conflicts such as this we can see the links between racism and class. Again, they are ambiguous: employers may use the racism of inferiorization to exploit migrant workers, while local workers, fearing competition, may use the racism of exclusion to keep them away. Debates on the White Australia policy in the late nineteenth century were full of such ambiguities (de Lepervanche 1975). It is here that we can see the core of rationality in certain racisms, which have their origins in the desire to protect class interests. Clearly, the distinction between exclusion/extermination and inferiorization/exploitation is important for analysing specific racisms. It is important to realize that racism does not depend on the characteristics of the dominated groups, but rather on the interests and culture of the dominant group.

Biology and culture

Until recently, the criteria for defining racism's Other were mainly biological: they focused on phenotypical features, especially skin colour (cf. Taguieff 1988). Anti-racists accordingly saw racism as being mainly about white practices towards non-white people. Recently, cultural factors (such as religion, language and national origins) have been more strongly emphasized. Sometimes these are linked to biology through assumptions on the genetic origins of cultural practices. Nazi propaganda claimed that the Jewish religion and lifestyles were an expression of some biological essence. The more invisible the Jewish characteristics, the more dangerous they were – a case of racism without phenotypical race. In fact, the reduction of racism to white racism against non-whites is recent and linked to post-1945 anti-colonial and civil rights movements. Many older forms of racism focused on culture and national origins (cf. Miles 1993b: ch. 3). Phenotypical and cultural racism have always existed side by side and have been closely linked.

The shift back to an emphasis on culture since the 1970s, which has led some observers to speak of a 'new racism' (Balibar 1991d; Barker 1981), has several causes. One was the increasing public unacceptability of biological racism after the defeat of Nazism. Another was the growth of ethnic minorities in Western Europe who could not sensibly be called black, but who were culturally distinct on the basis of religion (especially Islam), dress, lifestyle and values. Ironically, this led to problems for some British anti-racists, for whom it was axiomatic that the targets of racism were black: they went on tours of the Continent to identify 'the blacks' and were surprised to find that Turks and North Africans rejected the label. A third issue was the increasing evidence of racism against minority groups within African or Asian countries, which clearly could not be put in white–black terms.

Racism today is not just a 'colour' issue. Yet colour is not irrelevant since global power relations are still structured by the aftermath of colonialism: in a world split into rich North and poor South, being white is still an indicator of power and privilege. As Balibar (1991d: 44) points out, media discourses on the racisms of the Third World reinforce white racism by encouraging the idea that 'three-quarters of humanity are incapable of governing themselves'. When donor agencies like the World Bank today make 'good governance' a condition for loans, they are acting in the tradition of the 'civilizing mission' of the West.

What has been said so far implies that there is no difference in the essential character of racism, whether it is directed against a group defined on the basis of phenotypical characteristics (a 'race') or against a group defined on the basis of culture (an 'ethnic group'). Race and ethnicity are similar social constructions, serving to define Self and Other. The main difference, as Goldberg (1993: 76) points out, is that ethnicity uses a rhetoric of cultural content, whereas race uses a rhetoric of descent, but these are 'rhetorical tendencies, not fixed conceptualizations'. Indeed, race and ethnic group are sometimes used as alternatives, as with Jews, blacks or Hispanics in the USA. This does not imply that racists in a given location treat all minority groups in the same way: for instance, there is clear evidence that Australian racism is most virulent against Aboriginal peoples, then against Asians, and then other immigrant groups (HREOC 1991). Similarly, German racists targeted Turks more than European immigrants until recently. Significantly, after reunification in 1990, European immigrants of gypsy ethnicity came in for as much hostility as Turks. The point is that racism chooses its targets according to its own perverse inner logic, rather than on the basis of some fixed hierarchy.

The 'culturalization of racism' (Essed 1991: 14) is also linked to the new discourses of tolerance, which are so important for multiculturalism. Today, the term 'racism' is almost invariably pejorative: nobody admits to being a racist. Ideas of racial hierarchy are rejected, and the principle of equal opportunity is espoused by politicians of all persuasions. If some groups – especially people of non-European origin – are socio-economically and politically disadvantaged, this is attributed to cultural values which are seen as backward or inappropriate for a technologically advanced society. The acceptance of cultural pluralism is compatible with a belief in the superiority of the dominant culture. The very idea of tolerance for minority cultures implies a belief in the superiority of the dominant one: immigrants and ethnic minorities can keep their own values and cultures, but they cannot complain if this leads to their marginalization. Moreover, if black people do not do well despite all the welfare measures and equal opportunities policies, then it must be their own fault. Emphasis on cultural difference is therefore a new ideology of legitimation for a covert racism without claims of biological superiority (Essed 1991).

Fixation on older definitions of racism as notions of biologically based hierarchies allows more subtle racisms based on cultural markers to claim to be benign and progressive (Barker 1981). The 'new racism' is a 'racism without race' (Balibar 1991d: 23). It no longer speaks of superiority, but rather of immutable differences that make coexistence between varying cultural groups in one society impossible. Socio-biological theories of 'natural aggression' and 'inevitable conflict' within 'nations of tribes' provide a pseudo-scientific argument against immigration and multiculturalism. And even multiculturalism may be seen as a new and more sophisticated form of racism in the way in which it legitimates the power of the dominant group to proclaim and manage hierarchies of acceptable and unacceptable difference.

One way of dealing with this problem of constant change in the rhetoric of racism is to examine it as a form of culture. Goldberg (1993: 9) sees 'racist culture' as 'one of the central ways modern social subjects make sense of and express themselves about the world they inhabit and invent'. Racist culture has its expressions and objects, its meanings and values, which constitute a 'way of life'. Goldberg provides a powerful argument that racism is a central and enduring element of the modern world – however much its particular forms of expression may change. Racism has been intrinsic to the way of thinking of modernity. Moreover, although it has been important for centuries, the peak period of racism as a dominant ideology justifying European world conquest was only recent: the late nineteenth and early twentieth centuries. And let us not forget that racism was an accepted worldview, openly held by the majority of the population only thirty years ago.

Common-sense and everyday racism

Overt racism may be less frequent than in the past, but it remains deeply embedded in our traditions and culture. As van Dijk (1993: 7) argues:

> this undeniable progress has only softened the style of dominance of white Western nations. Far from abolished are the deeply entrenched economic, social and cultural remnants of past oppression and inequality; the modern prejudices about minorities; the economic and military power or the cultural hegemony of white over black, North over South, majorities over minorities.

Racism is still part of *common-sense*: the accumulated, taken-for-granted and often contradictory set of assumptions used by people to understand and cope with the complex social world around them. In ostensibly non-racist societies, the influence of past ideologies and practices makes itself felt indirectly through discourses in the media, politics and popular culture. The received ideas of racist culture are not expressed openly, but rather in the form of ahistorical common-sense notions about the character and achievements of specific groups, and about the inevitability of competitions and conflict between different races. This hidden and often unconscious power of racist discourse allows elite groups to claim enlightened and meritocratic views, while in fact applying racist definitions of social reality (van Dijk 1993).

People do not need to have conscious racist beliefs to act in a way which reinforces racist structures and ideologies. As Essed argues, racism has become part of the systematic, recurrent, familiar practices which make up everyday life. She defines 'everyday racism' as:

> a process in which (a) socialised racist notions are integrated into meanings that make practices immediately definable and manageable, (b) practices with racist implications become in themselves familiar and repetitive, and (c) underlying racial and ethnic relations are actualised and reinforced through these routine or familiar practices in everyday situations. (Essed 1991: 52)

Beliefs about racial hierarchies and ethnic differences are so much part of our culture and traditions that we continually learn them in all the different parts of the socialization process (in the family, school, peer groups and through the media). In our daily life, we tend to act on unconscious racist beliefs, and thus reproduce racist ideologies and practices as part of social structure and action.

A working definition

In the light of the above discussion, is it possible and useful to define racism? The danger of a formal definition is that it tends to simplify and fix something that is complex and constantly changing. On the other hand, a general definition of racism brings out the essential unity of certain types of normalization and differentiation of people. It is therefore a valuable yardstick for analysis and political action because it can help in assessing whether certain ideas, practices or situations can properly be seen as racist. I will provide a working definition here, on the understanding that it is only useful in the context of detailed analyses of specific racisms. The definition has three elements.

1 *Racism is not an aberration or a result of individual pathology.* It is a set of practices and discourses which are deeply rooted in the history, traditions and culture of modernity. Racism exists in a variety of forms in all modern societies, and plays a crucial role in consolidating nation-states by providing an instrument for defining belonging or exclusion. That is why increasing racism in decolonized nations is part of the process of modernization. Racism is linked to democracy in the sense that it reconciles ideologies of universalism and equality with the practices of hierarchization and segmentation which are central to the economic and social order. Racism is closely interrelated with other forms of social normalization and control, particularly sexism and class domination.

2 *Racism is the process whereby social groups categorize other groups as different or inferior on the basis of phenotypical characteristics, cultural markers or national origin.* This process involves the use of economic, social or political power, and generally has the purpose of legitimating

exploitation or exclusion of the group so defined. The dominant group constructs ideologies of the inherent difference and the inferiority of the dominated groups. The power of the dominant group is sustained by developing structures (such as laws, policies and administrative practices) that exclude or discriminate against the dominated group. This type of racism is generally known as *institutional racism*. More spontaneous types of prejudice or discrimination arising out of a racist culture are generally known as *informal racism*. These two types are closely related in that they are both expressions of group power or dominance. For this reason, as Essed (1991: 37) points out, the concept of individual racism is misleading: racism always implies a group process.

3 *Racism takes many forms of varying intensity, which may be seen as a continuum.* Acceptance of even the apparently milder forms – in the form of common-sense or everyday racism – can pave the way for the more violent ones. The forms include prejudiced attitudes, discrimination (in legal status, employment, housing, eligibility for services and access to public places), verbal or written abuse, incitement to hatred, discrimination or violence, harassment designed to intimidate or insult, physical violence, and genocide. All these practices may be seen as forms of violence, in the broad sense proposed by Galtung (1988: 281–2): violence should be taken to include any practices, whether carried out by individuals, social groups or institutions, which restrict the freedom or self-realization of human beings, and which are based on the ultimate threat of physical harm. In other words, all forms of racism are essentially violent, for they reduce people's life chances, and are ultimately based on the threat of physical harm.

The globalization of racism

Racism has increased in significance in many parts of the world in recent times. It is my hypothesis that the forms it takes are closely linked to processes of decolonization, modernization and international economic and cultural integration. In other words, most contemporary racisms are closely related to globalization and to the way in which this brings labour transformations – often of a disturbing or even traumatic nature – at national and local levels. In this section I will give a brief summary of some of the types of racism to be found in various settings.[2]

Oppression of indigenous peoples

The USA, Canada and Australia originated as white settler colonies, based on dispossession of indigenous peoples. In the USA, the destruction of Native American societies is part of the myth of nation-building and also an element in the widespread glorification of violence. In both the USA and Canada, indigenous people's movements since the 1960s have led to changes in public awareness and policies. However, most Native

Americans (0.8 per cent of the US population) and Native Canadians (2 per cent of total Canadian population) remain socio-economically marginalized and lacking in political power. The same applies to Australia's indigenous peoples.

Discrimination against indigenous peoples is also to be found in Latin America. In the Andean area and Central America, the rural peasant population is of Indian or *mestizo* (people of mixed European and Indian background) origin, while the urban population is of European immigrant background. Class and other power relations therefore have strong ethnic aspects. There have been many cases of serious human rights abuses, including massacres of indigenous people (for instance, in Guatemala) (US DoS 1992: 620).

Most Asian countries have long-standing national minorities – often marginalized through territorial expansion of dominant groups. For instance, the People's Republic of China has fifty-five designated ethnic minorities, making up 8 per cent of the total population. Most members of these groups are said to have living standards below the national average. In other Asian countries, minorities are categorized as 'tribal peoples' or 'hill tribes'. Such groups are to be found, for instance, in Bangladesh, India, Thailand and Vietnam. Minorities consisting of indigenous peoples overrun in the past by more powerful settler groups exist in Japan and Taiwan. All these groups experience some degree of socio-economic disadvantage and political exclusion (US DoS 1992: 1402–3).

Racism connected with decolonization and nation-building

Many forms of racism are part of the legacy of colonialism. European powers carved out new administrative entities with no regard for existing ethnic boundaries. Many post-colonial states include several ethnic groups, while members of a specific ethnic group may be citizens of two or more adjoining states. A further legacy of colonialism was the introduction of indentured workers from other areas (such as Indians in East Africa), who sometimes became economically successful but vulnerable minorities. Decolonization and the formation of new nation-states has frequently involved domination, discrimination or exclusion of minorities (Castles and Miller 1998: 124–7; Ricca 1990).

One consequence has been the rapid growth of refugee movements. An estimated 20 million people have had to seek refuge outside their countries, while at least the same number are internally displaced (UNFPA 1993: 31–4). The overwhelming majority of refugees have their origins in less-developed countries, and seek refuge in other such countries. Political upheavals are often linked to ethnic conflicts as well. In Africa, political and economic struggles frequently express themselves as battles for dominance between tribes. Many of the Indo-Chinese refugees are ethnic Chinese, who suffered racism as well as political persecution. Other refugee movements with this dual character include those of Tibetans to India and Nepal, East Timorese to Australia and Portugal, and

Burmese ethnic minority groups to Thailand and Bangladesh. Such refugees often find themselves also victims of racism while on the flight or in their new country of refuge (NPC 1991: 68–91).

Zolberg et al. (1989: 227–57) argue that the main cause of refugee movements is not poverty and under-development, but the generalized and persistent violence that has resulted from rapid processes of globalization. New states have been formed under conditions determined by colonial experience, as well as by neo-colonial power relations (domination of world trade by the industrialized countries). The result is weak states, under-developed economies and poor social conditions. This has been the context for ethnic conflicts and political struggles, leading to impoverishment and the denial of human rights. Moreover, during the Cold War, local conflicts became internationalized, with the major powers supporting opposing sides, and sending weapons and even troops to intervene in struggles in Africa, Asia and Latin America.

In the former Soviet Union over 60 million people lived outside their nationality's administrative region, creating an enormous potential for conflict as new nation-states are created. Such states are generally based on membership of specific ethnic groups, which often means discrimination against minorities. Some of these are in turn fighting to establish their own states, or seeking to link up with other states in which their own ethnic group has power. In Russia itself many ethnic minorities exist, and the political and economic unrest following the collapse of Soviet power has led to the emergence of nationalistic and anti-semitic movements. Conflicts have arisen as groups deported under Stalin have sought to regain their old territories (US DoS 1992: 1284–7; see also Brubaker 1992). The conflict in Chechnya in 1994–5 was one of the most extreme examples.

In Eastern and south-eastern Europe, the collapse of communist states has led to explosive ethnic conflicts based partly on long-suppressed historical issues and partly on current problems of rapid economic and political change (see Schierup 1993). Conflicts and refugee exoduses have affected Bulgaria, Romania and Albania. 'Ethnic cleansing' in the ruins of the former Yugoslavia has evoked widespread horror. The failure of supranational bodies like the European Union and the United Nations to stop the fighting shows vividly that racism can present a major threat to democratic states and to the international community.

Migrant labour

Recruitment of migrant labour frequently involves racist practices: the division between national and non-national, or between dominant ethnic group and minority, is a way of segmenting the labour market and forcing down wages. Migrant labour was a major factor in post-1945 economic growth in most industrial countries. Britain, France and The Netherlands encouraged labour migration from former colonies. Most immigrants were citizens of the immigration country, and differentiation was generally based on classical phenotypical racism. At the same time, nearly all Western European countries recruited foreign workers in southern Europe, Turkey and North Africa. Here the legal division between national and non-national was the basis of a whole set of discriminatory laws and practices against migrant workers.

In 1965, the USA abolished discriminatory immigration rules, leading to large-scale entries from Asia, Latin America and the Caribbean. Non-European immigrants have encountered considerable racism. The fear of mass Hispanic immigration has become a major factor in US politics, leading, for instance, to the 1994 invasion of Haiti. In contrast, most Asian immigrants come legally and have secure legal status as refugees or highly skilled workers. Their economic situation is therefore often better than that of Hispanics. None the less, Asians frequently report racial harassment and attacks.

Since the 1970s, foreign labour has been important for the Arab Gulf oil states, and since the 1980s for the newly industrializing countries of Asia. Labour movements are a result of growing capital mobility, uneven economic development, improving transport facilities and increasing awareness of opportunities in distant areas – all typical aspects of globalization (Castles and Miller 1998). The millions of foreign contract workers in the Gulf states lack civil, political and social rights, and are subject to economic exploitation, discrimination and arbitrary deportation. Such practices are even more severe in the case of undocumented (or illegal) workers, who are totally lacking in legal protection, even though their employment is often widespread and tacitly tolerated by the state (as in the USA, Italy, Japan and many other countries). In turn, the competition of rightless migrants often provokes a racist reaction from local workers.

Women play a growing part in labour migration: patriarchal stereotypes in both sending and receiving countries facilitate their exploitation, not only in traditional female occupations such as domestic service and the sex industry, but also in advanced industrial sectors such as electronics. Women in domestic service are frequently subjected to sexual abuse, as has been well documented in the case of the Gulf states. Here, again, we see the links between gender discrimination and racialization.

Racism against old and new minorities

Many forms of racism are continuations of long-standing patterns. However, they often take new forms due to new migrations which add additional elements to existing ethnic mixtures. In the USA, despite government action following the civil rights movement of the 1960s, racism against African-Americans (12 per cent of the US population) continues. Distinctions between whites and blacks in income, occupational status, unemployment rates, social conditions and education are still extreme (Hacker 1992; Marable and Mullings 1994). Racial violence and harassment remain serious problems (ADL 1988). Such phenomena have led some observers to regard racism as a permanent and unchangeable feature of US society, which blacks have to learn to live with (Bell 1992). The increasing complexity of inter-ethnic relations is leading to new types of conflict and to a politicization of issues of culture and ethnicity. The Los Angeles riots of 1992 were indicative of such trends.

Western European countries have a long history of ethnic conflict and a deeply entrenched culture of racism. Racism expresses itself in conflicts on the status of territorial minorities (such as Basques in Spain or Corsicans in France), discrimination against historical minorities (like Jews and gypsies), as well as in attitudes and practices towards the new ethnic minorities, which developed following post-1945 labour migrations. Racism has intensified since the late 1980s when the end of the Cold War coincided with a serious recession and with an increase in the entry of asylum-seekers. The most dramatic signs of tension are increasing racist violence, the rise of the extreme right and confrontations between ethnic minority youth and the police (Wrench and Solomos 1993). Growing cultural diversity feeds into a moral panic which portrays 'Fortress Europe' as under threat from unpredictable influxes from the East and the South, evoking the 'Mongol hordes' of a distant past. Neo-Nazis and skinheads now portray themselves as the 'defenders of the European idea' against invasion, while mainstream political leaders outdo each other in putting up barriers to stop immigration.

Explaining the racisms of globalization

There are many racisms throughout the world today, but they have an essential unity as a mode of exclusion based on socially constructed markers of biological or cultural variation and of national identity. In this section I will argue that contemporary racisms are closely linked to the process of globalization. The central question is: why does globalization give rise to new forms of racism, and in many cases to an increased prevalence and intensity of racism? My hypothesis is that globalization leads to fundamental societal changes, which are experienced as crises of the national economy and social relations, as crises of culture and identity, and as political crises. In turn, these shifts in the character and forms of expression of racism have led to a crisis of anti-racism. This section will concentrate on highly developed countries. The links between racism and the crisis of the South – characterized by decolonization, economic dependence, weak states and generalized violence – have already been hinted at in the last section.

Just as racism has always been an integral part of modernity, the current shifts in racism are linked to a general crisis of modernity. The French sociologists Wieviorka and Lapeyronnie and their collaborators argue that the recent rise of racism in Western Europe is the result of 'the decomposition of national industrial societies' (Wieviorka 1994: 25). The 'national industrial society' is the model which evolved in the nineteenth and twentieth centuries and became the norm for modern nation-states. It articulates three elements – society, state and nation – in a particular form.

The society refers to an economic and social system usually based on rational (as opposed to traditional or religious) principles, within a bounded national territory. The state refers to a political system based on secular (and usually democratic) principles, capable of regulating economic and political relations and change. The nation refers to a 'people' defined both on the basis of belonging to the territory of the state and having a common cultural and ethnic background (Lapeyronnie et al. 1990: 258–62).

Until recently, the social and political identities of citizens of highly developed countries were based upon the articulation of their own particular society, state and nation, within a world of nation-states. The whole of classical sociology takes this 'national society' for granted (Lapeyronnie et al. 1990: 259). Even the critics of capitalism based their politics on national units: social-democratic demands for economic reform and welfare policies addressed the state; communists called for world revolution, but were organized nationally. This helps to explain why the left was shattered by globalization: capital became international much sooner than its opponents did.

Globalization has destabilized the 'national industrial society'. The central dynamics of economic life now transcend national borders and have become uncontrollable for national governments. De-industrialization of the older industrial nations has led to profound social changes, and has eroded the political basis of the labour movement. This in turn has severely weakened one side in the political conflict between capital and labour, which was a central organizing element of society (Wieviorka 1991, 1992, 1993, 1995). Capital may appear to have won, but at the price of a social and political disorganization which is highly threatening. The same is true at the global level: the end of the Cold War seemed at first to offer the chance of a stable global order, but unpredictable and uncontrollable conflicts soon emerged. Such uncertainties apply to culture too: rapid communication, travel and mass media offer an enormous and often confusing range of choices. Cultural openness is enriching, but it also questions one of the basic elements which characterize integrated national societies: the myth of distinct and homogeneous national cultures (Anderson 1983; Gellner 1983). All these changes are ambivalent: they offer new horizons and possibilities of emancipation, but they can also lead to social and psychological insecurity, and threaten feelings of identity and community.

If we accept this idea of the 'decomposition of the national industrial society', the question is: how does this lead to new racisms? To answer this we need to look at the effects of restructuring on the societies of highly developed countries.

Economic and social crises

Globalization has been experienced initially as a process of economic and industrial restructuring. Until the 1960s, capitalist expansion was based mainly on investment in existing industrial countries, leading to a long economic boom, rising wages and upward social mobility for many. The stereotype of the 'affluent worker' was born. But from the 1970s, investment patterns changed: capital moved off-shore to establish factories in low-wage countries. Oil-rich countries and newly industrializing countries took an increasing share of world trade. Investment in the older industrial countries focused on labour-saving technologies. Full employment gave way to rising levels of joblessness. Qualified workers belonging to the old 'labour aristocracy' found their skills devalued by new technologies. The crisis of restructuring has occurred everywhere, but its effects have been felt most strongly in the older industrial areas with their outmoded heavy and mechanical industries.

The economic crisis is also always a social one. Housing and urban infrastructure have declined as fast as the industries which used to help finance them. The decaying cities of the North and Midlands of Britain – the oldest industrial country – symbolize the end of an epoch. The industrial city was a central site of modernity, serving as a focus for national capital, political power and national culture. This does not imply homogeneity and consensus: not only ruling-class political power and culture was centred in the city, but also the labour movement and its counter-culture. The post-industrial city is very different: manufacturing is declining, the ownership of productive and reproductive capital is integrated into complex international networks, political power is fragmented and opaque. At the same time, recent immigrations have made the big cities highly diverse in their ethnic composition. The spatial organization of the city is now based as much on ethnicity as class, the two combining in complex and conflictual forms (Cross and Keith 1993; Davis 1990; Sassen 1988).

The globalization of finance has led to a fiscal crisis of the state, which cannot be resolved at the national level. The welfare states which developed after 1945 were based on the need to maintain political legitimacy and ensure collective reproduction of labour power at a time of full employment. Their material basis and their ideologies of solidarity and compassion have been eroded by de-industrialization and limitations on national economic autonomy. The Thatcher and Reagan governments of the 1980s used the new ideology of economic rationality as a legitimation for changes designed both to privatize the crisis and to bolster the profits of international investors. The gradual roll-back of social-security policies has led to a high degree of insecurity for large sections of the population. The 'two-thirds society', in which a large part of the population is decoupled from real participation in society, creates the potential for marginalization and the exclusion of minorities.

These economic and social changes have coincided with the settlement of large numbers of immigrants in the cities. Many local people have seen the newcomers as the cause of the threatening changes – an interpretation encouraged by the extreme right, but also by many mainstream politicians. Paradoxically, disadvantaged local people often share a common fate with ethnic minorities. Both are subject to the same processes of polarization: a new middle class of highly trained managers, profession-als and technicians is growing, but so is a new lower class of low-skilled workers employed in casual and insecure jobs. Minorities are affected dis-proportionately, as are new immigrants, who can no longer find entry-level jobs in factory and construction work. These groups are often pushed into the ghettos of large public-housing projects. Here, marginal-ized members of the majority population are face to face with the immi-grants and minorities, whom they have come to blame for their own fate. The potential for racism is obvious, and it is indeed in such 'ghettos of the disadvantaged' (Dubet and Lapeyronnie 1992) that racist violence and extreme-right mobilization are most extreme.

Crises of culture and identity

The crisis of modernity also expresses itself in cultural terms. This happens at three levels. At the level of national culture, there is a feeling of uncer-tainty and loss, arising from the swamping of distinctive cultural prac-tices and forms by a commodified international culture, produced in global cultural factories like Hollywood. Nations which used to define their uniqueness through traditions of language, folklore and high culture now find all this slipping away. Intellectuals and governments combine to maintain the purity of the national language, and to restrict the import of foreign cultural artefacts: the resistance of the French government in 1993 to the opening of cultural markets to world trade in the GATT round was symbolic both of this struggle and of its futility.

A second level relates to the supposed threat to national culture from imported ethnic cultures. By maintaining their languages, folklore, cul-tural practices and religions, immigrants are seen as undermining national culture. Racists who attack women in Islamic dress claim to be defending the nation or even European culture – a stereotype which links up with older racist notions of the threat of the Other to Christianity and civilization. But this level is closely linked to the first: it is only because global influences make national culture so precarious that immigrant minorities appear as a serious danger.

The third level of culture is connected with the central role of the idea of superiority over non-European peoples in colonialism. If migrants from former colonies of France, Britain and The Netherlands have the same rights as local people that questions century-old traditions of hierarchy. The problem is all the more acute in a situation of decline: in Britain immi-gration from the Caribbean and the Indian sub-continent coincided with de-industrialization and social crisis, and with a rapid loss in significance on the international stage. Immigration could be portrayed as a revenge of the colonized peoples, which was undermining the nation (cf. Cohen and Bains 1988; Layton-Henry 1992; Solomos 1993). Similarly, the decline of French culture has been linked by the extreme-right *Front National* with the loss of the colonies and the immigration of North Africans.

In such situations, racism against minorities takes on a central role: it helps to recreate a threatened community. Racism is a form of white ethnic solidarity, in the face of the apparent cultural strength of immigrant groups (cf. Wieviorka 1995). If British workers lose their jobs, and find their social security and environment declining, they can blame the alien influences which are undermining the nation. Hating immigrants helps to maintain an illusion of national unity and pride. Racism can help strengthen group and personal identity in a situation of crisis.

It has become fashionable to claim that racism today is a working-class phenomenon. Extreme-right groups recruit mainly from working-class subcultures such as skinheads and football fans. Conflicts between local people and immigrants occur mainly in working-class neighbourhoods. Ruling-class racism, like the support of German industrialists for the Nazis, or the support of Australian elites for the White Australia policy, seems to be a thing of the past. Capital is international, and will chase profit regardless of colour, culture or creed. But caution is needed in accepting this judgement. First, racism should not be seen as a working-class phenomenon, but rather as one product of the current decline of working-class culture and organization. In the face of multinational cultural industries, popular cultures have lost much of their power to deal with change. Secondly, the absence of overt racism should not lead us to think that racism has declined in the middle or upper classes. As van Dijk (1993) shows so convincingly, racist discourses and beliefs have not lost ground among elites. Rather, they do not take open and violent forms because elites are not as directly threatened as workers, and because they have the power to contain threats in more subtle ways. When elites do feel threatened, the ugly face of racism can quickly reappear, as the Australian mine-owners have shown in their campaigns against Aboriginal land rights.

Political crises

Economic, social, cultural and identity crises are, of course, not separate phenomena but different facets of the crisis of modernity, as expressed in the dissolution of the national society. All these dimensions are political: the erosion of the nation-state through globalization leads to crises of both ruling-class and working-class politics. Racism should be seen not as a result of the crisis, but rather as one form of expression of the crisis (Balibar 1991c: 104–27). One aspect of the crisis is the *racialization of politics*, through which political discourses of many kinds are structured by attaching deterministic meanings to socially constructed physical and cultural characteristics. For example, the increasing role of ethnic difference in urban restructuring has led to a racialization of social relations and politics at the local level: every conflict of interest now has an ethnic dimension, and racism becomes a way of expressing group interests (Ball and Solomos 1990).

At the national level, too, social dislocation has been accompanied by a political crisis. The decline of working-class parties and trade unions, and the erosion of local communicative networks, have created the social space for the growth of racism (Wieviorka 1993, 1995). Disadvantaged groups have found themselves without political representation in mainstream parties, which has led to a decline in confidence in democratic institutions. Many people have turned to extreme-right groups which provide a monocausal explanation for the crisis: that the nation is being undermined by immigration and minorities. Thus organized racism – often leading directly to violence – is both a psychological and a political response to processes of rapid change, which are often incomprehensible and always uncontrollable for those most affected.

This points to the need to analyse the links between economic change, political ideologies and popular attitudes. In many cases, the political response to restructuring has been a neo-conservative model which emphasizes natural inequality, deregulation of markets, reduced state intervention, and a return to traditional values of family and nation. The attack on the welfare state helps to create the social conditions for racism, while the ideology of neo-conservatism provides a fertile climate for blaming 'deviant' minorities for social problems. These themes are taken up in the media and in popular discourse, helping to create a new 'common-sense' racism.

Extreme-right organizations take this ideology a step further by reinterpreting it as a call to violence. They recruit urban 'poor white' youth, who seek to overcome their own powerlessness through violence against minorities with even less social power. At the same time, ideologies of equality and tolerance help legitimate elite racism. In this 'racism without race', powerful groups maintain that there is equal opportunity for all irrespective of ethnic background. Those groups which are disadvantaged or excluded must therefore be the victims of their own 'inferior cultures', and of their refusal to adapt to the superior majority culture.

The crisis of anti-racism

Racism is an integral part of the crisis of modernity, in all its economic, social, cultural and political facets. The failure to realize this is an important factor in the crisis of anti-racist thinking, which is still often fixated on older forms of racism – above all on the biological racism which was a central part of Western culture until at least 1945 (see Taguieff 1988). Even more serious, most anti-racists still see racism as something peripheral to social and political life – what Paul Gilroy has called the 'coat-of-paint theory of racism' (Gilroy 1992: 52). The idea is that racism is an unpleasant anomaly which is alien to the basic notions of humanism and liberal democracy. Racism can therefore be combated by legal, educational and psychological strategies which will deal with the ugly aberration without changing the overall social and political system. This approach has two main aspects, which may be called official anti-racism and critical anti-racism.

Official anti-racism refers to the role of the state. Throughout the history of modernity the state has had a crucial role in constructing racism. In more recent times – since the international struggle against Nazism – the state has also had a role in combating racism. Most modern states have signed UN human rights declarations and have a whole gamut of anti-racist laws and policies. Australia is a case in point with its Federal Racial Discrimination Act, Human Rights and Equal Opportunity Commission, State Anti-discrimination Boards and so on. Sometime there is a tongue-in-cheek cynicism about such institutions: for instance, the strong German anti-racist laws do not apply to non-citizens, while strict naturalization rules stop most of the 7 million foreign residents from becoming citizens. But on the whole, anti-racism based on the UNESCO declarations of the post-war period has become part of the ruling consensus.

And yet, as discussed above, exclusion and exploitation based on racist criteria are as widespread and serious as ever, though they may have changed in form. Clearly, official anti-racism is ineffective. There are several reasons for this. One is the weakness and unwieldiness of laws on vilification and discrimination. Prosecutions are rare, and the effects on social behaviour are peripheral; the rules are often merely symbolic gestures. More important is the fact that official anti-racism is generally based on outmoded concepts of overt, biological racism. It is blind to the more subtle and pervasive expressions of cultural racism, as embodied in dominant political and economic institutions, everyday life and common-sense discourses. This is not surprising, for to recognize that racism is a central part of our social and political life would imply the need for radical changes, and thus undermine existing power relations. Official anti-racism has therefore an ambivalent character. It does represent a break with the overtly racist ideologies of the past, but it sometimes serves as an alibi for new forms of exclusion and exploitation of minorities.

Critical anti-racism refers to movements which have developed since the 1960s, generally linked to ethnic communities as well as to left-wing political organizations, trade unions and church groups. Critical anti-racists have pointed to the hollowness of official policies, and have shown how laws and institutions have been inadequate in combating the widespread discrimination and marginalization of minorities. But most anti-racist groups have concentrated on old-style biological racism, especially in its neo-Nazi guise. Racism has been analysed as something peripheral to capitalist society, and therefore excisable without other basic changes. Anti-racists have courageously fought against racist groups and exposed official hypocrisy. But their demands have generally been for better legislation, stronger anti-racist institutions, and more comprehensive community strategies. All these things are needed, but they will not in themselves alter the basic causes of racism, which are deeply embedded in our social order and culture.

Moreover, the fixation of anti-racism on legislation and rules for securing equality have opened the door to a new conservative critique, based on the slogan of 'political correctness'. By exposing and caricaturing alleged excesses of affirmative action and quota systems, especially in the USA, the new right has endeavoured (with some success) to label anti-racists as opponents of equality and democracy. The powerful critique of 'political correctness' is designed to legitimate inequality and racism, by appealing to the principle of individual rights and equality.

Anti-racism therefore needs to re-invent itself in response to the transformation of racism. It is essential to understand that racism is a basic element of our society, and has played a crucial role in its evolution, from the very beginnings of modernity. It is equally important to realize that globalization has not interrupted the continuity of racism, but has led to a whole gamut of new racisms. These are closely linked to the crises connected with restructuring, which are occurring everywhere, albeit in a variety of specific forms. The culturalization of race, and the idea of 'racism without race', are widespread expressions of these developments. At the same time some of the older forms of racism, such as discrimination against indigenous peoples and ethnic nationalism in new nations, continue unabated. Anti-racism therefore needs a multi-faceted strategy, which takes account of the strength, diversity and mutability of racism, as well of its fundamental importance in modern society.

Notes

1 For a discussion of definitions of ethnicity and the ethnic group, see Castles and Miller (1998: 29–36).

2 It is important to remember that any attempt at classification is arbitrary for the boundaries between categories could be drawn in various ways, while many racist practices fit into a number of the categories used. For more detail and sources, see Castles (1993). The annual country reports on human rights practices published by the US Department of State are a valuable source of information on racist practices in every country (except the USA!).

12

CITIZENSHIP AND THE OTHER IN THE AGE OF MIGRATION

In the past half-century, the democratic nation-state has become the global norm as the principal unit of political organization. Within it, people are defined as citizens with rights and obligations laid down by constitutions and laws. There is, of course, a gap between the principle and the reality: the majority of the 185 states within the United Nations cannot claim to be stable democracies in which all citizens are truly equal before the law. Where democracy does not yet exist those in power claim that this is due to economic deprivation or histories of colonialism, foreign domination and internal conflict. Democratic citizenship is the goal.

The paradox is that, just as the nation-state has achieved almost universal acceptance, it appears increasingly precarious: globalization is eroding national boundaries and breaking the nexus between territory and power. This challenge has multiple dimensions:

- The emergence of global markets and transnational corporations with economic power greater than many states.
- The increasing role of supranational bodies in regulating inter-state relations and individual rights.
- The emergence of global cultural industries based on new communication techniques.
- The growth in international migration since 1945 and especially since about 1980.

This last dimension of globalization is my main theme. In the age of migration (Castles and Miller 1998) a major problem arises: if the citizen is a person who belongs both culturally and politically to one specific nation-state, what of migrants who settle in one country without abandoning their cultural belonging in another? The migrant has always been the 'Other' of the nation. National identity is often asserted through a process of exclusion – feelings of belonging depend on being able to say who does not belong. But if the Other is part of society (as a worker, parent or tax-payer, for example), how can national distinctiveness be maintained? Moreover, the increase in the number of people with transnational

This chapter was first published in A. Davidson and K. Weekley (eds), *Globalization and Citizenship in the Asia-Pacific* (London, Macmillan, 1999), pp. 27–48.

identities – as shown by multiple citizenship, and by family, social and economic connections in more than one country – questions the principle of nation-state exclusivity (Basch et al. 1994).

Globalization makes it necessary to work out new modes of inclusion for 'the citizen who does not belong'. The problem is all the more acute in that cultural difference within nation-states is increasing at a time when new forms of economic and social polarization are also emerging. Ethnic exclusion and social exclusion are linked in complex ways. These are the issues that I will address in this chapter.[1]

Citizenship and nationality

It is necessary first to discuss some of the inherent contradictions of the nation-state and of citizenship. It is significant that today's global association of *states* is actually called the United *Nations*, indicating that we find it hard today to conceive of a state that is not also a nation. A *state* refers to a legal and political organization which controls a certain territory. A *nation* is a cultural community of people who believe that they have a common heritage and a common destiny (see Seton-Watson 1977; Smith 1991). Both are of great antiquity, but their linking as a *nation-state* is relatively new, dating from the eighteenth and nineteenth centuries. The juxtaposition of nation and state has many problems which I cannot go into here (see Castles 1998b). I will focus on just two key issues: the contradiction between citizenship and nationality, and the contradiction between the active and the passive citizen.

An essential feature of a democratic nation-state is the integration of all its inhabitants into the political community and their equality as citizens. As a political community, the nation-state claims to be inclusive of all people in its territory, while those outside are excluded. In the 'universal state', all citizens are meant to be free and equal persons, who, as citizens, are homogeneous individuals (Rawls 1985: 232–4). This requires a separation between a people's political rights and obligations and their membership of specific groups, based on ethnicity, religion, social class or regional location.

The notion of the free citizen goes back to medieval towns, which developed as places of refuge from feudal servitude and as the location of the new classes of merchants and artisans. But in the era of modernity, citizenship no longer referred to the city, but to the nation-state. Becoming a citizen depended on membership of a specific national community (for example, being French, German, Italian). A *citizen* was always also a member of a nation, a *national*. So citizenship is meant to be universalistic and above cultural difference, yet it exists only in the context of a nation-state, which is based on cultural specificity – on the belief in being different from other nations.

Since very few nation-states actually start off with a single national group, the question is how the varying ethnic groups in a territory are to be moulded into one nation. This *obliteration of difference* may take place by means of the forcible imposition of the culture of the dominant group; for instance, through the prohibition of minority languages, schools and festivals. The process may be a more gradual and consensual one, in which groups grow together through economic and social interaction and the development of a common language and shared institutions, such as schools, church and military service. Most nation-states have elements of both repression and evolution.

States vary in the degree to which ethnic nationalism is subordinated to universalism. The ultra-nationalism of the nineteenth-century German *Kulturnation* was in strong contrast to the French *Staatsnation* created by the democratic revolution of 1789. This civic nation was regarded as a political project capable of transcending the tension between universalism and particularism and of assimilating ethnic or religious minorities (Schnapper 1994: 83–114). Yet the claim of transcending culture was dubious: even in France, nation-state formation involved linguistic homogenization, political centralization and compulsory assimilation. The key to success was the long duration of the process of conquering and homogenizing surrounding peoples, starting in the fifteenth century, and only completed towards the end of the nineteenth century. This, in the famous formulation of Renan (1992), gave people 'time to forget' the history of their own oppression, which had made them into one nation. But, even over centuries, some people did not forget, which is why there have been separatist movements in Corsica and Languedoc.

This fundamental contradiction between citizen and national is at the root of many of the conflicts that tore Europe apart in the nineteenth and twentieth centuries, such as anti-semitism, racism and nationalism. It was never fully overcome within the nation-state model: the wars triggered by rival nationalisms were only ended through *supranational* approaches after 1945 – and even then not completely, as the example of former Yugoslavia has shown.

The passive and the active citizen

The contradiction between citizen and national cuts across another crucial dichotomy: that between the passive and the active citizen. According to seventeenth-century social-contract theory, a sovereign could only rule with the consent of the people, but once this consent was given the people had a duty to obey the constitutionally enacted laws. In the pre-1914 German *Rechtsstaat*, the passive citizen had obligations towards the state and rights to protection from unlawful state action, but had no right to question state authority.

By contrast, the French Revolution of 1789 led to a notion of citizenship as an assertion of political will, which has to be constantly renewed through participation in the process of law-making (summed up in Renan's designation of the nation as 'the daily plebiscite'). The essence of citizenship was a set of procedures designed to guarantee equal participation in the expression of political will. This popular sovereignty was the basis for the legal rights laid down in the Declaration of the Rights of Man and the Citizen. Citizenship meant participation as an equal in the public sphere, while protecting the right to be different in the private sphere. In principle there was no link between being a citizen and belonging to the French cultural community: the 1793 Constitution virtually gave citizenship at will to resident foreigners (Davidson 1997: 45).

The principle of equal citizenship was always incomplete – above all, women were excluded. Moreover, it was linked to the exclusion of the external Other: the democratic citizen was always also the 'warrior-citizen'. The right to vote was explicitly linked to conscription. Nevertheless, the conflict between active and passive notions of the citizen was – and remains – one of the great political divides within modern nation-states. Democratic movements have struggled for the enfranchisement of previously excluded groups, such as workers and women. Conservatives have always opposed popular sovereignty because it restricts the rights of those with wealth and power. Today, the growing complexity of society and state make it difficult for the popular will to control the decisions of experts and technocrats.

What is important in our context is that the notion of the active citizen inevitably leads to demands for broadening the rights of citizenship. A person cannot participate in political processes without a certain minimum standard of education and of economic and social well-being. Political rights are meaningless in the long run unless they are linked to social rights. This principle was asserted by European labour movements from the late nineteenth century, and given real substance in the post-war European welfare states.

The roll-back of social citizenship since the 1970s is the expression of an ideological offensive against the idea of the active citizen with social rights. New right ideologies are reasserting the notion of the citizen as a person who fits into the community by working and obeying the law. The task of the state is to guarantee the private realm by maintaining law and order and minimizing intervention in economic and social affairs (Mead 1986). Underlying this ideology is the economic and social crisis brought about by global economic restructuring. The question is how high wages and the welfare state can be maintained in a world where the old industrial countries are no longer dominant.

The immigration of the irreducible Other

Globalization and international migration exacerbate the contradictions of citizenship. Today, there are at least 100 million people resident outside their country of birth. This is only a small proportion of the world's population, yet the consequences are much broader, affecting migrants' families, their communities of origin, and the places where they settle. Moreover, the effects of migration are felt most in areas already undergoing rapid change. Economic and social transformation in poor areas lead to emigration, while the destinations may be global cities with burgeoning service economies, or new industrial countries undergoing rapid urbanization.

The significance of migration for citizenship is felt at the intersection between the two basic contradictions discussed above. The principle of citizenship for all members of society demands the inclusion of new ethnic minorities into the political community; the principle of national belonging demands their exclusion. Similarly, the principle of active citizenship demands giving minorities the economic and social rights needed for full participation. But the current roll-back in the welfare state makes it difficult to admit new groups and to provide the conditions they need to achieve full societal membership.

Immigration and growing cultural diversity poses a dual challenge to nation-states. First, admitting the Other into the national community through citizenship and equal rights appears as a threat to national cohesion and identity. The process of immigration has become so rapid that there is no time to obliterate difference, let alone to forget it. This problem is all the more acute when the Other comes from former colonies, where their otherness (expressed both through phenotypical and cultural difference) has been constructed both as inferiority and as a danger to 'Judeo-Christian civilization'.

Secondly, at a time of economic decline, sharing a shrinking social cake with new groups appears as a threat to the conditions of the local working class. The social polarization brought about by economic restructuring and policies of privatization and deregulation leaves little room for minority rights. It is much easier to turn these groups into the scapegoats for the social crisis, by blaming them not only for their own marginality, but also for the decline in general standards. Migration is therefore seen as a central aspect of the North–South conflict, and migrants may be perceived as infiltrators who will drag the rich countries down to Third-World poverty. The 'enemy within' is the racialized 'underclass' in the new urban 'ghettos'.

The immigration of the irreducible Other creates a dilemma for Western countries because it exacerbates the existing contradictions of the nation-state model at the very moment when this model is in any case being undermined by globalization. To what extent does this also apply to the new immigration countries of Asia? There are clearly some important differences. The long historical process which led to the emergence of the democratic citizenry in Europe has no parallel in Asia. The idea of popular sovereignty is relatively new and untried, while the practice of achieving political objectives through negotiation within complex authoritarian structures has a long tradition. The Western model of the nation-state and citizenship came to Asia mediated through the distorting mirror of colonialism. France offered citizenship to some of the colonized people of Indo-China; Britain and The Netherlands made colonized people into subjects of their monarchs; the USA preached democratic values in the Philippines. But such ideals were always tarnished by the realities of dispossession, exploitation and racism.

Yet at the same time colonialism was so effective in destroying previous state-forms that liberation movements usually set out to take over the Western model – often with the ideal of giving reality to democratic principles that had been mere hypocrisy in their colonial guise. The new post-colonial states were largely based on the Western form, but without the historical process that had led to its emergence. Above all, the democratic citizen was absent. Anti-colonial trade unions, parties and movements tried to create a democratic-nationalist consciousness. They often failed: military rule or other forms of authoritarianism quickly became the norm, although there has been a shift towards greater democracy in some countries in the past twenty years (see Rodan 1996).

Post-colonial nation-states developed so quickly that there was no 'time to forget'. Ruling elites were incapable of homogenizing the various ethnic and national groups brought together by colonialism into one people. In some cases, colonialism had cut across traditional ethnic boundaries; in others long-standing ethnic divisions were exacerbated by colonialism (such as the situation of the Chinese in South-east Asia); in yet others, colonial labour recruitment had created new minorities (for example, the Indians in Malaysia). Where there were cleavages of religion, ethnicity, culture or economic interests, the rule of a dominant group was often imposed by force.

This is not to argue that there have not been successful examples of nation-building: Singapore, Indonesia and Malaysia all provide models for building unity on diversity. Rather, the point is that the development of national consciousness is a difficult and as yet incomplete process. The national and the citizen are not generally emerging in parallel, as was the experience in at least some European countries. The strains arising from attempts to develop a single national community out of diverse cultures may make it all the harder to include immigrants into the nation. 'Late nations' are generally the most nationalistic ones.

Becoming a citizen

How have immigration countries dealt with the dilemmas outlined above? Becoming a citizen is clearly of crucial importance to an immigrant. But gaining formal *access to citizenship* – symbolized by getting the passport of the country of residence – is only one aspect of this. Equally important is the extent to which people belonging to distinct groups of the population actually achieve *substantial citizenship*: that is equal chances of participation in various areas of society, such as politics, work and social security. This section deals with access to citizenship while the following one will examine substantial citizenship. The discussion concentrates on older immigration countries (Western Europe, North America and Australia) due to lack of information on newer immigrant-receiving countries.

Rules for formal access to citizenship are highly complicated and are in a state of flux. Laws on citizenship or nationality derive from two competing principles: *ius sanguinis* (literally, law of the blood), which is based on descent from a national of the country concerned, and *ius soli* (literally, law of the soil), which is based on birth in the territory of the country. *Ius sanguinis* is often linked to an ethnic or folk model of the nation state (the German *Kulturnation*), while *ius soli* generally relates to a nation-state built through incorporation of diverse groups on a single territory (as in the case of the United Kingdom). *Ius sanguinis* has been seen historically as appropriate for an emigration country (like Germany, Spain or Greece) which wished to retain the allegiance of people who had settled elsewhere. A 'law of return' to reintegrate former emigrants may be based on this principle, as in the case of contemporary Germany and its *Aussiedler* (ethnic Germans from Eastern Europe). *Ius soli*, on the other hand, is particularly useful for integrating immigrants of diverse national origins into a new nation, which is why it has been adopted in the former British colonies (USA, Australia and so on) and former Spanish colonies in Latin America. In practice, all modern states have citizenship rules based on a combination of *ius sanguinis* and *ius soli*, although one or the other may be clearly predominant. For instance, *ius soli* countries use the *ius sanguinis* principle to confer citizenship on children of their citizens born overseas. A further principle is growing in significance at present: *ius domicili* (law of residence) according to which people may gain an entitlement to citizenship through residence in the territory of a country.

However, some general trends can be made out (Çinar 1994; Guimezanes 1995). Half a century of large-scale immigration to Western nations is leading to a grudging realization that people of diverse ethno-cultural backgrounds are there for good, and that there is no real alternative to incorporating them as citizens. This recognition has been easier for some countries than others. Classical immigration countries like the USA, Canada and Australia have been able to continue their traditions of incorporating newcomers as citizens, although they have had to drop practices of racial selectivity and find new ways of dealing with cultural difference. Immigrants are encouraged to become citizens with automatic citizenship for their children. These countries seem highly inclusive. However, it may be argued that the real decision on citizenship is made when immigration applications are rejected or accepted, rather then later on when settlers apply for naturalization. Selectivity of immigrants according to economic, social and humanitarian criteria may be based on (possibly unconscious) political and cultural biases.

European countries, with their strong historical links between imagined cultural community and political belonging, have found it more difficult to change their access criteria. None the less, naturalization rules have been gradually relaxed to grant citizenship to long-standing foreign residents. Many observers speak of a cross-national convergence of rules, but a comparison of actual practices and outcomes shows that major differences still exist. Table 12.1 presents a comparison of naturalization figures. Naturalization rates are still very low in the *ius sanguinis* countries which used to recruit guest-workers: Germany, Austria and Switzerland. Countries with models combining elements of *ius soli* and *ius sanguinis* – France, Belgium, the UK – have intermediate rates. Sweden and The Netherlands have done most to change rules to include immigrants and now have naturalization rates close to those of Australia or Canada.

Measures are also being introduced to facilitate access to citizenship for the second and subsequent generations through the extension of *ius soli* or through various combinations of *ius soli, ius sanguinis* and *ius domicili*. Immigrants' children are automatically citizens in the USA, Australia, Canada and the UK. The overwhelming majority become citizens on reaching adulthood in France, Sweden, The Netherlands, Belgium and Italy. Despite recent changes, rules are still restrictive in Germany, Austria and Switzerland, so that many young people remain foreigners in their country of birth and upbringing.

Another general trend is that towards dual or multiple citizenship. Although many governments reject this due to fears of 'divided loyalties', there are now millions of people with two or more passports. The rapid increase reflects both the reality of migrants' dual national affiliations and

Table 12.1   *Naturalizations in selected countries 1988 and 1995*

Country	1988		1995	
	No. of naturalizations	Naturalization rate[1]	No. of naturalizations	Naturalization rate[1]
Australia	81,218	57	114,757	74
Belgium	8,366	10	26,109	29
Canada	58,810	n.a.	227,720	n.a.
France	46,351	13	59,988	17
Germany (FR)	16,660	4	31,888	5
Japan	5,767	6	14,104	10
Netherlands	9,110	14	71,440	98
Sweden	17,966	43	31,993	60
Switzerland	11,356	11	16,795	12
UK	64,600	35	40,500	19
USA	242,063	n.a.	445,853	n.a.

n.a. = not available.

[1]The naturalization rate is defined as the number of naturalizations per thousand foreign residents. The calculated naturalization rate for Australia is based on an estimate for foreign resident population, assuming that 60 per cent of overseas-born persons are Australian citizens. The naturalization rate for France is calculated using the foreign resident population figure for 1990. The German naturalization figure excludes naturalization based on legal entitlement, which applies mainly to 'ethnic Germans' from Eastern Europe. The comparison has only indicative value, as definitions and procedures vary from country to country.

Sources: Australian census 1996, preliminary figures; OECD (1997: Table III. 1, Tables A.1, B3, and C5)

the growth in bi-national marriages. This contributes to the erosion of notions of exclusive national belonging.

Several states have created systems of quasi-citizenship, through which long-term residents are granted some but not all of the rights of citizenship (for instance, local but not national voting rights) (Hammar 1990). Such measures do improve the legal and psychological security of settlers but seem fundamentally unstable because they create a two-class system of citizenship which is inconsistent with democratic principles. However, once immigrants have civil and social rights, they are in a better position to demand political rights. Citizenship of the European Union (EU) is a special form of quasi-citizenship. It is linked to citizenship of a member-state and confers only limited political rights, though quite considerable social rights. EU citizenship does nothing for the millions of 'extra-communitarians' and is seen by some as one aspect of the construction of an exclusionary European identity. But, like other types of quasi-citizenship, EU citizenship could be an important stepping-stone towards full membership. The question is whether this will be membership of an exclusionary nation-state or of a new type of transnational democratic entity (Martiniello 1994).

Issues of formal access to citizenship for immigrants are thus far from resolved. Large numbers of people still have ambiguous and disadvantaged legal positions. In some countries, a generation of young people is reaching maturity without equal rights in their country of birth. Populations can be divided up into *full citizens, denizens* (people with limited citizenship rights) and *margizens* (undocumented immigrants or other people with insecure legal status) (Martiniello 1994). Such legal differentiation reinforces social divisions and racism against minorities.

Minorities and rights

The rise of the welfare state after 1945 led to debates on the contradiction between formal political membership and persistence of severe economic and social disadvantage. Welfare state theorists in Britain, Scandinavia and other European countries (Townsend 1979; Turner 1992) argued that a bundle of social rights, including the rights to work, education and certain basic social standards, were essential for members of the working class to be full citizens. On this basis, T.H. Marshall (1950, 1964) developed his famous notion of three types of citizenship rights, which had developed in historical progression: *civil rights, political rights* and *social rights*.

Such debates have become all the more significant today. In all the old industrial countries, certain social groups are becoming spatially segregated and cut off from mainstream economic and social frameworks. Some US urban sociologists (for example, Wilson 1987, 1994) refer to such groups as the 'underclass', while most European observers prefer the concept of 'social exclusion' (Cross and Keith 1993; Mingione 1996). A high proportion of the socially excluded in Western countries belong to ethnic minorities, defined on the basis of race, culture or origins. There is a clear trend towards the *racialization* or *ethnicization of poverty* (Schierup 1997).

It would be useful to review the rights of ethnic minorities according to Marshall's triad of civil, political and social rights. This task cannot be carried out adequately here, but a few key issues can be mentioned. In principle, *civil rights*[2] are guaranteed by law for everyone (including non-citizens) in a democratic state. Moreover, as Soysal (1994) has pointed out, the rights of non-citizens have in many cases been expanded through supranational legal norms laid down by such bodies as the United Nations, the International Labour Organization and the Council of Europe. However, civil rights guaranteed by law to ethnic minorities are frequently violated in practice, often by powerful institutions such as the police, prisons and courts. For instance, indigenous peoples such as Australian Aborigines suffer extremely high rates of incarceration and of death in custody (HREOC 1991). Police brutality against African-Americans is also well documented.

The prevalence of racist violence can in itself be seen as a constraint on civil rights, for it severely reduces minority members' chances of equal participation in society. In the USA, 'hate organizations', such as the Ku Klux Klan, neo-Nazi groups and 'militia' organizations, carry out campaigns of violence and intimidation against African-Americans and other minorities. European countries have also experienced growing racist violence since the 1970s. The situation deteriorated further as the end of the Cold War coincided with a serious recession. 'By the early 1990s, many groups of people have had to face racist violence and harassment as a threatening part of everyday life' (Björgo and Witte 1993: 1). These groups included immigrants and asylum-seekers, but also long-standing minorities such as Jews and gypsies.

The situation with regard to *political rights*[3] is highly complex: many resident non-citizens are denied political rights, while others have been granted limited rights, such as the vote in local elections. On the other hand, minorities which do have formal citizenship may have little real chance of political participation. In Australia, indigenous people make up less than 2 per cent of the population, and there are few constituencies where they have a chance of securing representation. Their only way of making their voice heard is through special representative bodies, such as the Aboriginal and Torres Strait Islander Commission (ATSIC). However, its prerogatives are limited and insecure, as was shown in 1996 when the Liberal–National government took steps to curtail its autonomy in financial matters.

Different categories of rights are interdependent. Criteria of exclusion based on socio-economic position and on minority status may be mutually reinforcing: in the USA, large numbers of the poor and of ethnic minorities are not even registered as voters. Even in presidential elections, only about half the population votes, while the proportion is far lower in congressional and state elections.

Current trends are leading to a weakening of *social rights*[4] for many ethnic minority members. Two main situations may be distinguished. First, the majority of immigrants and their descendants do not live in enclaves nor find employment in workplaces separate from those of the majority populations. Yet their position is frequently precarious: the combination of only partial incorporation into mainstream economic and social systems with continuing processes of racialization makes them highly vulnerable. This situation may be referred to as *social segmentation* (Cross 1995).

Secondly, some minority groups are highly vulnerable due to their weak legal position, racial stigmatization, lack of human capital and specific historical conditions of conflict. These groups include indigenous peoples in North America and Australia, African-Americans in the USA, Afro-Caribbeans and South Asians in Britain and asylum-seekers everywhere. Groups on the verge of such situations include Muslim immigrants in most countries, some (but not all) Hispanics in the USA, and certain Asian groups (especially those of refugee origin). These groups are likely to suffer *social exclusion*. As Mingione (1996: 12) argues, their disadvantage is so severe as to weaken the social bond and to question the strength of citizenship as an integrating force in contemporary society.

However, Marshall's triad of civil, political and social rights is inadequate to understand fully the situation of ethnic minorities today. It is necessary to add the additional categories of gender rights and cultural rights. In Western countries, women were excluded from formal citizenship and legal equality until quite recently (Pateman 1988): women got the vote in 1902 in Australia, 1918 in Britain,[5] 1920 in the USA, and in 1944 in France. Although explicit legal discrimination had disappeared in most places by the 1970s, the legacy of historical subordination remains: women have worse jobs, lower incomes, low rates of participation in political decision-making processes, and are still seen as primarily responsible for the domestic sphere (Gregory 1987; Meehan 1993: 101–20; Vogel 1994: 85).

Ethnic minority women are in a double bind: they are marginalized both through subordinating constructions of gender and through ethnic and racial stigmatization. These are not simply additive processes, where two forms of discrimination reinforce each other. Rather, racialization of minority women takes specific forms within the reproduction of gendered social relations (Anthias and Yuval-Davis 1989; Brah 1993; Lutz et al. 1995). These interlocking processes can be observed in many social arenas, including:

- ideological discourses on nation and community;
- notions of sexuality;
- legal rules on immigration and nationality;
- mechanisms of labour market segmentation;
- the spatial ordering of social relations;
- the construction of socio-cultural norms.

Minority women cannot become full citizens simply by achieving formal equality because this will not overcome sexist and racist discourses. Rather they need specific rights, which recognize the historical forms in which their oppression and exclusion have been constructed. Iris Young (1989) argues that this can only be achieved, first, through 'mechanisms for group representation' of previously excluded groups, and, secondly, through 'the articulation of special rights that attend to group differences in order to undermine oppression and disadvantage'.

A similar point can be made with regard to cultural rights. Since the nation-state is based on the obliteration of minority cultures, the maintenance of immigrant cultures and languages can become a stigma used to justify the inferiority of minorities. On the other hand, giving up the original culture and accepting assimilation can lead to even greater marginalization for minorities because it means losing the self-esteem and the community solidarity needed to survive in an often hostile environment. Therefore, minorities demand the rights both to the maintenance of their original culture and to social equality within the country of settlement. This duality of social and cultural rights is accepted in countries with policies of multiculturalism, like Australia, Canada and Sweden. It seems an essential aspect of citizenship in a culturally diverse society (Castles 1994).

Racialization and community formation

Until quite recently, the prevailing view in most immigration countries was that the problem of cultural diversity would solve itself over time through the assimilation of minorities. This is still the dominant ideology in some countries, most notably France. But the belief in assimilation is becoming harder to sustain. The capability of the nation-state to 're-socialize' immigrants is being undermined both by globalizing tendencies and by a decline in social solidarity (Schnapper 1994). At the same time, immigrants find it easier to maintain their cultural and other links with their areas of origin through better communication and frequent visits.

This situation gives rise to two closely linked phenomena: racialization (or ethnicization) of minorities and community formation. Racialization arises from the combined effects of all the exclusionary effects already discussed in this chapter. Racial discrimination and violence, spatial segregation, economic disadvantage and social exclusion all work together to create ethnic or racial minorities which are clearly identifiable. Racialization as a discursive process goes a step further by blaming the minorities for their social isolation, and by portraying them as a threat to society. For example, Susan Smith has shown how residential segregation in Britain was presented as the choice of immigrants, who wanted to live together in a 'black inner city'. The development of minority neighbourhoods then appeared as the result of 'natural processes' of racial differentiation, rather than as the consequence of economic and social exclusion. Minority areas were portrayed as a threat to morality and public order. Welfare dependency, crime, vice and dangerous religious and political ideologies were seen as cancers which developed in such areas, and might spread to threaten the whole society. This laid the ground for a racialization of politics in the 1960s: extreme-right groups and sections of the Conservative Party mobilized public opinion around demands to stop immigration and curtail the rights of existing immigrants (Smith 1993).

The response by minorities to racialization is to maintain their cultures and languages, and to develop community solidarity. In the early stages of a migratory process, immigrant groups normally cluster together and develop their own infrastructure – businesses, religious institutions, associations – as a way of coping with the new social situation. In time, successful immigrants make links with mainstream economic and social frameworks, and move out into other areas. When such shifts are blocked by racial discrimination and violence, and by lack of economic opportunities, members of minorities have to focus their activities within the ethnic community, and this stimulates the development of religious, political and economic institutions. This in turn increases the suspicions of the majority population that 'alien enclaves' are developing. Ethnic segregation is thus a self-fulfilling prophecy, originating in exclusionary discourses. However, extreme separatism – such as Islamic fundamentalist groups in France, Germany and Britain – is very much the exception. In most cases, ethnic mobilization, especially by members of the second generation, is concerned with combating discrimination and achieving equal treatment within mainstream society.

In France, Catherine Wihtol de Wenden (1988, 1995) has shown how forms of ethnic mobilization changed at different stages of migration and settlement:

1   Immigrants as foreigners and workers (1950s and 1960s). Migrant workers originally became politicized with reference to home-country issues, as well as with regard to industrial and trade-union action.
2   Immigrants as purveyors of traditional culture (from the 1970s). Both European and African workers of the first generation formed religious and cultural associations concerned with maintaining the traditions of the area of origin. These associations contributed to the internal cohesion of immigrant families and groups without necessarily integrating them into French society.
3   The second generation of immigrants as political actors (1980s and 1990s). Associations were formed to fight against racism, to lobby for civic rights and for new citizenship laws, to promote socio-cultural integration in the suburbs, to organize help with home work, and to offer help with work-seeking and new business ventures.

The movement of the *beurs* (youth of North African origin) has become an important cultural and political force in France (Bouamama 1994). New forms of citizenship appeared in urban struggles when *beurs* asserted that they were 'citizens by participation' without necessarily being nationals. The notion of a 'new citizenship' was viewed as the answer to a crisis in democracy caused both by the rise of individualism and the growth of collective identities. Members of the second generation demanded participatory citizenship in a multicultural society, based on residence rather than nationality or descent (Wihtol de Wenden 1995). Cultural symbols and ethnic community solidarity play an important part in the development of movements for equal participation in the wider society without loss of identity. This presents a major challenge to traditional forms of national belonging (Bouamama et al. 1992).

Towards post-national belonging

My central conclusion is that the nation-state model, which asserts (or seeks to create) congruity between nationality and citizenship, cannot offer an adequate basis for societal belonging in the age of globalization and migration. The continuing attempt to base citizenship on membership of an imagined cultural community leads to political and social exclusion and the racialization of difference. Such trends do not just disadvantage minorities – they also lead to social divisions and political conflicts for the societies concerned. Three sets of principles arise from this conclusion.

1 The need for citizenship rules which guarantee formal inclusion of all permanent residents of a given country. A notion of *porous borders* is required, with admission rules and rights based on people's real societal membership (cf. Bauböck 1994). Where people belong to more than one society there may need to be differential or segmented forms of citizenship, which recognize the different modes of participation.
2 The need for economic and social policies which make social citizenship possible for all, and which overcome trends to racialization of social exclusion and poverty. Since there can be no political equality without certain basic social standards, there is a need for a social safety-net for all, as well as affirmative action policies to facilitate the inclusion of previously excluded groups. Here the principle of interdependence of civil, political, social, gender and cultural rights must be stressed.
3 The need for institutional change. Existing constitutions, laws, political parties and economic organizations all embody the dominant cultural values of the era in which they were constructed. These cultural values are based on the idea of a distinctive national community, with fixed boundaries to the outside world. If belonging is uncoupled from nationality, new members of society are likely to question and change existing structures (Habermas 1994).

It is very easy to put forward such principles, but much harder to achieve them in practice. It is important to examine actual political tendencies, which are in fact quite contradictory: on the one hand, attempts are being made to shore up the old nation-state model, while, on the other, certain changes point to the possibility of devising new modes of belonging. I will conclude by giving a few examples.

With regard to formal inclusion, it may be argued that significant changes are gradually eroding the link between citizenship and nationality. Every major immigration country has altered its naturalization rules in recent times. There is a trend towards easier naturalization for immigrants and stronger entitlement to citizenship for their children. Dual citizenship is also burgeoning. This has often meant relaxing the requirement for prior cultural assimilation: the new citizens are not yet nationals, and may never become so. Moreover, many immigrants unable to secure full citizenship are obtaining some crucial rights through national and supranational legal norms. Regional political integration (above all the European Union) is creating new forms of political belonging decoupled from nationality. But there are also countervailing tendencies: the tightening of immigration and refugee rules is leading to an increase in the number of illegal residents. Moreover, minority members are often unable to obtain their formal rights in practice.

The picture is far less positive with regard to social citizenship. Current trends towards the economic polarization of Western societies and the dismantling of welfare systems make it much more difficult for minorities to achieve the minimum standards necessary for genuine participation. The racialization of social exclusion creates both the material and the ideological conditions for deep societal divisions. Anti-discrimination laws and affirmative action policies have not been very effective in preventing such developments. Here the key to change may lie in social movements, in which ethnic solidarity is used as an instrument to achieve societal inclusion and equality.

Finally, the question of institutional change is the one which rouses most resistance from dominant groups. The idea of changing time-honoured institutions is a threat both to identity and vested interests. Here the need of minorities for the removal of cultural biases has to be linked to the need of the wider population for greater participation. Under existing political arrangements, popular sovereignty has been steadily eroded by the power of experts and the decline of the public sphere. In response, citizens' groups and social movements have demanded 'more democracy in more places' – that is, the decentralization of decision-making to the lowest possible level. New technological developments – such as 'electronic democracy' – could be used to allow much wider participation by citizens. Within such a general movement for democratization, minority demands for a new citizenship may play an important part.

Notes

1 Many of the ideas in this chapter arise from joint work with Alastair Davidson.

2 Civil rights include freedom and inviolability of the person; freedom of expression; freedom of religion; protection from unlawful acts by the state, such as imprisonment or forced labour; equality before the law; prohibition of discrimination on grounds of gender, origins, race, language or beliefs.

3 Political rights include the right to vote and to stand for office at the various levels of government; freedom of assembly and of association; freedom of information (including access to the information needed to understand complex issues in contemporary societies).

4 Social rights include the right to work; equality of opportunity (in education, the labour market, etc.); entitlement to welfare benefits and social services in the event of unemployment or inability to work; entitlement to health services; entitlement to a certain standard of education.

5 But British women got the vote only from the age of 30 in 1918; enfranchisement on the same terms as men came ten years later.

13

POSTSCRIPT: THE NEXT THIRTY YEARS

Looking back over the past thirty years, one cannot help being struck by the dramatic social and cultural changes brought about by migration. When I began research on the theme in Europe in the late 1960s, large numbers of migrant workers and their families had already arrived, but to many members of the receiving populations they were barely visible. Often they were housed on building sites, in hostels or *bidonvilles*, and they did not compete for scarce housing with the local population. They worked long hours and had little social contact outside the workplace. They only became apparent to most citizens at the weekends when they came to the main railway stations to buy homeland newspapers, or when they sought relaxation in bars or dance-halls. Sensationalist headlines portrayed them as strange, exotic and somewhat threatening (for instance, when 'dashing' young Italian workers proved more popular with girls than the local men), but as peripheral to mainstream life. Immigration had not yet shaken insular lifestyles nor questioned myths of national cultural homogeneity. Admittedly, matters were rather different in the USA, where the white–black divide was a stark feature of most cities; this became a burning issue in the mid-1960s due to the Black Power movement and urban riots. The ethnic neighbourhoods created by older European immigrants were also a visible presence in the cityscape. Despite the ideal of Americanization, the third and fourth generations were in the midst of an 'ethnic revival' by the late 1960s. None the less, the diversity was far less pronounced than it would become through later Asian and Hispanic inflows.

How different our cities have become in the meantime! Whether in Europe, North America or Australasia, you have only to take a local bus or train to encounter people of every conceivable ethnic appearance. Distinct ethnic neighbourhoods circle the city centres, and their shops offer a wide range of imported foods, religious symbols and cultural artefacts. Dozens of languages can be heard in the streets, while schools, public offices and hospitals have to cater for a wide range of cultural and linguistic needs. Mainstream cultural and culinary habits have become far more cosmopolitan, and lifestyles have become more varied. Indeed, the notions of majority and minority are themselves becoming eroded, through cultural interaction and intermarriage. In Australia, which has the largest immigrant population share of any developed country, the majority of the population now has mixed ethnic ancestry if one goes back just three generations. Matters have not gone so far elsewhere, but trends are in the same direction. For many people this is deeply threatening: everywhere, immigration and cultural diversity have become pre-eminent sites of contestation.

Moreover, the very nature of population mobility has changed as a result of new technologies of transport and communication. In the past, most transcontinental migration was one way and permanent, while much short-distance migration (for example, from Italy to Germany) was temporary. Today, such differences have become blurred. Remote places like Australia are now so well connected to the rest of the world that they have become hosts to self-styled 'astronauts': people who commute regularly over very long distances. A family of Hong Kong origin may live in Sydney, while the breadwinner works back in Hong Kong, and comes down every weekend. Countries which recruited temporary migrant workers now have millions of permanent settlers. All these types of migrants are affected by the emergence of migration networks, which span countries and continents, and allow people to maintain linkages with people of similar origins everywhere. Personal, religious, cultural and business communities have become truly transnational – a further factor questioning the integrity of nation-states already weakened by economic and political globalization.

So what has happened to those Moroccan and Spanish workers whom Godula Kosack and I interviewed back in 1969? Some have passed away no doubt, while others have managed to return to their homelands, perhaps to enjoy the houses they built with so much sacrifice during their years of exile. But many have remained in France, Switzerland or Germany. Most of them would now be at or close to the end of their working lives. Now a new problem is emerging: how to provide appropriate aged care for older immigrants, who often become socially isolated and revert to their original language late in life. Of course, many older immigrants are fortunate enough to live among their children and grandchildren. These new generations have grown up in situations of ambiguity: are they Germans or Turks, Moroccans or French, both or neither? Many have experienced lack of legal security, unclear citizenship status, discrimination and racism. Anti-immigrant attitudes and frequent changes in laws and policies have compounded the difficulties. Yet the second and third generations have coped with these problems, and in the process many have acquired educational credentials, multi-lingual skills, cross-cultural competencies and a great deal of social and political experience. These are the people who built the anti-racist campaigns of the 1970s and 1980s, and who are now heading movements for new forms of citizenship which are not tied to a certain cultural or national background.

All that has been said so far applies to the highly developed countries that experienced large-scale immigration during the post-war boom years from 1945 to 1973. Since then, new areas of immigration have developed. The southern European emigration countries went through economic and demographic transitions which transformed them into immigration countries by the 1980s. Now they attract workers from Africa, Asia and Eastern Europe. One might think that countries with a long tradition of emigration would be more competent and humane in dealing with immigration, but there is no evidence that this is the case: lack of rights, bureaucratic control and exploitation affect migrants in southern Europe just as much as elsewhere.

Other new immigration areas include the oil-producing countries of the Persian Gulf, other oil economies like Libya, Nigeria and Venezuela, and the newly industrializing countries of Asia and Latin America. Large flows of workers and refugees are to be found throughout the less-developed world. Whether migration takes place through rigid contract systems as in the Gulf states, through the activities of migration agents, or in spontaneous and undocumented forms, there is usually scant regard for the human rights of the migrants. As in Europe in the 1960s, migrant workers are not intended to bring in dependants and settle. Yet there is considerable evidence, even in the Gulf states, that migrants are staying for longer periods, and that family formation is occurring. Perhaps we should not expect a repetition of the settlement patterns typical of Europe, North America or Australasia a generation ago, but nor does it seem likely that all the migrants will return to their countries of origin. The Asian crisis of 1997–8 has already shown that migrants do not simply depart when demand for their labour declines. Community ties, social networks and lack of viable alternatives at home may lead to settlement. The Asian crisis may well prove to be a turning-point from temporary migration to the emergence of multicultural societies in the same way as the 1973 oil crisis was in Europe.

As the main source countries for migrant labour back in the 1960s have become immigration countries, new labour reserve areas have emerged. In Africa, poor areas with large and still fast-growing populations already linked into international mobility chains include North Africa, West Africa and large parts of southern Africa. Turkey, much of Eastern Europe, Russia and many of the Central Asian successor states to the Soviet Union have large labour reserves. The whole of South Asia and large parts of South-east Asia (notably Indonesia, the Philippines, Indo-China and Burma) are already major participants in regional and global migration. In Latin America, migratory streams involve Mexico, the Central American countries, parts of Brazil and the Andean states. The world's largest potential labour reserve is in China: so far the state has kept migration under quite rigid control, permitting only small flows of officially recruited labour, although some irregular movement has begun to emerge. Any major economic or political change in China could unleash huge migratory flows. Emigration from less-developed areas arises from the massive economic and social changes caused by increasing integration into the global economy. In turn the migrants send remittances which accelerate economic change, and bring back new experiences, skills and attitudes. They become agents of social and cultural transformation in their home communities. Where emigration becomes an integral part of economic and social life, change is likely to spill over into the political arena too.

If the past thirty years have changed the world so much, what is likely to happen in the next thirty? No prediction is likely to be accurate – after all, who would have predicted today's multicultural societies and transnational communities back in 1970? However, we can say a few things with some confidence. The most obvious is that there are likely to be dramatic changes, and that the ethnoscape of 2030 will be at least as different from that of today as today is from 1970. A second statement that can be made with some confidence is that the changes of the past thirty years cannot be reversed: there is no way back to the relatively autonomous and homogeneous national societies of the past. It must be added that these had been more myth than reality for a long time, but at least they were sustainable myths, while in the future it will be very hard to make such claims.

But what changes can we expect? Perhaps answers may be found by extrapolating the trends of recent years. More people are likely to migrate more frequently. Just as the rapid technological shifts in modern economies require workers to change their occupations several times in a working life, it will become more and more common for people to spend periods working in different countries. This already applies to highly skilled people who sell their labour-power in international labour markets. Lower-skilled workers will migrate either because they cannot gain a livelihood at all at home or because the opportunities are greater elsewhere. Transport and communication techniques are likely to go on improving, so that migration will become relatively cheaper and easier. In addition, the globalization of the media and improvements in education will give more people the cultural capital needed to migrate. The social networks that have become such a feature of migration will continue to facilitate and structure migratory movements. Forced migration is likely to continue too: political, religious and ethnic conflicts will go on producing streams of refugees, while environmental catastrophes linked to overuse of resources and global warming may generate large flows of environmental refugees. Some new types of migration are likely to expand, such as retirement migration: already senior citizens from Britain, Scandinavia and Germany are repopulating Tuscany, the Costa del Sol and the Greek islands, while elderly Japanese and Koreans are moving to Australia and New Zealand. Posthumous migration may also grow, for many migrants have indicated that they want their bodies flown home to rest in their native soil after death. In summary, international migration looks likely to grow at least as rapidly as in the past whatever governments do to restrict it.

Similarly, trends towards the emergence of multicultural societies are likely to continue. At the same time, there will be a further growth in flexible forms of migration with frequent multi-directional movements. Together, these trends will encourage the development of transnational communities. Borders will become even more porous, and more and more people will have multiple identities, transnational affiliations and dual (or multiple) citizenships. The cultural diversification of populations within state boundaries is likely to have significant effects on legal frameworks and political institutions. Already, many immigration countries have changed their citizenship laws (sometimes repeatedly). This process is certainly not complete. Obviously, change in this area is likely to be uneven and conflictual because it goes to the heart of national myths and entrenched political and economic interests. It seems possible that change will be easiest in traditional immigration countries which are already moving towards pluralist models of belonging. Change may be hardest in post-colonial nations which are still struggling to build national identities under the difficult conditions of globalization. Overall, population mobility will be one of the major forces of globalization, which is challenging the position of the nation-state as the pre-eminent political unit. Migration will contribute to the development of infra- and supranational levels of political identity, making it necessary to re-think the meaning of democracy.

The big question is whether democratic frameworks for the peaceful negotiation of economic interests, social difference and cultural identity can be constructed, or whether such processes will take on divisive or even violent forms. Another trend which, unfortunately, is likely to persist is that of the growing politicization of ethno-cultural difference. This may well take the form of a political backlash against minorities, and demands for the restriction of their rights. In the 1990s, movements against immigration and multiculturalism developed in many highly developed countries. Scapegoating of minorities for economic and social problems has also been a prominent feature of the Asian crisis, especially in Indonesia and Malaysia. Anti-immigrant slogans are often the rallying-point for parties and movements seeking to mobilize groups which feel threatened by globalization and economic change. Again, there is every reason to fear that trends towards increasing economic polarization and social exclusion will continue in many societies, and immigrants and minorities will bear the main brunt.

All these expectations may prove false. The period ahead may see dramatic economic, environmental or political changes which may make all extrapolation of past trends irrelevant. None the less, it seems highly probable that the world in thirty years' time will be even more mobile and cosmopolitan than today, but just as contradictory and conflictual. Despite the many problems examined in this book, the past thirty years of migration and the emergence of multicultural societies can also be interpreted as a triumph of the human agency of millions of ordinary people over deprivation, exploitation and discrimination. While many politicians, administrators and academics conspicuously failed to understand what was going on, migrant workers, families and communities were busy building new lives for themselves. In doing so they changed the world in unpredicted ways. This too may be the case in future.

REFERENCES

Abella, M. (1992) 'The troublesome gulf: research on migration to the Middle East', *Asian and Pacific Migration Journal*, 1 (1): 145–67.

Abella, M. (1995) 'Asian migrant and contract workers in the Middle East', in R. Cohen (ed.), *The Cambridge Survey of World Migration*. Cambridge: Cambridge University Press. pp. 418–23.

Adelman, H., Borowski, A., Burstein, M. and Foster, L. (eds) (1993) *Immigration and Refugee Policy: Australia and Canada Compared*, 2 vols. Melbourne: Melbourne University Press.

ADL (1988) *Hate Groups in America*. New York: Anti-Defamation League of B'nai B'rith.

Aguilar Jr, F.V. (1996) 'The dialectics of transnational shame and national identity', *Philippine Sociological Review*, 44 (1–4): 101–36.

Akpinar, U., Lopez-Blasco, A. and Vink, J. (1977) *Pädagogische Arbeit mit ausländischen Kindern und Jugendlichen*. Munich: Juventa Verlag.

Alba, R. and Nee, V. (1997) 'Rethinking assimilation theory for a new era of immigration', *International Migration Review*, 31 (4): 826–74.

Ålund, A. and Schierup, C-U. (1991) *Paradoxes of Multiculturalism: Essays on Swedish Society*. Aldershot: Avebury.

Amjad, R. (1996) 'Philippines and Indonesia: on the way to a migration transition', *Asian and Pacific Migration Journal*, 5 (2–3): 339–66.

Anderson, B. (1983) *Imagined Communities*. London: Verso.

Andric, I. (1994) *The Bridge over the Drina*. London: Havill.

Anon. (1969) 'L'insertion sociale des étrangers dans l'aire métropolitaine Lyon-Saint-Étienne', *Hommes et Migrations*, 113.

Anthias, F. and Yuval-Davis, N. (1983) 'Contextualising feminism: gender, ethnic and class divisions', *Feminist Review*, 15: 62–75.

Anthias, F. and Yuval-Davis, N. (1989) 'Introduction', in F. Anthias and N. Yuval-Davis (eds), *Woman–Nation–State*. Basingstoke and London: Macmillan. pp. 1–15.

Australian Bureau of Statistics (ABS) (1995) *National Aboriginal and Torres Strait Islander Survey 1994: Detailed Findings*. Canberra: AGPS.

Australian Council of Trade Unions (ACTU) (1995) *Combating Racism: Discrimination and Racism during 1994: How Far in Fact Have We Come?* Melbourne: ACTU.

Bader, V. (ed.) (1997) *Citizenship and Exclusion*. London: Macmillan.

Bagley, C. (1970) *Social Structure and Prejudice in Five English Boroughs*. London: Institute of Race Relations.

Balibar, E. (1991a) '*Es gibt keinen Staat in Europa*: racism and politics in Europe today', *New Left Review*, 186: 5–19.

Balibar, E. (1991b) 'Racism and crisis', in E. Balibar and I. Wallerstein (eds), *Race, Nation, Class: Ambiguous Identities*. London: Verso. pp. 217–27.

Balibar, E. (1991c) 'Class racism', in E. Balibar and I. Wallerstein (eds), *Race, Nation, Class: Ambiguous Identities*. London: Verso. pp. 204–16.

Balibar, E. (1991d) 'Is there a neo-racism?', in E. Balibar and I. Wallerstein (eds), *Race, Nation, Class: Ambiguous Identities*. London: Verso. pp. 17–28.

Balibar, E. (1991e) 'Racism and nationalism', in E. Balibar and I. Wallerstein (eds), *Race, Nation, Class: Ambiguous Identities*. London: Verso. pp. 37–67.

Ball, W. and Solomos, J. (eds) (1990) *Race and Local Politics*. London: Macmillan.

Barker, M. (1981) *The New Racism*. London: Junction Books.

Barrett, M. (1980) *Women's Oppression Today*. London: Verso.

Basch, L., Glick-Schiller, N. and Blanc, C.S. (1994) *Nations Unbound: Transnational Projects, Post-colonial Predicaments and Deterritorialized Nation-states*. New York: Gordon and Breach.

Battistella, G. and Assis, M. (1998) *The Impact of the Crisis on Migration in Asia*. Manila: Scalabrini Migration Center.

Battistella, G. and Paganoni, A. (1992) *Philippine Labor Migration: Impact and Policy*. Quezon City: Scalabrini Migration Center.

Bauböck, R. (1994) 'Changing the boundaries of citizenship: the inclusion of immigrants in democratic polities', in R. Bauböck (ed.), *From Aliens to Citizens*. Aldershot: Avebury. pp. 199–232.

Bauböck, R. and Rundell, J. (eds) (1998) *Blurred Boundaries: Migration, Ethnicity, Citizenship*. Aldershot: Ashgate.

Becker, R., Dörr, G. and Tjaden, K.H. (1971) 'Fremdarbeiterbeschäftigung im deutschen Kapitalismus', *Das Argument*, December.

Bell, D. (1992) *Faces at the Bottom of the Well: the Permanence of Racism*. New York: Basic Books.

Berger, J. and Mohr, J. (1975) *A Seventh Man*. Harmondsworth: Penguin.

Beschluss der Kultusministerkonferenz (1976) *Neufassung der Vereinbarung 'Unterricht für Kinder ausländischer Arbeitnehmer' 8 April 1976*. Bonn: Kultusministerkonferenz.

Bielefeld, U. (ed.) (1990) *Das Eigene und das Fremde*. Hamburg: Junius.

BIMPR (Bureau of Immigration, Multicultural and Population Research) (1995) *Immigration Update: June Quarter 1995*. Canberra: AGPS.

Birks, J.S., Sinclair, C.A. and Seccombe, I.J. (1986) 'Migrant workers in the Arab Gulf: the impact of declining oil revenues', *International Migration Review*, 20 (4): 799–814.

Björgo, T. and Witte, R. (1993) 'Introduction', in T. Björgo and R. Witte (eds), *Racist Violence in Europe*. London: Macmillan. pp. 1–16.

Blanc, C.S. (1996) 'Balikbayan: a Filipino extension of the national imaginary and of state boundaries', *Philippine Sociological Review*, 44 (1–4): 178–93.

Blaschke, J. (1990) 'Foreigners' work in Germany: demographic patterns, trends and consequences'. Unpublished manuscript.

Böhning, W.R. (1998) *The Impact of the Asian Crisis on Filipino Employment Prospects Abroad*, SEAPAT working paper 1. Geneva: International Labour Office.

Boos-Nünning, U. and Hohmann, M. (1976) 'Probleme des Unterrichts in der Grund-und Hauptschule aus der Sicht der Lehrer in Vorbereitungs-und Regelklassen', in M. Hohmann (ed.), *Unterricht mit ausländischen Kindern*. Dusseldorf.

Borjas, G.J. (1989) 'Economic theory and international migration', *International Migration Review*, 23 (3): 457–85.

Borjas, G.J. (1990) *Friends or Strangers: the Impact of Immigration on the US Economy*. New York: Basic Books.

Bouamama, S. (1994) *Dix ans de marche des beurs*. Paris: Desclée de Brouwer.

Bouamama, S., Cordeiro, A. and Roux, M. (1992) *La Citoyenneté dans tous ses états*. Paris: CIEMI l'Harmattan.

Boyd, M. (1989) 'Family and personal networks in migration', *International Migration Review*, 23 (3): 638–70.

Boyle, P., Halfacree, K. and Robinson, V. (1998) *Exploring Contemporary Migration*. Harlow, Essex: Longman.

Brah, A. (1991) 'Difference, diversity, differentiation', in J. Donald and A. Rattansi (eds), *'Race', Culture and Difference*. London, Newbury Park and New Delhi: Sage. pp. 126–45.

Brah, A. (1993) 'Difference, diversity, differentiation: processes of racialisation and gender', in J. Wrench and J. Solomos (eds), *Racism and Migration in Western Europe*. Oxford: Berg. pp. 195–214.

Breton, R., Isajiw, W.W., Kalbach, W.E. and Reitz, J.G. (1990) *Ethnic Identity and Equality*. Toronto: University of Toronto Press.

Briggs Jr, V.M. (1986) 'The "albatross" of immigration reform: temporary worker policy in the United States', *International Migration Review*, 20 (4): 995–1019.

Brubaker, W.R. (1990) 'Citizenship and nationhood in France and Germany'. PhD thesis, Columbia University.

Brubaker, W.R. (1992) 'Citizenship struggles in Soviet successor states', *International Migration Review*, 26 (2): 269–91.

Bundesanstalt für Arbeit (1970) *Ausländische Arbeitnehmer 1969*. Nüremberg: Bundesanstalt für Arbeit.

Bundesanstalt für Arbeit (1971) *Ausländische Arbeitnehmer 1970*. Nüremberg: Bundesanstalt für Arbeit.

Bundesminister für Arbeit und Sozialordnung (1977) *Vorschlädge der Bund-Länder Kommission zur Fortentwicklung einer umfassenden Konzeption der Ausländerbeschäftigungspolitik*. Bonn: Bundesminister für Arbeit und Sozialordnung.

Bundesvereinigung Deutscher Arbeitgberverbände (1966) *Magnet Bundesrepbulik*. Bonn: Köllen Verlag.

Butterwegge, C. and Jäger, S. (eds) (1992) *Rassismus in Europa*. Cologne: Bund Verlag.

Carnoy, M. (1994) *Faded Dreams: the Politics and Economics of Race in America*. Cambridge: Cambridge University Press.

Castells, M. (1996) *The Rise of the Network Society*. Oxford: Blackwell.

Castles, S. (1968) 'Social aspects of the mobility of labour: foreign workers in the German Federal Republic'. Masters thesis, University of Sussex.

Castles, S. (1985) 'The guests who stayed – the debate on "foreigners policy" in the German Federal Republic', *International Migration Review*, 19 (3): 517–34.

Castles, S. (1990) 'Sozialwissenschaft und ethnische Minderheiten in Australien', in E.J. Dittrich and F-O. Radtke (eds), *Ethnizität: Wissenschaft und Minderheiten*. Opladen: Westdeutscher Verlag. pp. 43–72.

Castles, S. (1993) *Racism: a Global Analysis*, occasional paper no. 28. Wollongong: University of Wollongong, Centre for Multicultural Studies.

Castles, S. (1994) 'Democracy and multicultural citizenship: Australian debates and their relevance for Western Europe', R. Bauböck (ed.), *From Aliens to Citizens*. Aldershot: Avebury. pp. 3–27.

Castles, S. (1995) 'How nation-states respond to immigration and ethnic diversity', *New Community*, 21 (3): 293–308.

Castles, S. (1996) 'A German dilemma: ethnic identity and citizenship', in G. Fischer (ed.), *Debating Enzensberger: 'Great Migration' and 'Civil War'*. Tübingen: Stauffenberg. pp. 169–86.

Castles, S. (1998a) 'New migrations in the Asia-Pacific region: a force for social and political change', *International Social Science Journal*, 156: 215–27.

Castles, S. (1998b) 'Globalisation and the ambiguities of national citizenship', in R. Bauböck and J. Rundle (eds), *Blurred Boundaries: Migration, Ethnicity, Citizenship*. Aldershot: Avebury. pp. 223–44.

Castles, S. and Davidson, A. (2000) *Citizenship and Migration: Globalisation and the Politics of Belonging*. London: Macmillan.

Castles, S. and Kosack, G. (1973) *Immigrant Workers and Class Structure in Western Europe*. London: Oxford University Press. 2nd edn, 1985.

Castles, S. and Kosack, G. (1974) 'How the trade unions try to control and integrate immigrant workers in the German Federal Republic', *Race*, 15 (4): 497–514.

Castles, S. and Miller, M. (1993) *The Age of Migration: International Population Movements in the Modern World*. London: Macmillan.

Castles, S. and Miller, M.J. (1998) *The Age of Migration: International Population Movements in the Modern World*, 2nd edn. London: Macmillan.

Castles, S. and Wüstenberg, W. (1979) *The Education of the Future: an Introduction to the Theory and Practice of Socialist Education*. London: Pluto Press.

Castles, S., Booth, H. and Wallace, T. (1984) *Here for Good: Western Europe's New Ethnic Minorities*. London: Pluto Press.

Castles, S., Cope, B., Kalantzis, M. and Morrissey, M. (1988) 'The bicentenary and the failure of Australian nationalism', *Race and Class*, 29 (3): 53–68.

Castles, S., Kalantzis, M., Cope, B. and Morrissey, M. (1992) *Mistaken Identity: Multiculturalism and the Demise of Nationalism in Australia*. Sydney: Pluto Press.

Centre for Contemporary Cultural Studies (1982) *The Empire Strikes Back*. London: Hutchinson.

Çinar, D. (1994) 'From aliens to citizens: a comparative analysis of rules of transition', in R. Bauböck (ed.), *From Aliens to Citizens*. Aldershot: Avebury. pp. 49–72.

Cohen, P. and Bains, H.S. (1988) *Multi-racist Britain*. Basingstoke and London: Macmillan.

Cohen, R. (1987) *The New Helots: Migrants in the International Division of Labour*. Aldershot: Avebury.

Cohen, R. (ed.) (1995) *The Cambridge Survey of World Migration*. Cambridge: Cambridge University Press.

Cohen, R. (1997) *Global Diasporas: an Introduction*. London: UCL Press.

Cohn-Bendit, D. and Schmid, T. (1993) *Heimat Babylon: Das Wagnis der multikulturellen Demokratie*. Hamburg: Hoffmann und Campe.

Collins, J. (1991) *Migrant Hands in a Distant Land: Australia's Post-war Immigration*. Sydney: Pluto Press.

Connell, R.W. (1997) 'Why is classical theory classical?', *American Journal of Sociology*, 102 (6): 1511–57.

Cox, O.C. (1959) *Caste, Class and Race*. New York: Monthly Review Press.

Cross, G.S. (1983) *Immigrant Workers in Industrial France: the Making of a New Laboring Class*. Philadelphia: Temple University Press.

Cross, M. (1995) 'Race, class formation and political interests: a comparison of Amsterdam and London', in A. Hargreaves and J. Leaman (eds), *Racism, Ethnicity and Politics in Contemporary Europe*. Aldershot: Edward Elgar. pp. 47–78.

Cross, M. and Keith, M. (1993) *Racism, the City and the State*. London: Routledge.

Dacanay, M.L.M. (1997) 'Citizenship in an era of globalisation: a view from the Philippines', paper presented at the Conference on Globalisation and Citizenship, United Nations Research Institute for Social Development and Swinburne University of Technology, Melbourne.

Daniels, W.W. (1968) *Racial Discrimination in England*. Harmondsworth: Penguin.

Davidson, A. (1993) 'Understanding citizenship in Australia', in Public Affairs Research Centre (ed.), *Beyond the Headlines: Politics, Australia and the World*. Melbourne: Public Affairs Research Centre. pp. 1–13.

Davidson, A. (1997) *From Subject to Citizen: Australian Citizenship in the Twentieth Century*. Cambridge: Cambridge University Press.

Davidson, A. and Weekley, K. (eds) (1999) *Globalization and Citizenship in the Asia-Pacific*. London: Macmillan.

Davis, M. (1990) *City of Quartz: Excavating the Future in Los Angeles*. London: Verso.

Dohse, K. (1981) *Ausländische Arbeiter und bürgerliche Staat*. Konistein/Taunus: Hain.

Dubet, F. and Lapeyronnie, D. (1992) *Les Quartiers d'exil*. Paris: Seuil.

Engels, F. (1962a) 'The condition of the working class in England', in K. Marx and F. Engels (eds), *On Britain*. Moscow: Foreign Languages Publishing House.

Engels, F. (1962b) 'Preface to the English edition of "The condition of the working class in England"', in K. Marx and F. Engels (eds), *On Britain*. Moscow: Foreign Languages Publishing House.

Engels, F. (1962c) 'The English elections', in K. Marx, and F. Engels (eds), *On Britain*. Moscow: Foreign Languages Publishing House.

Esman, M. (1992) 'The political fallout of international migration', *Diaspora*, 2 (1): 3–42.

Esman, M. (1994) *Ethnic Politics*. Ithaca and London: Cornell University Press.

Essed, P. (1991) *Understanding Everyday Racism*. Newbury Park, London and New Delhi: Sage.

European Parliament (1985) *Committee of Inquiry into the Rise of Fascism and Racism in Europe: Report on the Findings of the Inquiry*. Strasbourg: European Parliament.

Fahin and Seidel-Pielen (1992) *Rechtsruck: Rassismus im neuen Deutschland*. Berlin: Rotbuch.

Fawcett, J.T. (1989) 'Network linkages and migration systems', *International Migration Review*, 23 (3): 671–80.

Featherstone, M. (ed.) (1990) *Global Culture: Nationalism, Globalization and Modernity*. Newbury Park, London, New Delhi: Sage.

Fries, T. (1975) 'Auszug aus einem Info des BV Frankfurt – 40% aller Grundschulanfänger Ausländerkinder', *Hessische Lehrerzeitung*, January– February.

Galtung, J. (1988) 'On violence in general and terrorism in particular', in J. Galtung (ed.), *Transarmament and the Cold War: Essays in Peace Research*, vol. 6. Copenhagen: Christian Ejlers. pp. 281–97.

Gavi, P. (1970) *Les Ouvriers*. Paris.

Gellner, E. (1983) *Nations and Nationalism*. Oxford: Blackwell.

Gienanth, Ulrich Freiherr von (1996) 'in', *Der Arbeitgeber*, 18 (20 March).

Gilroy, P. (1987) *There Ain't no Black in the Union Jack*. London: Hutchinson.

Gilroy, P. (1992) 'The end of antiracism', in J. Donald and A. Rattansi (eds), *Race, Culture and Difference*. Newbury Park, London, New Delhi: Sage. pp. 49–61.

Glyn, A. and Harrison, J. (1980) *The British Economic Disaster*. London: Pluto Press.

Goldberg, D. (1993) *Racist Culture: Philosophy and the Politics of Meaning*. Oxford: Blackwell.

Goldberg, D. (1994) *Multiculturalism: a Critical Reader*. Cambridge, MA: Blackwell.

Golini, A., Gesano, B. and Heins, F. (1990) 'South–north migration with special reference to Europe', paper presented at the International Organization for Migration Seminar on Migration, Geneva.

Gordon, M. (1964) *Assimilation in American Life: the Role of Race, Religion and National Origins*. New York: Oxford University Press.

Grahl, J. (1983) 'Restructuring in West European industry', *Capital and Class*, 19 (Spring): 118–41.

Gregory, J. (1987) *Sex, Race and the Law*. London: Sage.

Guimezanes, N. (1995) 'Acquisition of nationality in OECD countries', in OECD (ed.), *Trends in International Migration: Annual Report*. Paris: OECD. pp. 157–79.

Gutmann, A. (ed.) (1994) *Multiculturalism: Examining the Politics of Recognition*. Princeton, NJ: Princeton University Press.

Habermas, J. (1994) 'Struggles for recognition in the democratic constitutional state', in A. Gutmann (ed.), *Multiculturalism: Examining the Politics of Recognition*. Princeton, NJ: Princeton University Press. pp. 107–48.

Habermas, J. (1996) *Die Einbeziehung des Anderen: Studien zur politischen Theorie*. Frankfurt am Main: Suhrkamp.

Hacker, A. (1992) *Two Nations: Black and White, Separate, Hostile, Unequal*. New York: Charles Scribner's Sons.

Hammar, T. (1985) 'Sweden', in T. Hammar (ed.), *European Immigration Policy: a Comparative Study*. Cambridge: Cambridge University Press. pp. 17–49.

Hammar, T. (1990) Democracy and the *Nation-state: Aliens, Denizens and Citizens in a World of International Migration*. Aldershot: Avebury.

Hammar, T. (1993) 'Political participation and civil rights in Scandinavia', in J. Wrench and J. Solomos (eds), *Racism and Migration in Western Europe*. Oxford: Berg. pp. 115–28.

Hartmann, H. (1979) 'The unhappy marriage of Marxism and feminism: towards a more progressive union', *Capital and Class*, 8 (Summer): 1–33.

Hawthorne, L. (1994) *Labour Market Barriers for Immigrant Engineers in Australia*. Canberra: AGPS.

Hepple, B. (1968) *Race, Jobs and the Law in Britain*. London: Penguin.

Hoffmann, L. (1990) *Die unvollendete Republik*. Cologne: Pappy Rossa Verlag.

HREOC (Human Rights and Equal Opportunity Commission) (1991) *Racist Violence: Report of the National Inquiry into Racist Violence in Australia*. Canberra: AGPS.

HREOC (Human Rights and Equal Opportunity Commission) (1993) *State of the Nation 1993: a Report on People of Non-English Speaking Backgrounds*. Canberra: AGPS.

HREOC (Human Rights and Equal Opportunity Commission) (1994) *State of the Nation 1994: a Report on People of Non-English Speaking Backgrounds*. Canberra: AGPS.

Hugo, G. (1994) *Migration and the Family*. Vienna: United Nations Occasional Papers Series for the International Year of the Family, no. 12.

Hugo, G. (1998) 'The demographic underpinnings of current and future international migration in Asia', *Asian and Pacific Migration Journal*, 7 (1): 1–25.

Huguet, J.W. (1995) 'Data on international migration in Asia: 1990–94', *Asian and Pacific Migration Journal*, 4 (4): 517–27.

Husband, C. (1982) 'Introduction: "race", the continuity of a concept', in C. Husband (ed.), *Race in Britain: Continuity and Change*. London: Hutchinson. pp. 11–23.

International Organization for Migration (IOM) (1990) 'Background document', presented at the IOM Seminar on Migration, Geneva.

Jayasuriya, L. (1993) 'The idea of citizenship for a multicultural Australia', paper presented at the Seminar on Ideas for Australia, Sydney.

Jones, K. and Smith, A.D. (1970) *The Economic Impact of Commonwealth Immigration*. Cambridge: Cambridge University Press.

Kalpaka, A. and Räthzel, N. (eds) (1990) *Die Schwierigkeit, nicht rassistisch zu sein*, 2nd edn. Leer: Mundo.

Kassim, A. (1998) 'The case of a new receiving country in the developing world: Malaysia', paper presented at the Technical Symposium on International Migration and Development, The Hague.

Kindleberger, C.P. (1967) *Europe's Post-war Growth: the Role of Labor Supply*. Cambridge, MA: Harvard University Press.

King, A.D. (ed.) (1991) *Culture, Globalization and the World-system*. London: Macmillan.

King, R. (1996) 'Review article. Of free movement and the fortress: recent books on European migration', *West European Politics*, 19 (1): 176–81.

Komai, H. (1998) 'Migrants in Japan', paper presented at the Technical Symposium on International Migration and Development, The Hague.

Korfes, G. (1992) 'Rechtsextreme Bewegungen und rechtslastige Jugendkulturen in Ostdeutschland', in C. Butterwegge and S. Jäger (eds), *Rassismus in Europa*. Cologne: Bund Verlag. pp. 71–85.

Kritz, M.M., Lin, L.L. and Zlotnik, H. (eds) (1992) *International Migration Systems: a Global Approach*. Oxford: Clarendon Press.

Kuhn, T.S. (1962) *The Structure of Scientific Revolutions*. Chicago: University of Chicago Press.

Kymlicka, W. (1995) *Multicultural Citizenship: a Liberal Theory of Minority Rights*. Oxford: Clarendon Press.

Lapeyronnie, D., Frybes, M., Couper, K. and Joly, D. (1990) *L'Intégration des minorités immigrées étude comparative: France – Grande Bretagne*. Paris: Agence pour le Développement des Relations Interculturelles.

Layton-Henry, Z. (1992) *The Politics of Immigration*. Oxford: Blackwell.

Lenin, V.I. (1966) *Imperialism: the Highest Stage of Capitalism*. Moscow: Foreign Languages Publishing House.

de Lepervanche, M. (1975) 'Australian immigrants 1788–1940: desired and unwanted', in E.L. Wheelwright and K. Buckley (eds), *Essays in the Political Economy of Australian Capitalism* vol. 1 Sydney: Australia and New Zealand Book Co. pp. 72–104.

Light, I. and Bonacich, E. (1988) *Immigrant Entrepreneurs*. Berkeley, CA: University of California Press.

Lim, L.L. and Oishi, N. (1996) 'International labor migration of Asian women', *Asian and Pacific Migration Journal*, 5 (1): 85–116.

Lutz, H., Phoenix, A. and Yuval-Davis, N. (1995) 'Introduction: nationalism, racism and gender', in H. Lutz, A. Phoenix and N. Yuval-Davis (eds), *Crossfires: Nationalism, Racism and Gender in Europe*. London: Pluto Press. pp. 1–25.

Maaz, H.J. (1992) *Der Gefühlsstau: ein Psychogramm der DDR*. Munich: Knaur.

Marable, M. and Mullings, L. (1994) 'The divided mind of Black America: ideology and politics in the post-Civil Rights era', *Race and Class*, 36 (1): 61–72.

Marshall, T.H. (1950) *Citizenship and Social Class*. Cambridge: Cambridge University Press.

Marshall, T.H. (1964) 'Citizenship and social class', *Class, Citizenship and Social Development: Essays by T.H. Marshall*. New York: Anchor Books.

Martin, J. (1986) 'Non-English speaking migrant women in Australia', in N. Grieve and A. Burns (eds), *Australian Women: New Feminist Perspectives*. Melbourne: Oxford University Press.

Martin, P. (1991) 'Labor migration in Asia: conference report', *International Migration Review*, 25 (1): 176–93.

Martin, P., Mason, A. and Nagayama, T. (1996) 'Introduction to special issue on the dynamics of labor migration in Asia', *Asian and Pacific Migration Journal*, 5 (2–3): 163–73.

Martiniello, M. (1994) 'Citizenship of the European Union: a critical view', in R. Bauböck (ed.), *From Aliens to Citizens*. Aldershot: Avebury. pp. 29–48.

Marx, K. (1961) *Capital*, vol. 1. Moscow: Foreign Languages Publishing House.

Marx, K. and Engels, F. (1962) *On Britain*. Moscow: Foreign Languages Publishing House.

Massey, D.S., Arango, J., Hugo, G., Kouaouci, A., Pellegrino, A. and Taylor, E. (1993) 'Theories of international migration: a review and appraisal', *Population and Development Review*, 19 (3): 431–66.

Massey, D.S., Arango, J., Hugo, G. and Taylor, J.E. (1994) 'An evaluation of international migration theory: the North American case', *Population and Development Review*, 20: 699–751.

Mead, L. (1986) *Beyond Entitlement: the Social Obligations of Citizenship*. New York: Free Press.

Meehan, E. (1993) *Citizenship and the European Community*. London: Sage.

Messina, A.M. (1996) 'The not so silent revolution: postwar migration to Western Europe', *World Politics*, 49: 130–54.

Miles, R. (1989) *Racism*. London: Routledge.

Miles, R. (1993a) 'The articulation of racism and nationalism: reflections on European history', in J. Wrench and J. Solomos (eds), *Racism and Migration in Western Europe*. Oxford: Berg. pp. 35–52.

Miles, R. (1993b) *Racism after 'Race Relations'*. London: Routledge.

Mingione, E. (1996) 'Urban poverty in the advanced industrial world: concepts, analysis and debates', in E. Mingione (ed.), *Urban Poverty and the Underclass*. Oxford: Blackwell. pp. 3–40.

Ministère de l'Intérieur (1970) 'Statistiques du Ministère de l'Intérieur', *Hommes et Migrations*, 788.

Ministry of Labour Sweden (1990) 'The pre-requisites for and the direction of a comprehensive refugee and immigration policy', paper presented at the International Organization for Migration Seminar on Migration, Geneva.

Mitter, S. (1986) 'Industrial restructuring and manufacturing homework: immigrant women in the UK clothing industry', *Capital and Class*, 27 (Winter): 37–80.

Montagu, A. (1974) *Man's Most Dangerous Myth: the Fallacy of Race*. New York: Oxford University Press.

Mori, H. (1997) *Immigration Policy and Foreign Workers in Japan*. London: Macmillan.

Mörshäuser, B. (1992) *Hauptsache Deutsch*. Frankfurt am Main: Suhrkamp.

Nairn, T. (1980) *The Break-up of Britain*. London: New Left Books.

Netherlands Scientific Council for Government Policy (1979) *Ethnic Minorities*. The Hague: Netherlands Government.

Nicoladze, R.D., Rendu, C. and Millet, G. (1969) 'Coupable d'être malades', *Droit et Liberté*, 280 (March).

Nirumand, B. (1992) 'Vorwort', in B. Nirumand (ed.), *Angst vor den Deutschen: Terror gegen Ausländer und der Zerfall des Rechtstaates*. Reinbek bei Hamburg: Rowolt.

NMAC (National Multicultural Advisory Council) (1995) *Multicultural Australia: the Next Steps – Towards and Beyond 2000*, 2 vols. Canberra: AGPS.

Noiriel, G. (1988) *Le creuset français: histoire de l'immigration XIXe–XXe siècles*. Paris: Seuil.

NPC (National Population Council) (1991) *Refugee Review*. Canberra: National Population Council.

Oberndörfer, D. (1993) *Der Wahn des Nationalen*. Freiburg: Herder.

OECD (Organization for Economic Cooperation and Development) (1978) *Migration Growth and Development*. Paris: OECD.

OECD (Organization for Economic Cooperation and Development) (1995) *Trends in International Migration: Annual Report 1994*. Paris: OECD.

Office of Multicultural Affairs (1989) *National Agenda for a Multicultural Australia*. Canberra: AGPS.

Office of Multicultural Affairs (1992) *Access and Equity: Evaluation Report*. Canberra: AGPS.

Office National d'Immigration (1968) *Statistiques d'Immigration*. Paris: ONI.

Park, R.E. (1950) *Race and Culture*. Glencoe, IL: The Free Press.

Pateman, C. (1985) *The Problem of Political Obligation: a Critique of Liberal Theory*. Cambridge: Polity Press.

Pateman, C. (1988) *The Sexual Contract*. Cambridge: Polity Press.

Pfahlmann, H. (1968) *Fremdarbeiter und Kriegsgefangene in der deutschen Kriegswirtschaft 1939–45*. Darmstadt: Wehr und Wissen.

Phizacklea, A. (1985) 'Minority women and restructuring: the case of Britain, France and the Federal Republic of Germany', paper presented at the Conference on Racial Minorities, Economic Restructuring and Urban Decline, University of Warwick.

Phizacklea, A. (1990) *Unpacking the Fashion Industry: Gender, Racism and Class in Production*. London: Routledge.

Piore, M. (1980) *Birds of Passage: Migrant Labor and Industrial Societies*. Cambridge: Cambridge University Press.

Portes, A. and Böröcz, J. (1989) 'Contemporary immigration: theoretical perspectives on its determinants and modes of incorporation', *International Migration Review*, 28 (4): 606–30.

Portes, A. and Rumbaut, R.G. (1990) *Immigrant America: a Portrait*. Los Angeles: University of California Press.

Potts, L. (1990) *The World Labour Market: a History of Migration*. London: Zed Books.

Purcell, J.N. (1990) 'Statement by the Director General of the IOM', presented at the International Organization for Migration Seminar on Migration, Geneva.

Rath, J. (1993) 'The ideological representation of migrant workers in Europe: a matter of racialisation?', in J. Wrench and J. Solomos (eds), *Racism and Migration in Western Europe*. Oxford: Berg. pp. 215–32.

Rawls, J. (1985) 'Justice as fairness: political not metaphysical', *Philosophy and Public Affairs*, 14 (3): 223–51.

Reich, R.B. (1991) *The Work of Nations*. London: Simon and Schuster.

Renan, E. (1992) *Qu'est-ce qu'une nation? et autres essais politiques*, introduced by J. Roman. Paris: Presses Pocket, Agora.

Rex, J. and Mason, D. (eds) (1986) *Theories of Race and Ethnic Relations*. Cambridge: Cambridge University Press.

Ricca, S. (1990) *Migrations internationales en Afrique*. Paris: L'Harmattan.

Robertson, R. (1992) *Globalisation: Social Theory and Global Culture*. London, Newbury Park, New Delhi: Sage.

Rodan, G. (ed.) (1996) *Political Oppositions in Industrialising Asia*. London: Routledge.

Rose, E.J.B., Deakin, N., Abrams, M., Jackson, V., Peston, M., Vanags, A.H., Cohen, B., Gaitskell, J. and Ward, P. (1969) *Colour and Citizenship*. London: Oxford University Press.

Salowsky, H. (1972) 'Sozialpolitische Aspekte der Auslanderbeschaftigung', *Berichte des Deutschen Industrie instituts zur Sozialpolitik*, 6 (2).

Sassen, S. (1988) *The Mobility of Labour and Capital*. Cambridge: Cambridge University Press.

Sassen-Koob, A. (1985) 'Capital mobility and labour migration: their expression in core cities', paper presented at the Conference on Racial Minorities, Economic Restructuring and Urban Decline, University of Warwick, Centre for Research in Ethnic Relations.

Schierup, C.-U. (1993) 'Prelude to the inferno – economic disintegration and the political fragmentation of Yugoslavia', *Migration*, 19 (93): 5–40.

Schierup, C.-U. (1997) *Multipoverty Europe: Reflections on Migration, Citizenship and Social Exclusion in the European Union and the United States*. Umeå: unpublished manuscript.

Schnapper, D. (1991) 'A host country of immigrants that does not know itself', *Diaspora*, 1 (3): 353–64.

Schnapper, D. (1994) *La Communauté des citoyens*. Paris: Gallimard.

Sekine, M. (1990) *Guest Workers in Japan*, occasional paper no. 21. Wollongong: University of Wollongong, Centre for Multicultural Studies.

Seton-Watson, H. (1977) *Nations and States*. London: Methuen.

Sivanandan, A. (1979) 'Imperialism and disorganic development in the silicon age', *Race and Class*, 21 (Autumn): 111–26.

Sivanandan, A. (1982) *A Different Hunger*. London: Pluto Press.

Skeldon, R. (1992) 'International migration within and from the East and South-east Asian region: a review essay', *Asian and Pacific Migration Journal*, 1 (1): 19–63.

Skeldon, R. (1997) *Migration and Development: a Global Perspective*. Harlow, Essex: Addison Wesley Longman.

Skeldon, R. (1998) *The Impact of the Current Economic Crisis in Asia on Population Migration in the Region*. Geneva: International Organization for Migration.

Smith, A.D. (1991) *National Identity*. London: Penguin.

Smith, S. (1993) 'Residential segregation and the politics of racialisation', in M. Cross and M. Keith (eds), *Racism, the City and the State*. London: Routledge. pp. 128–43.

Solomos, J. (1993) *Race and Racism in Contemporary Britain*, 2nd edn. London: Macmillan.

SOPEMI (1984) *SOPEMI Continuous Reporting System on Migration*. Paris: OECD.

SOPEMI (1990) *OECD Continuous Reporting System on Migration Report 1989*. Paris: OECD.

SOPEMI (1991) *OECD Continuous Reporting System on Migration Report 1990*. Paris: OECD.

SOPEMI – Netherlands (1985) *SOPEMI – Netherlands: Migration, Minorities and Policy in The Netherlands*. Amsterdam: University of Amsterdam, Department of Human Geography.

Soysal, Y.N. (1994) *Limits of Citizenship: Migrants and Postnational Membership in Europe.* Chicago and London: University of Chicago Press.

Spaeter-Bergamo, R. (1974) 'Kinder zweiter Klasse – Lehrer zweiter Klasse', *Hessische Lehrerzeitung*, October.

Stark, O. (1991) *The Migration of Labour.* Oxford: Blackwell.

Taguieff, P.-A. (1988) *La Force du préjugé.* Paris: La Découverte.

Tapinos, G.P. (1990) *Development Assistance Strategies and Emigration Pressure in Europe and Africa.* Washington DC: Commission for the Study of International Migration and Co-operative Economic Development.

Taylor, C. (1994) 'The politics of recognition', in A. Gutmann (ed.), *Multiculturalism: Examining the Politics of Recognition.* Princeton, NJ: Princeton University Press. pp. 25–74.

Taylor, E.J. (1987) 'Undocumented Mexico–US migration and the returns to households in rural Mexico', *American Journal of Agricultural Economics*, 69: 616–38.

Thompson, E.P. (1968) *The Making of the English Working Class.* Harmondsworth: Penguin.

Todaro, M. (1976) *Internal Migration in Developing Countries.* Geneva: International Labour Office.

Touraine, A. (1998) 'Social transformations of the twentieth century', *International Social Science Journal*, 156: 165–71.

Townsend, P. (1979) *Poverty in the United Kingdom.* London: Penguin.

Turner, B. (1992) 'Outline of a theory of citizenship', in C. Mouffe (ed.), *Dimensions of Radical Democracy: Pluralism, Citizenship, Community.* London and New York: Verso. pp. 33–62.

UNFPA (United Nations Population Fund) (1993) *The State of World Population.* New York: United Nations.

UNHCR (United Nations High Commissioner for Refugees) (1989) *Assessment of Global Resettlement Needs and Priorities for Refugees in 1990.* Geneva: UNHCR Resettlement Service.

UNHCR (United Nations High Commissioner for Refugees) (1995) *The State of the World's Refugees: in Search of Solutions.* Oxford: Oxford University Press.

United Nations Economic Commission for Europe (1968) *Economic Survey of Europe 1967.* Geneva: United Nations.

US DoS (US Department of State) (1992) *Country Reports on Human Rights Practices for 1990.* Washington, DC: US Government Printing Office.

van Dijk, T.A (1993) *Elite Discourse and Racism.* Newbury Park: Sage.

Vasta, E. (1993a) 'Rights and racism in a new country of immigration: the Italian case', in J. Wrench and J. Solomos (eds), *Racism and Migration in Western Europe.* Oxford: Berg. pp. 83–98.

Vasta, E. (1993b) 'Immigrant women and the politics of resistance', *Australian Feminist Studies*, 18: 5–23.

Vasta, E. and Castles, S. (eds) (1996) *The Teeth are Smiling: the Persistence of Racism in Multicultural Australia.* Sydney: Allen and Unwin.

Vogel, U. (1994) 'Marriage and the boundaries of citizenship', in B. van Steenbergen (ed.) *The Condition of Citizenship.* London: Sage, pp. 76–89.

Vuddamalay, V. (1998) *Specificities of French Migration Research. Intercultural Relations, Identity and Citizenship: a Comparative Study of Australia, France and Germany.* Paris: CERI.

Waldinger, R., Aldrich, H. and Ward, R. (1990) *Ethnic Entrepreneurs: Immigrant Business in Industrial Societies*. London, Newbury Park, New Delhi: Sage.

Wallerstein, I. (1991) 'The ideological tensions of capitalism: universalism versus racism and sexism', in E. Balibar and I. Wallerstein (eds), *Race, Nation, Class: Ambiguous Identities*. London: Verso. pp. 29–36.

Weil, P. (1991) *La France et ses étrangers*. Paris: Calmann-Levy.

Wieviorka, M. (1991) *L'espace du racisme*. Paris: Seuil.

Wieviorka, M. (1992) *La France raciste*. Paris: Seuil.

Wieviorka, M. (1993) 'Tendencies to racism in Europe: does France represent a unique case, or is it representative of a trend?', in J. Wrench and J. Solomos (eds), *Racism and Migration in Western Europe*. Oxford: Berg. pp. 55–66.

Wieviorka, M. (1994) 'Introduction', in M. Wieviorka, P. Bataille, K. Couper, D. Martuccelli and A. Peralva (eds), *Racisme et xénophobie en Europe: une comparaison internationale*. Paris: La Découverte. pp. 7–25.

Wieviorka, M. (1995) *The Arena of Racism*. London: Sage.

Wihtol de Wenden, C. (1988) *Les immigrés et la politique: cent-cinquante ans d'évolution*. Paris: Presses de la FNSP.

Wihtol de Wenden, C. (1995) 'Generational change and political participation in French suburbs', *New Community*, 21 (1): 69–78.

Wilson, W.J. (1987) *The Truly Disadvantaged: the Inner City, the Underclass and Public Policy*. Chicago: University of Chicago Press.

Wilson, W.J. (1994) 'Citizenship and the inner-city ghetto poor', in B. van Steenbergen (ed.), *The Condition of Citizenship*. London: Sage. pp. 49–65.

Wong, D. (1996) 'Foreign domestic workers in Singapore', *Asian and Pacific Migration Journal*, 5 (1): 117–38.

Wrench, J. and Solomos, J. (eds) (1993) *Racism and Migration in Western Europe*. Oxford: Berg.

Young, I.M. (1989) 'Polity and group difference: a critique of the ideal of universal citizenship', *Ethics*, 99: 250–74.

Zolberg, A.R. (1989) 'The next waves: migration theory for a changing world', *International Migration Review*, 23 (3): 403–30.

Zolberg, A.R., Suhrke, A. and Aguayo, S. (1989) *Escape from Violence*. New York: Oxford University Press.

INDEX